The Curious World of Carnivorous Plants

THE CURIOUS WORLD OF
Carnivorous Plants

A Comprehensive Guide to
Their Biology and Cultivation

by Wilhelm Barthlott, Stefan Porembski,
Rüdiger Seine, and Inge Theisen

Timber Press
Portland • London

Contents

Cephalotus follicularis
W. Barthlott

Preface

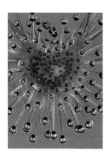

The notion of plants that catch and eat animals seems almost implausible. Indeed, when the great botanist Carl Linnaeus first heard of the Venus flytrap at the end of the eighteenth century, he considered it "against the order of nature as willed by God." Hence, it is not surprising that it was only in 1875 that the great freethinker Charles Darwin first documented the existence of carnivorous plants in scientific terms.

Today, some 650 known species of carnivorous plants are the subject of current research. They are draws for visitors to gardening centers and botanical collections, and there are a number of specialist societies and associations for carnivorous plants worldwide. The existence of these "flowers of evil" (to borrow a famous title from the French poet Charles Baudelaire) has also found its way into comic strips, horror films, and musicals. Meanwhile, new details are coming to light, such as the evidence in 1998 of the carnivorous plant *Genlisea* that chemically attracts and traps unicellular animals, or in 2000 of an animal-trapping liverwort, and in 2006 of the smallest genome of flowering plants found in the bladderwort family (Lentibulariaceae), with chromosomes of bacterial size (Greilhuber et al. 2006). Since 2000, about seven new species of carnivorous plants have been described each year.

This book first appeared in German in 2004. It was the first account to provide a complete overview of the biology, diversity, and cultivation of carnivorous plants. We are pleased to present an updated and revised English edition of the original German text. Written in popular science style, it covers leading-edge research from a wealth of specialized scientific publications, as well as the results of a special symposium on carnivorous plants held at the XVII International Botanical Congress in Vienna, Austria in 2005 (Porembski and Barthlott 2006). Previous excellent books on the topic include Juniper et al. (1989), Slack (2000), and Schnell (2002), McPherson (2006), and Rice (2006).

We have worked together as professional botanists at the University of Bonn in Germany for many years. The senior author, Wilhelm Barthlott, has researched carnivorous plants for three decades. In his role as head of the Nees Institute of Plant Biodiversity, he has built up one of the largest specialist collections of carnivorous plants in the world, in the botanical gardens of the University of Bonn. Stefan Porembski is primarily concerned with the ecology of tropical carnivorous plants, and he is currently director of the botanical garden and chair of the Institute of Biodiversity Research (General and Systematic Botany) at the University of Rostock, Germany. Rüdiger Seine completed his doctorate on the topic of tropical ecology and has worked on the systematics of the sundews. Inge Theisen completed her doctorate in systematics and is coordinating a project in Bonn supported by the German Research Foundation (DFG) on the bladderworts (Lentibulariaceae), covering a wide spectrum from the molecular genetics to the evolution and ecology of this, the largest of all carnivorous plant families.

We would like to express our special gratitude to numerous professional colleagues, plant enthusiasts, collaborators, and institutions. The most important of these are (listed in alphabetical order): Dr. Nadja Biedinger (University of Rostock: illustrative materials); Prof. Wilhelm Boland (Max-Planck Institute

of Chemical Ecology, Jena: chemistry of the attracting substances of the Lentibulariaceae); Dr. Thomas Borsch (University of Bonn: molecular systematics and evolution); Prof. Gerhard Bringmann (University of Würzburg: *Triphyophyllum*); Dr. Brigitte Buchen and Prof. Andreas Sievers (University of Bonn: cell biology of *Utricularia* and *Dionaea*); Thomas Carow (Nüdlingen: illustrative and plant materials); Prof. Jost Casper and Prof. Helga Dietrich (University of Jena: *Pinguicula*); Prof. Eberhard Fischer (University of Koblenz: systematics of the Lentibulariaceae); Prof. Jan-Peter Frahm (University of Bonn: mosses); Dr. M. Janarthanam (Goa University, India: *Utricularia*); Dr. Laurent Legendre (University of Saint Etienne, *Pinguicula*); Dr. Kai Müller (University of Bonn: molecular systematics); Christoph Scherber (University of Jena: illustrative materials); Dr. Jan Schlauer (University of Tübingen: *Triphyophyllum*); our graduates Jan Schnitzler and Andreas Worberg (University of Bonn); Prof. Richard Sikora (University of Bonn: illustrative materials, fungi); Dr. Jürg Steiger (University of Bern: *Pinguicula*); Dr. Heike Vibrans (Colegio de Postgraduados en Ciencias Agrícolas, Montecillo, Mexico: *Pinguicula*); Dr. Aparna V. Watve (University of Pune, India: *Utricularia*); Prof. Anton Weber (University of Vienna: illustrative materials, *Nepenthes*); and Prof. Georg Zizka (Senckenberg, Frankfurt). Many of our research projects have been supported by the German Research Foundation and the Mainz Academy of Sciences and Literature, and we express our considerable gratitude to both these institutions.

An important basis for our research, and a constant source of wonder, is our living collection of remarkable carnivorous plants, which is probably the largest in the world. Accordingly, we would like to express our special thanks to Otto Kriesten, Werner Höller, Dr. Wolfram Lobin, and all the other dedicated staff of the botanical gardens of the University of Bonn. We are also delighted that the highly respected publishing house Timber Press has now issued an English-language edition of our book. It was a pleasure to cooperate with them. Last, but not least, we are indebted to Dr. Donald Schnell for his review and most valuable comments on the manuscript.

Wilhelm Barthlott
Stefan Porembski
Rüdiger Seine
Inge Theisen

Utricularia campbelliana
C. Scherber

The Flowers of Evil: An Introduction

Over many millions of years of evolution, nature has produced some rather bizarre and abstruse creations. Perhaps among the most remarkable of these are plants that attract, trap, and digest animals. Such a notion runs contrary to our idea of the passive, vegetative role of plants, breaking rules that would otherwise seem to be set in stone. They are "nervous plants that already go a little beyond the mysterious and probably imaginary ridge that separates the vegetable from the animal kingdom," wrote the Nobel Prize laureate Maurice Maeterlinck in 1907, in his *The Intelligence of the Flowers*. Symbolist poet Ernst Stadler captured our ambivalent relationship with what might be termed "another botany" in a poem of 1904, which can be translated, in part:

Flecked mosses, brightly colored lichens sway
around the fanlike banners of high palms,
and between smooth yew plants creep
pale and lasciviously trembling vines.

Let us first attempt to define carnivorous plants. There are some 650 different species of plants that attract, trap, and digest animals with the aid of specialized structures. We will examine these in detail in the following chapters—but first, some comments to begin with.

The carnivorous plants' prey serve nutritional requirements, and the ecological specialization of carnivory makes it possible for these plants to colonize even extremely low-nutrient sites. The diversity of prey is enormous; in fact, anything that can fit into the traps can be caught and digested, if it is digestible at all. Insects, including anything from flies to butterflies, are probably the most com-

mon victims, as in the case of Venus flytraps (*Dionaea*) and sundews (*Drosera*). Some pitcher plants (such as *Sarracenia*) can occasionally trap small vertebrates, and even rats have been found in the pitchers of *Nepenthes*, which can have a capacity of up to 3 L. Bladderworts (*Utricularia*), on the other hand, catch nematodes, water fleas, and other small crustaceans, but up to 50 percent of their catch may consist of planktic algae. Other bladderworts and the corkscrew plant (*Genlisea*) are specialized to capture unicellular animals, such as *Paramecium*. Butterworts (*Pinguicula*) mainly trap small insects on their sticky leaves, but they are also not averse to pollen, which may make up as much as 70 percent of their catch. As diverse as the prey animals are, so, too, are the trapping organs, which always take the form of modified leaves. These can be anything from sticky adhesive traps to sliding pitfall traps, closing traps, and the extremely complicated suction traps of *Utricularia*.

And what should we call this fascinating group of plants? Perhaps Charles Darwin (1875) coined the best-known term, *insectivorous plants*. However, this is applicable to only some of the species or prey involved. The terms *carnivorous plants* or *carnivores*, which by definition include all potential prey animals, are therefore much more appropriate, and these are the terms that we use in this book. The special cases of bladderworts that consume algae or butterworts that digest pollen hardly justify the use of the terms *herbivorous* or *phytophagous*; such terms conjure up somewhat incongruous images of grazing cows or sucking aphids. For true carnivores, however, there are two terms that should be avoided at all costs: *animal-trapping plants* or *insect-trapping plants*. In fact, many plants trap insects for pollination purposes. Perhaps the best-known examples are the lords-and-ladies (*Arum maculatum*) of the forests of central Europe and the Jack-in-the-pulpit (*Arisaema triphyllum*) in North America, which catch insects with their pitfall flowers but then release them again after pollination. Such trapping clearly has nothing to do with "carnivorous" plants.

The approximately 650 species of carnivorous plants are found virtually all over the world, and many of them have been known for a very long time. The herbal books of the late Middle Ages mentioned most of the species that are native to Europe. The sundew, which was used for medicinal purposes and for curdling milk, was probably the best-known example. It was mentioned in an incunabulum by Matthaeus Plataerius Salernitanus (1120–1161) that was printed in 1493. Matthaeus Merian's copperplate engraving from 1626 is one of the most beautiful early illustrations of these plants (Fig. 1). We believe that we have found what may be the oldest illustration of a carnivorous plant, in the mysterious *Cypher Manuscript* (also known as the *Voynich Code*, now in the Beinecke Library at Yale University). It is believed that this is a text by Roger Bacon (*c.* 1214–1292), written in a code that remains undeciphered even to this day. Even more mysterious are the fantastic illustrations that the manuscript contains. On page 56 of the manuscript, however, there is quite clearly a depiction of a sundew (Fig. 2): the growth form, leaves, and the characteristically rolled-up (involute) inflorescence leave hardly any doubt as to the plant's identity.

In 1576, Lobelius described and illustrated the first non-European carnivorous plant, the North American pitcher plant *Sarracenia*. In 1658, a description followed of the pitcher plant *Nepenthes* of tropical Madagascar, which Gouverner de Flacourt named "anramitaco."

Fig. 1.
Round-leaved sundew (*Drosera rotundifolia*), engraving by Matthaeus Merian (1626).

In our brief overview of the early history of carnivorous plant discovery, however, we have neglected to mention one vital thing: at the time, it was not known that all these plants are carnivorous. Quite understandably it may be assumed that plants are plants, and animals are animals. Even when we observe carnivory in sundews in our own backyard, we do not take in something that cannot be, even when we can see it right in front of us. The real sensation came around 1759, with the discovery of the North American Venus flytrap (*Dionaea muscipula*) and the subsequent exchange of letters between the naturalist who described them, John Ellis, and the father of modern botany, Carl Linnaeus. Anyone who has ever seen a live Venus flytrap catch a butterfly in a flash with its "gin trap" (see Figs. 81–83) will be left with no doubt that the plant is carnivorous. And yet, the story of the plant's discovery and its reception by the scientific community reads

Fig. 2
One of the earliest illustrations of a sundew (*Drosera*), taken from Roger Bacon's thirteenth-century *Voynich Code*.

something like an adventure novel (see Nelson 1990).

Venus flytraps have an extremely restricted area of natural distribution, in the border region between North and South Carolina. Despite this, they are not exactly rare—quite the opposite, in fact. They colonize open coastal plains in vast stands that contain thousands of individual plants. The first written reference to the Venus flytrap was in a letter of April 2, 1759, by Governor Arthur Dobbs to the English naturalist Peter Collinson. The amazing plant also attracted the attention of William Young, a German-American born in Kassel, Germany, who journeyed through the Carolinas in 1768 as the Queen's botanist, taking with him live specimens of "tipitiwitchet" back to England. Some of these plants came into the possession of the London merchant John Ellis (1710–1776), who was also active in the coffee trade and had a keen interest in natural history. In 1768, in a letter to the editor of the *St.*

James Chronicle, Ellis described the plant using the botanical name that is still valid today, *Dionaea muscipula*. The epithet *muscipula* actually means "mousetrap," and *Dionaea* refers to the goddess Dione, the mother of Venus-Aphrodite. Thus, there is a rather overt sexual innuendo behind the name, given the half-closed leaves (see Fig. 82), which is something we botanists naturally keep quiet about. Ever since that time, the plant has been commonly known as the "Venus flytrap."

The scientific world was electrified. John Ellis sent material and detailed descriptions to the botanical world's highest authority, Carl Linnaeus (1707–1778), in Uppsala, Sweden. From 1770, translations of his famous letter were published in nearly every language (Ellis 1770): the "botanical description of the *Dionaea muscipula*, a newly-discovered sensitive plant, in a Letter to Sir Charles Linnaeus, Knight of the Polar Star, . . . from John Ellis" also featured a colored copperplate engraving of a flowering *Dionaea* catching a fly and an earwig with its leaves (Fig. 3). Linnaeus's reaction to this *miraculum naturae*, or "wonder of nature," was predictable. Naturally, he was not offended by the plant's lewd name; as the inventor of the sexual system of plants, he himself had thought of many other such names in the past, everything from *Orchis* to *Phallus*. However, there was one aspect that he could not accept—that the plant was supposed to be insectivorous. For Linnaeus, that was simply outrageous. As a product of his time, he stated quite plainly that such a notion was "against the order of nature as willed by God." This was a decree, *ex cathedra*, of the highest authority.

With that, for more than a century after 1770, the controversy over so-called carnivorous plants and any scientific discussion of them came to an end. No provincial botanist would ever have succeeded in refuting Linnaeus; instead, it was a revolutionary new biologist who dared to make the attack. It was no less a figure than Charles Darwin (1809–1882), who proposed the theory of evolution, who began to address the topic in the summer of 1860. His most important study object was the round-leaved sundew (*Drosera rotundifolia*), which he found growing in large numbers on the heaths of Sussex, England. He began to experiment and make measurements, identifying the number and species of insects that were caught on the sticky leaves and observing their digestion. He fed *Drosera* plants salts of ammonia, egg white, and small pieces of cheese. And then he began to speak of "digestion," called the glands "tentacles," and included Venus flytraps, bladderworts, and other suspicious candidates in his experiments. Sir Joseph Hooker, the highly influential director of the Royal Botanic Gardens at Kew, became his comrade-in-arms. On July 3, 1875, *Scientific American* promptly reported on Darwin and Hooker's first lecture in Belfast, Northern Ireland, with an illustration entitled "Carnivorous Plants" that occupied almost an entire page. The scientific fact of carnivory in the plant kingdom had been proven at last. Darwin's 400-page monograph, which remains exemplary to this day, was first published in London in late 1875; translations into nearly all languages followed.

This was an outrageous provocation. In St. Petersburg, the botanist Eduard von Regel described Darwin's work as "scientific garbage." In 1878, in Breslau (Wrocław), Poland, Franz Lorinser, the prince-bishop counselor of justice, stated, "The conclusions that credit the plant with a kind of predatory character are so fantastic, and so contrary to the entire organism of plants, that they quite obviously reveal themselves to be tendentious fiction and require no serious refutation." Even as late as 1920, the existence of carnivorous plants was still contested among some natural historians.

However, the notion of animal-trapping plants, at least, and even carnivory had been

BOTANICAL DESCRIPTION
OF THE
DIONÆA MUSCIPULA,
OR
VENUS's FLY-TRAP.
A NEWLY-DISCOVERED SENSITIVE PLANT:

In a LETTER to Sir CHARLES LINNÆUS,
Knight of the Polar Star, Physician to the King of Sweden, and Member of most of the Learned Societies of Europe,

From JOHN ELLIS, Fellow of the ROYAL SOCIETIES of LONDON and UPSAL.

F 2

Fig. 3.
Venus flytrap (*Dionaea muscipula*), illustration from the letter by John Ellis to the Swedish botanist Carl Linnaeus (1770).

around long before Darwin. John Gerarde had depicted insects caught on sundew leaves in his herbal book of 1597, although he did not interpret what he had illustrated. In 1750 suspicions were raised that pitcher plants, such as *Nepenthes* and *Sarracenia*, might be carnivorous. In the latter case, in 1791 W. Bartram showed that the fluid in the pitchers had digestive properties. The notion of carnivory was not long in coming, along with its elucidation. John Ellis himself, in a September 24, 1768, letter to Dr. Skene concerning *Dionaea*, posed the question, "Do you think Sir that the plant receives any nourishment from insects it catches?" (Nelson 1990, p. 37). In 1778 the encyclopedist Denis Diderot, too, welcomed the Venus flytrap: "Voilà, une plante presque carnivore!" he exclaimed (Diderot 1774–1784), thus coining the term *carnivorous plants* for the first time.

It was not just Diderot whom the Venus flytrap fascinated, and thus the plant soon became widely known. Following in the footsteps of Arthur Dobbs, the first governor of Carolina, Thomas Jefferson collected this most remarkable of all plants in its natural habitat, shortly after 1800. In London, the plant had been cultivated since 1768, and soon after in the Jardin Royal des Trianon in Versailles.

Fig. 4.
The man-eating tree ("L'Arbre anthropophage"), title page of the French magazine *Journal des Voyages et des Aventures de Terre et de Mer* (1878, no. 61). W. Barthlott

Fig. 5.
Nepenthes melamphora, from Ernst Haeckel's *Art Forms in Nature* (1899).

Could it be that Louis XVI and Marie-Antoinette saw the Venus flytrap growing there before the storms of the French Revolution bore them away? Napoleon, at least, very probably knew the plants, because the Empress Josephine, a keen plant enthusiast, grew them in the garden of Malmaison. The great plant illustrator Pierre-Joseph Redouté painted them, while the major encyclopedias, such as the third edition of the *Dictionaire d'Histoire Naturelle* by Valmont de Bomare (Lyon, 1791), described the plants in great detail and even gave instructions on how to grow them. Surprisingly enough, there seems to have been no reaction from Goethe—it is perhaps in keeping with his character that he did not want to acknowledge the Venus flytrap's existence. Around 1800, the Königlich-Preussische Porzellan Manufaktur china company in Berlin manufactured dessert plates with an excellent depiction of a Venus flytrap in flower, for which John Ellis's often-reproduced original illustration quite obviously served as a basis.

It is no coincidence that one of these very plates fetched the highest sum at auction at Christie's in London on May 1, 2002, when it was sold to an American collector for 9000 euros. Evidently this collector loved carnivorous plants as well as fine Prussian chinaware.

Dionaea remains a subject of scientific research to this day. More than 200 years after its discovery, Hodick and Sievers (1986, 1988) demonstrated that it even has a molecular clock, accurate to within seconds, to optimize the trapping of prey.

Even before Maurice Maeterlink, whom we quoted above, carnivorous plants appeared in art and literature in grotesque forms. The notion of "carnivorous monsters" was indeed both fascinating and profound (Baffray et al. 1992). The boundaries between facts and fiction became blurred. Soon after Darwin's seminal publication (1875), reports of the "man-eating tree" of Madagascar made the headlines (Prior 1939). On September 8, 1878, a picture of the horrible monster killing a group of native Madagascans filled the title page of the French magazine *Journal des Voyages et des Aventures de Terre et de Mer*. We have reproduced it in Figure 4, next to a stylized Art Nouveau depiction of pitcher plants in Ernst Haeckel's *Art Forms in Nature* from 1899 (Fig. 5). The great surrealist Max Ernst, too, could not resist using the grandiose illustration of "l'arbre anthropophage" in 1930, for one of his most beautiful collages.

Today, carnivorous plants remain as popular as ever. Hardly any comic strip manages to do without them, and they have also appeared in horror films and Broadway musicals (most famously *Little Shop of Horrors* by Howard Ashman). Many postage stamp series (Figs. 6, 7) also bear witness to the fascinating impact that these plants have. In spring 2001, Wilhelm Barthlott once spent a night in the Hotel Nepenthes in Fort Dauphin, while on an expedition to Madagascar.

Today, there are hundreds of specialized

Carnivorous plants on postage stamps.

Fig. 7.
Ivory Coast:
Triphyophyllum peltatum.
W. Barthlott

nurseries and market gardens around the world that sell carnivores. About a dozen societies keep their enthusiastic membership informed about carnivorous plants and are dedicated to their research. A wealth of published scientific literature has been devoted to carnivores (for example, Cheers 1992; Pietropaolo and Pietropaolo 1996; Schnell 2002; Labat 2003); nevertheless, we hope that we have managed to list the most relevant publications in our comprehensive bibliography. In 1942, the emeritus professor of botany Francis Ernest Lloyd, a former pupil of the great morphologist Karl von Goebel, compiled the first great monograph since that of Charles Darwin, entitled *The Carnivorous Plants*; today, it is published in reprint form. The Oxford botanist Barrie E. Juniper and his two coauthors, R. J. Robins and D. M. Joel, chose the same title for

Fig. 6.
United States: *Darlingtonia californica, Drosera anglica, Dionaea muscipula, Sarracenia flava*.
Illustrations by S. Buchanan

the most recent comprehensive scientific monograph (Juniper et al. 1989), which concentrates on physiological aspects in particular.

New details are still coming to light. Green et al. (1979) demonstrated carnivory in the unusual western African hookleaf (*Triphyophyllum*) of the hitherto unsuspicious family Dioncophyllaceae. Among the monocotyledons, Givnish et al. (1984) demonstrated that the bromeliad *Brocchinia reducta* from the table mountains of Venezuela catches and presumably also digests insects. In a study of *Genlisea*, Barthlott et al. (1998) showed that these highly specialized plants catch protozoans, using chemical attractants to lure their prey. Later, we were able to prove the existence of a liverwort of the genus *Colura* that catches protozoans (Barthlott et al. 2000). Meanwhile, taxonomic research on carnivorous plants is continuing. Here, milestones have included the monumental *Pinguicula* monograph by Jost S. Casper (1966). In 1989, Peter Taylor of the Royal Botanic Gardens at Kew issued an exemplary 725-page monograph on *Utricularia*, the largest of all the carnivore genera.

Some 650 carnivorous plants are known today, comprising just a small fraction of the more than 250,000 known vascular plants. Since 2000, however, an average of seven new species have been described each year. Unexpected new finds are still being made, in particular Mexican species of *Pinguicula* and Australian species of *Drosera*. Finally, since 1993, the field of molecular genetics has revolutionized our view of vascular plant systematics. Long-contested kinship relationships are now regarded as incontrovertible. We know now, for example, that sundews (Droseraceae), Asian pitcher plants (Nepenthaceae), and the hookleaf family (Dioncophyllaceae) are closely allied to one another, and that, contrary to conventional opinion, all of them belong to the so-called caryophyllids, which means that they are related to the carnations and cacti. This notion is not a new one: in 1791, even Valmont de Bomare believed the Venus flytrap to be related to the carnations. And so we have come full circle. Both the status of the families in the system and the evolution of the genera within the families have been elucidated; we need only to refer to the molecular genetic analyses of the Droseraceae (Rivadavia et al. 2003) and Lentibulariaceae (Müller et al. 2000, 2004, 2006). The latest findings about carnivorous plants are summarized in a special edition of the journal *Plant Biology* (Volume 8, 2006). But these are just a few of the details of the following chapters, which deal with the diversity, biology, and cultivation of carnivorous plants—perhaps the most fascinating plants of all.

Habitats

Carnivorous plants colonize a wide range of habitats that are characterized by particular environmental conditions. These are predominantly open, low-nutrient sites that are moist to wet for at least part of the year, as well as water bodies and watercourses.

Unable to compete with other plants, carnivorous plants only seldom grow on mineral-rich soils, and they are also uncommon in dense forests. In addition, most carnivores are sensitive to desiccation, and so they are largely absent from deserts and semideserts, where the shortage of water would make their existence impossible. The intermittently moist sites in the semi-arid southwest of Australia, where several *Drosera* species are found, are an exception. There is strong evidence that the evolution of carnivorous plants (which occurred several times independently within the angiosperms) took place on open, moist, and low-nutrient sites such as white-sand savannas and bogs (Givnish 1989). The colonization of water bodies and watercourses and the occasional transition to an epiphytic lifestyle came only during a later evolutionary phase. In the following, we present the most important carnivorous plant habitats (bogs and swamps, water bodies and watercourses, sandy sites, rocky sites, and forests), describing them in terms of the occurrence of specific representatives of this plant group. In fact, the habitats of carnivorous plants are as diverse as the roughly 650 species that make up the group.

Bogs and Swamps

Bogs and swamps occupy extensive tracts of land in many parts of the Arctic tundra, the Nordic coniferous forests (taiga), and the deciduous broadleaved forest zone. Human impacts have greatly reduced their extent, however. Bogs and swamps are species-rich, moist biotopes that, among other things, owe their existence to the silting up of lakes. They are particularly widespread in the temperate and cold climatic zones, where they cover large areas. Bogs are habitats characterized by peat formation, and they can be classified into different types according to their water and mineral supply (for details, see Gore 1983; Succow and Jeschke 1990).

Central Europe

In central Europe, a primary distinction can be made between ombrogenic bogs and lowland bogs, whereby the former are supplied by precipitation water only, but the latter also receives mineral-rich groundwater. In addition, there are intermediate or transitional bogs, which have characteristics of both the main bog types.

With their exclusive water supply from precipitation and their low pH values, ombrogenic bogs are extremely poor in nutrients, whereas lowland bogs have high nutrient levels. Ombrogenic bogs are often almost tree-

Fig. 8.
A transitional bog with reddish, cushionlike stands of the oblong-leaved sundew (*Drosera intermedia*) in the Murnauer Moos nature reserve in Bavaria, Germany.
C. Scherber

less and feature dwarf shrub–cotton grass–sphagnum moss communities, among others. Sphagnum mosses (*Sphagnum* species) may cover a large proportion of the bog area, and their water-retention function makes these mosses very important for the overall water

regime of the habitat. Dependent on the water supply, sphagnum mosses grow steadily at the tips, while the lower parts die off and become transformed into peat in the absence of air. Depending on the predominant vegetation elements, a distinction can be made between sphagnum moss peat, pine bog peat, and cotton grass peat. A typical species occurring on sphagnum moss cushions is the round-leaved sundew (*Drosera rotundifolia*), which, with its leaf rosette, can keep pace with the growth of the moss. The oblong-leaved sundew (*Drosera intermedia*) grows on waterlogged sites of ombrogenic bogs and on acidic transitional bogs in central Europe (Fig. 8). The great sundew (*Drosera anglica*) is found mainly on transitional bogs, where it grows in bog hollows together with several bladderwort species (*Utricularia intermedia, U. minor*, and *U. vulgaris*). The standing water in the bog hollows has a characteristic brownish tealike color, is rich in dissolved humus matter, and has a very low pH value.

Pinguicula vulgaris, the common butterwort, is a typical species of limestone transitional bogs in North America and temperate Eurasia. This species is also present in alpine and subalpine limestone spring meadows and in the Scandinavian mountain ranges, where it also often grows on slopes over which seepage water rich in lime (calcium carbonate) flows only occasionally.

In central Europe, most of the bogs that are currently still growing in extent are the lowland bogs, which have a relatively good mineral supply. The most common sites are inundated river floodplains (such as, until several decades ago, the Spreewald region southeast of Berlin) and coastal environments. Here, the peat-forming vegetation consists of highly productive reedlands, sedgelands, and alder swamp forests, in which carnivorous plants generally do not thrive.

In dry weather, more or less open pine forests on sandy soils (pine savannas) are greatly at risk of fire. The plants in the undergrowth of this forest type (including the carnivorous species), however, are well adapted to frequent outbreaks of forest fire. Especially in the pine savannas of the southwestern United States, *Sarracenia* species in particular readily withstand regular forest fires, thanks to their rhizomes. In fact, carnivorous plants growing in open habitats actually benefit from the consequences of fire, because it eradicates competing plants and it leads to an enrichment of minerals in the soil, promoting plant growth.

Fig. 9.
The natural habitat of *Sarracenia flava* and *Dionaea muscipula* in North Carolina. A. Sievers

North America

The cobra lily, *Darlingtonia californica* (Fig. 145), which is native to the coastal parts of the Pacific Northwest, grows mainly on very wet serpentine (heavy-metal-containing) soils. *Sarracenia* species are mainly distributed throughout the Southeast and are primarily found in savanna and sand-peat soils associated with sphagnum moss (Fig. 9). Summer droughts dry out the vegetation, which means that fire caused by lightning strikes can quickly spread over the entire savanna. *Sarracenia* plants can easily recover from fire, and in particular they benefit from the eradication of competing species in what were formerly dense, shaded plant stands. Some *Sarracenia* species (including *S. minor*) grow in *Sphagnum* cushions that drift on the water, as in the Okefenokee Swamp in Florida, for example.

Australia and Asia

The Australian pitcher plant, *Cephalotus follicularis* (Fig. 56), is native to the winter-rain regions of southwestern Australia, where it grows in bogs in which the peat is largely formed by the root mass of plants of the locally dominant family, Restionaceae, which are grasslike herbs of the Southern Hemisphere. Although we know relatively little about the extent of bogs in the tropics, extensive areas are known in Malaysia and Indonesia (mainly in Sumatra and Borneo), which include a range of *Nepenthes* species. Bogs were once also widespread on the moist, eastern side of Madagascar. The best-known element of these bogs is the endemic pitcher plant *Nepenthes madagascariensis* (Figs. 130, 131).

Water Bodies and Watercourses

Especially in temperate latitudes, where there are standing waters, barely flowing streams, and oxbow lakes characterized by a paucity of nutrients (oligotrophy) and in part also by low pH values, aquatic bladderwort (*Utricularia*) species dominate the habitats, together with *Aldrovanda vesiculosa*, the waterwheel plant (Figs. 85, 86). These carnivores are typically found in free-floating stands at the lake margins; often, however, bog hollows and ditches of human origin (such as turf cuts) are also colonized.

The trapping organs of aquatic *Utricularia* are submerged, and only their inflorescences project above the water. The rootless bladderworts can form extensive stands in still waters that are often an impressive sight during the warmest time of the year, when they are in

conspicuous, and even larger stands are difficult to locate. In Europe, waterwheel plant stands have sharply declined during the last 200 years due to human impacts. According to Adamec and Lev (1999), about 150 sites were still known about 200 years ago. Today, this figure has dropped to fewer than 40, found mainly in Poland, the Ukraine, and Russia (Fig. 11).

In the tropics and warm temperate regions as well, aquatic *Utricularia* species often form dense stands, colonizing not only oligotrophic standing waters (such as *U. purpurea* in the Okefenokee Swamp in Florida), but also relatively nutrient-rich lakes, dams, ponds, and pools that sometimes dry out during rainless periods. Together with *Aldrovanda vesiculosa*, aquatic *Utricularia* species are also common in rice paddies.

The rocky substrates of fast-flowing tropical streams provide a habitat for certain *Utricularia* species in tropical Africa and in South America. In these streams, which carry water only during the rainy season, highly specialized *Utricularia* species (such as *U. neottioides* in South America and *U. rigida* in Africa) are firmly rooted to the substrate with the aid of rhizoids; on first glance, the plants betray their presence only by their inflorescences projecting above the water surface. The algaelike, modified plant bodies of these bladderworts, which are little known and not cultivated, are flattened and closely appressed to the rocky streambed (see *U. rigida*, Fig. 121). The plants are notable for having a small number of bladders or in many cases none at all.

Sandy Sites

Low-nutrient sandy sites that are moist for at least part of the year provide a habitat for carnivorous plants worldwide. In principle, we

Fig. 10.
A bog pond in the Bernrieder Filz nature reserve in Bavaria, Germany, with *Utricularia australis*. C. Scherber

Fig. 11.
The gently flowing Nogat River, a tributary of the Weichsel in Poland, with extensive water lily stands, a refuge for waterwheel plants and bladderworts. The Marienburg (Malbork) Castle is in the background. W. Barthlott

flower (Fig. 10). These bladderworts withstand the cold season, during which the water freezes over large areas, with the aid of their winter buds (turions) that sink into the lake or pond substrate in the fall, only to reappear the following spring. The bladder traps of these *Utricularia* species are mostly only a few centimeters below the water surface, occasionally reaching deeper (such as *U. foliosa*). Compared with the bladder traps of terrestrial *Utricularia* species, they are relatively large (5 mm) and easy to see with the unaided eye, often together with their trapped prey. In some aquatic bladderworts, the number of bladders that the plant develops seems to depend on the nutrient supply of the water body or watercourse.

In contrast to the strikingly flowering *Utricularia* species, *Aldrovanda vesiculosa* is quite in-

Fig. 12.
Drosera graniticola
growing in the
western Australian
bush. R. Seine

can distinguish between open, forest-free sites (such as dunes, quartz sand, savannas, and Australian "heathland"; Fig. 12) and open forest communities (including pine forests in the southeastern United States and Spain, the eucalyptus forests of Australia, and, in part, the *fynbos* of South Africa). For example, a whole range of sundew and butterwort species are found on open, humus-poor sandy soils in the undergrowth of open pine forests and on dune sands.

A number of *Drosera* species (such as *D. filiformis*) have been recorded in the longleaf pine (*Pinus palustris*) savannas of the southeastern United States, occasionally also growing in mass stands along road edges. The Venus flytrap (*Dionaea muscipula*) has been recorded in grassland communities on more or less permanently moist, sandy soils in the coastal zone of North and South Carolina. These latter sites can sometimes be completely inundated with water, with the Venus flytrap still catching its prey while submerged (Schnell 2002).

In southwestern Spain, Portugal, and Morocco, the Portuguese sundew, *Drosophyllum lusitanicum*, also grows mainly near the coast on sandy, acidic soils, often on open, rocky slopes that are exceptionally dry during the summer months (April to October). The plant is sometimes also found in open pine forests.

There are also extensive sandy sites in southwestern Australia, where the vegetation ranges from very open, heathlike formations to low scrub and eucalyptus savanna woodlands. The open heathland and scrub communities contain many species of sundew (*Drosera*), and the rainbow plant (*Byblis gigantea*). These carnivores are perfectly adapted to the seasonal climate of the region, with its alternation between a winter rainy season and a summer dry season. The rainbow plant has a fleshy rootstock from which it sprouts anew each year after the dry season.

In the Australian species of *Drosera*, two strategies have evolved for surviving the dry season: tuber-forming species such as *D. erythrorhiza* (Figs. 68, 71) and *D. zonaria* die off completely above the ground and are dormant during the summer months. The tubers are buried about 10–30 cm deep in the sand, where they are protected from extremes of temperature and desiccation. By contrast, pygmy sundews undergo a summer dormancy above the ground. They lose their leaves and form a resting bud that is surrounded by light-reflecting, papery stipules.

In various tropical regions, and less commonly in temperate latitudes, the mostly scattered and isolated white-sand areas are an im-

Fig. 13.
Savanna in Comoé
National Park, Ivory
Coast. W. Barthlott

Fig. 13.
Savanna in Comoé
National Park, Ivory
Coast. W. Barthlott

Fig. 14.
The small bladder-
wort *Utricularia
pubescens* can be
found growing at
ground level
between the grasses
(detail from Fig. 13).
W. Barthlott

portant habitat for carnivorous plants. These areas are of varying extent that, due to their coloration, are conspicuous even from a distance and clearly stand out from the surrounding areas because of their sparse vegetation cover. White-sand areas are characterized by quartz sand at the surface that is almost pure, strongly acidic, and extremely low in nutrients (Splett 1996), while strongly reflecting incoming sunlight. White-sand areas are often found on the lower slopes of quartzite hills, from which the quartz sand is released by weathering processes.

The plant life of white-sand areas has been examined particularly closely in Brazil, where comparative studies have been conducted in the Amazon rainforest, the central Brazilian Campo-Rupestre vegetation, and along the Atlantic coast (Restinga vegetation). Our knowledge of the central Brazilian white-sand areas is especially detailed; they feature a large number of species, including many endemics, that Splett (1996) studied in the Serra do Espinhaço (in the state of Minas Gerais) and elsewhere. Here, the quartz sand layer can be several meters deep, and the proportion of humus compo-

nents in the soil is generally small. Site-specific species predominate here, and these plants are well adapted to the paucity of nutrients and the sites' intermittent dryness. In addition to a large number of carnivorous plants (especially Lentibulariaceae and Droseraceae), there are species of the Eriocaulaceae and Xyridaceae as well as spherical cacti, such as the bizarre genus *Uebelmannia* (sometimes with large mucilaginous ducts in the shoot periphery) and *Discocactus* (including *D. horstii*, with water uptake via the thorns), and completely desiccation-tolerant species of the genus *Vellozia* (Velloziaceae). The Lentibulariaceae grow on white-sand areas with numerous terrestrial *Utricularia* and *Genlisea* species. Some *Utricularia* species are remarkable in that they have extraordinarily small foliage leaves that are partially buried in the snow-white quartz sand. The trapping organs of the *Utricularia* and *Genlisea* species penetrate several centimeters into the quartz sand, in which the interstitial spaces are filled with water at least during the rainy season, providing a habitat for various microorganisms.

Carnivorous species are also found in the white-sand areas of other tropical regions, in-

cluding Madagascar (Rauh 1995; Fischer et al. 2000) and tropical Africa (such as the Fouta Djalon Mountains in Guinea). However, our knowledge of the site conditions in these sometimes highly inaccessible regions is extremely rudimentary. We know more about the white-sand areas in the south of Venezuela and in neighboring Guiana. Here, near the sandstone table mountains, known as *tepuis*, can be found the bromeliad *Brocchinia reducta*. This terrestrial species is a characteristic element of the savannas in this region, which is known as the Gran Sabana.

Wet, sandy grassland formations of the tropics and subtropics are also the preferred habitat of many terrestrial bladderwort species. These are mostly low growing and hidden in the lowest grass stratum of the seasonally inundated savannas (such as *Utricularia pubescens*, Figs. 13, 14). The large-flowering bladderwort *Utricularia reniformis* can attain a height of 60 cm and has large blue-violet flowers, which can be up to 5 cm across. This species is found in Brazil not only as a hyper-epiphyte in water-filled bromeliad cisterns, but also as a prominent associated species of the tussock grasslands (Figs. 15, 16) in the southern coastal mountains (Organ and Itatiaia Mountains).

While most *Nepenthes* species are found in forests of Southeast Asia (often in so-called heath forests, locally known as *kerangas*), some species, such as *N. albomarginata* and *N. reinwardtiana*, sometimes grow near the beach on pure sand. These plants may even be exposed to the effects of sea spray and are subject to considerable stress from the wind and sun. A whole range of *Nepenthes* species (including *N. macrovulgaris* and *N. burbidgeae* on Mount Kinabalu) are found on heavy-metal-containing (serpentine) soils with very high nickel and iron concentrations.

Rocky Sites

The rocky sites on which carnivorous plants grow include the rock faces of inselbergs, steep mountain slopes, and laterite plateaus that are supplied by runoff water.

Fig. 17.
The Sugerloaf, the
famous landmark of
Rio de Janeiro, is a
typical inselberg.
W. Barthlott

Fig. 17.
The Sugerloaf, the famous landmark of Rio de Janeiro, is a typical inselberg.
W. Barthlott

Rock Faces of the Inselbergs and Tepuis Supplied by Runoff Water

Inselbergs, which are made up of granites and gneisses and are characterized by their rounded forms (such as the Sugarloaf of Rio de Janeiro; Fig. 17). They are widespread on the crystalline continental plates, especially in the tropics (see the overview in Porembski and Barthlott 2000). Table mountains consisting of Precambrian sandstones are another kind of rocky site, of which the *tepuis* in the north of South America (southern Venezuela, southeastern Colombia, Guiana, and northern Brazil) are the best known (Fig. 18).

The inselbergs, which mostly rise abruptly out of the surrounding landscape, are very old, typically many millions of years. These are extreme sites, characterized by high temperatures (daily maxima regularly over 50°C, 122°F), intense incoming solar radiation, and, for the most part, an absence of fine soil. Due to these special microclimatic and edaphic conditions, the inselberg vegetation is starkly different than that of the surrounding landscape and includes a large proportion of site-specific species (Barthlott and Porembski 2000).

On the lower slopes of rock faces and in the ecotones of plant communities growing on the rock faces, ephemeral seepage zones develop, particularly on inselbergs in intermittently moist tropical regions. This vegetation type depends on the presence of seepage water over a period of several months during the rainy season. Low-growing annual species are predominant in this seasonal habitat, which is typified by a paucity of nutrients (Richards 1957; Hambler 1964). Most of the plants are characteristic of low-nutrient sites, with many species of the Cyperaceae, Eriocaulaceae, Xyridaceae, and the carnivorous Lentibulariaceae. The last family is represented by many terrestrial *Utricularia* species, as well as several *Genlisea* species in the seepage zones (Figs. 19, 20). Often, several *Utricularia* species may be found growing together in close proximity, which, in

Some *Nepenthes* species show a preference for rocky sites. *Nepenthes pervillei*, for example, is found on the sometimes-bare granite rock faces of the inselbergs of the Seychelles (see Fig. 129). According to Phillipps and Lamb (1996), *N. campanulata* and *N. northiana* are found exclusively on steep limestone rock faces in Borneo.

Fig. 18.
Roraima Tepui, at
2800 m above sea
level, is the highest
table mountain in
Venezuela's Gran
Sabana region.
W. Barthlott

terms of their rooting depth, occupy different ecological niches. Occasionally, climbing *Utricularia* species (including *U. tortilis*) grow in the seepage zones, climbing up the culms of neighboring grasses and sedges with the aid of winding shoots.

Utricularia subulata is one of the most common carnivorous species in the seepage zones of nearly all tropical regions, and hence also the inselbergs. This species mainly colonizes shallow sites where the substrate is only a few millimeters deep. Often, *U. subulata* will also colonize mats of blue-green algae in the transition zone to bare, open rock. Especially on inselbergs in the savannas of tropical Africa, ephemeral seepage zones are among the most species-rich plant communities, with carnivorous plants among the typical elements (Dörrstock et al. 1996).

On tropical inselbergs, mats of blue-green algae up to several millimeters thick develop on very steep rocky slopes that are supplied by runoff water. During the rainy season, these mats provide a habitat for several bladderwort species (including *Utricularia amethystina*, *U. subulata*, and *U. striatula*; see Fig. 114), whose presence depends on this extremely shallow organic substrate. In addition, small representatives of the families Eriocaulaceae, Xyridaceae, and Cyperaceae are found here.

A particular habitat is that of the tepuis, which are table mountains in the north of South America. Because rain has been washing away their soils for millions of years, the tepuis are among the most nutrient-poor sites in the world. At the same

Fig. 19.
Seepage zone of
an inselberg, Ivory
Coast. R. Seine

Fig. 20.
Utricularia juncea
(detail from Fig. 19).
R. Seine

Fig. 21.
A Brazilian inselberg, the natural habitat of the epiphytic bladderwort *Utricularia nelumbifolia* in the leaf cisterns of the bromeliad *Vriesea pardalina*.
W. Barthlott

Fig. 22. *Utricularia campbelliana*, an epiphytic bladderwort found in the upland rainforests of the Sierra de la Neblina (Venezuela and Brazil).
C. Scherber

time, this entire habitat is covered with huge numbers of individual carnivores. Restricted in their distribution to the high elevations of the tepuis are some species of *Heliamphora* (such as *H. nutans* from Mount Roraima), which grow there in the midst of plant cushions with a continuous supply of runoff.

Steep Mountain Slopes and Cliffs

Rocky sites supplied by runoff water are not just restricted to inselbergs, but are also found on steep mountain slopes and on isolated cliffs. In Europe, particularly in the Mediterranean, and in Japan, such sites are known to be habitats for different *Pinguicula* species. If there is a sufficient water supply, these plants are often found in large numbers, even on very steep slopes (primarily on limestone). Under these site conditions, some *Pinguicula* species (such as *P. longifolia* and *P. vallisneriifolia*) develop leaf rosettes appressed against the rocky substrate, sometimes with long, extended, and spirally twisted leaves that may hang down against the rock walls.

Some *Nepenthes* species show a preference for rocky sites. On the Seychelles Islands, for example, *N. pervillei* grows on granite rock, which can sometimes be completely bare (see Fig. 129). According to Phillipps and Lamb (1996), *N. campanulata* and *N. northiana*, which are endemic to Borneo, are exclusively restricted to steep limestone cliffs.

Laterite Plateaus

In some tropical regions, such as the western African savanna zone and the Western Ghats of India, conspicuous flat laterite plateaus can determine the local landscape character, sometimes extending over an area of several square kilometers. They have a characteristic brownish red coloration, due to an iron laterite crust near the surface. This crust is as hard as concrete and is almost completely impermeable to water. Fine soil is present only in scattered places. During the dry season, these plateaus present a barren picture, dominated by the gray remains of died-off herbaceous plants.

Bare upon first glance, laterite crusts are exposed to extremes of sun and high temperatures and lack any plant growth. During the rainy season, however, these sites are transformed into a true wonderland of flowers. Because precipitation water cannot seep into the ground, the laterite plateaus are constantly covered by runoff water during this time. Aquatic plants (including species of *Aponogeton*) are found in places that are completely inundated by water. Under these conditions, in addition to numerous grasses and sedges, there are typical representatives of low-nutrient habitats, including members of Eriocaulaceae and numerous carnivorous species.

Epiphytic plants are exposed to particular site conditions. The tree crown habitat is characterized by a greater paucity of nutrients and exposure to the sun. Accordingly, the greatest numbers of epiphytes are found in more or less continuously moist tropical montane rainforests that are often enveloped in fog.

Among the latter, mainly terrestrial *Utricularia* species are found in dense stands on laterite plateaus; these include *U. albocaerulea*, *U. lazulina*, and *U. reticulata* (Fig. 24) in the Western Ghats region of the Indian federal states of Maharashtra, Goa, and Karnataka.

Forests

While small and mostly herbaceous carnivorous species are widespread in open forests on sandy soils (savannas), dense forests only rarely provide suitable sites for small carnivorous plants, since here the carnivores are often unable to compete against other plants, such as large, shading trees and giant herbs. Instead, the dominant growth forms of carnivorous plants in forests are epiphytes and lianas.

The hookleaf (*Triphyophyllum peltatum*; see Figs. 60, 61) is found on low-nutrient soils in western African rainforests, in an area extending from the southwest Ivory Coast to Liberia and Sierra Leone. This vine, which is a member of the family Dioncophyllaceae (hookleaf), is the only carnivorous plant found in these forests, where it grows on moist sandy soils in the middle of dense rainforest. *Triphyophyllum peltatum* develops glanduliferous leaves to catch prey, but only during the juvenile stage of its development. The older plants then develop into large woody lianas that ascend into the tree crowns.

Several Asian pitcher plants (*Nepenthes*) are among the few carnivorous plants that grow in forests, sometimes in relatively dense stands. This genus, which is represented by a particularly large number of species in Borneo, grows in rainforests and features several climbers and epiphytes. The pitcher traps of *Nepenthes* are often embedded in leaf litter (such as *N. ampullaria*; see Fig. 136), to which their color is well matched. *Nepenthes* species are particularly widespread in so-called heathland forests

Fig. 23.
A tree trunk covered with numerous epiphytes in the Amazon rainforest of eastern Ecuador.
W. Barthlott

Fig. 24.
Vast stands of the large-flowering, terrestrial bladderwort *Utricularia reticulata* extend as far as the eye can see on a laterite plateau in Karnataka, India. I. Theisen

Fig. 25.
Utricularia humboldtii growing in a leaf cistern of *Brocchinia tatei*. W. Barthlott

(such as *N. sanguinea*, Fig. 142). In these open forests, *Nepenthes* grow on podsolized (acidic and nutrient-poor) sandy soils and can be found along road edges. Due to the widespread deforestation of primary rainforest in Southeast Asia in recent decades, the area of distri-

bution of some *Nepenthes* species in the remaining secondary forests has increased, thanks to the greater availability of open sites.

As in the genus *Nepenthes*, the bladderwort family also includes epiphytic species. *Pinguicula casabitoana* and *P. lignicola* and about fifteen species of *Utricularia*, such as *U. jamesoniana* and *U. campbelliana* (Fig. 22) in Central and South America and *U. mannii* in western Africa, grow in the canopies of tropical forests (Fig. 23). Most of these species grow on cushions of moss or humus that are mainly found in montane or cloud forests at elevations over 500 m above sea level. The butterwort *P. lignicola*, which is endemic to Cuba, is remarkable in that it is confined to pines as the support trees (Fig. 93). Highly specialized bladderworts such as *Utricularia nelumbifolia* or *U. humboldtii* are usually found in the constantly water-filled cisterns of certain bromeliads (including *Brocchinia* and *Vriesea pardalina*; Fig. 25). These species, which grow in Brazil and Venezuela, can spread from one bromeliad to another by aerial runners.

Catopsis berteroniana (Fig. 53), a member of the pineapple family, is found as an obligatory epiphyte over a region that extends from Florida to the Caribbean and Brazil. This carnivorous cistern bromeliad colonizes a wide range of forest types, including mangrove trees (such as *Rhizophora mangle*) right next to the ocean.

Biogeography and Diversity

Biogeography is concerned with the spatial distribution of ecosystems and their associated plant and animal species. Today's distribution patterns are largely the result of the specific climatic requirements of individual species, although they can also have historical origins.

If we compare the areas of distribution of different plant species, we recognize that they do not coincide arbitrarily, but rather in relation to the uniform climatic and edaphic conditions in the regions concerned. The result is that floristic boundaries often coincide with vegetation boundaries, which may be called climate-typical habitats, or zonobiomes (Walter and Breckle 1983).

During the Cretaceous period (144–65 million years B.P.), the southern continents (South America, Africa, and Australia) began to split apart as a result of continental drift, while the land masses of the Northern Hemisphere (America, Eurasia) remained interlocked, with only the shallow and narrow Bering Strait separating them. This global geological development is clearly mirrored in the Earth's classification into six floral kingdoms of terrestrial flora, as opposed to marine flora (Fig. 26). The northernmost and largest floral kingdom, the Holarctic kingdom, covers the arctic to subtropical regions of the entire Northern Hemisphere. The Paleotropical kingdom of the Old

Fig. 26. World map showing the species diversity of vascular plants. The different colors indicate the species numbers per 10,000 square kilometers: the darker the color, the higher the biodiversity. The global biodiversity centers are almost red, and the gray lines delineate the six floral kingdoms. W. Barthlott, G. Kier, H. Kreft, W. Küper, D. Rafiqpoor & J. Mutke 2005 after W. Barthlott, W. Lauer & A. Placke 1996

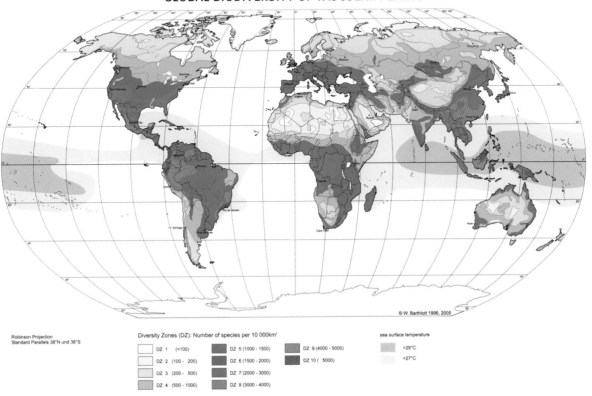

GLOBAL BIODIVERSITY OF VASCULAR PLANTS

© W. Barthlott 1996, 2005

Robinson Projection
Standard Parallels 38°N und 38°S

Diversity Zones (DZ): Number of species per 10 000km²

DZ 1 (<100)	DZ 5 (1000 - 1500)
DZ 2 (100 - 200)	DZ 6 (1500 - 2000)
DZ 3 (200 - 500)	DZ 7 (2000 - 3000)
DZ 4 (500 - 1000)	DZ 8 (3000 - 4000)

DZ 9 (4000 - 5000)
DZ 10 (5000)

sea surface temperature
>29°C
>27°C

World and the Neotropical kingdom of the New World cover the tropics. The three floral kingdoms in the Southern Hemisphere are the Cape kingdom at the southernmost tip of Africa; the Australian kingdom, which largely coincides with the Australian continent; and the Antarctic kingdom, which also includes the southernmost tip of South America and New Zealand's South Island.

If we examine the classification of floral kingdoms, we can characterize the individual continents in terms of their carnivorous plants—excluding Antarctica, which is largely ice-covered and characterized by a rich moss and lichen flora only in isolated places.

Europe

The continent of Europe, from a global geographic perspective, is merely the westernmost tip of a Eurasian continental plate. It is characterized by Holarctic floral elements, such as forests of beech (*Fagus*), birch (*Betula*), and willow (*Salix*). Europe is also distinguished by four large vegetation zones, or zonobiomes: tundra, boreal coniferous forests, deciduous hardwood forests, and sclerophyllous vegetation of the Mediterranean.

There are only a few carnivorous plants to be found in the treeless tundra of Lapland and Iceland, which has a flora of few species and is typified by dwarf shrubs (such as plants of the heather family, Ericaceae). Nor are there many carnivores in the uniform, boreal coniferous forests (*taiga*) of Norway, Sweden, and Finland. There are only seven species in the European tundra and taiga, belonging to three genera: *Pinguicula* (*P. alpina* and *P. villosa*), *Utricularia* (*U. intermedia*, *U. minor*, and *U. stygia*), and *Drosera* (*D. anglica* and *D. rotundifolia*), all of which are also found in the Holarctic parts of Asia and the Americas.

Characteristic elements of the deciduous

forests predominate in the temperate, oceanic regions of Europe, namely the beeches (*Fagus*), oaks (*Quercus*), lindens (*Tilia*), maples (*Acer*), and pines (*Pinus*). Special edaphic sites in this zone feature a greater proportion of carnivorous species (twenty-five species, especially those of the genus *Pinguicula*). Such sites include the mountain ranges (Pyrenees, Alps, and Carpathians) and their forelands, with their many bog and rocky sites that are poor in nutrients.

The Mediterranean, which includes northern Africa, is rich in species, including endemics (species that are found only in that region). The region and is typified by evergreen sclerophyllous vegetation and winter rains. The sclerophyllous vegetation includes oak and pine forests and olive groves. There are relatively few carnivorous plants in this zone (twenty species of the genera *Pinguicula*, *Utricularia*, and *Drosera*). Here, we should make special mention of the Portuguese sundew (*Drosophyllum*), which is the sole genus of the monotypic Drosophyllaceae and grows exclusively along the western margins of the Mediterranean (Spain, Portugal, and Morocco).

Asia

As in the arctic tundra and boreal coniferous forests of Europe, which are characterized by a paucity of species, there are only a few carnivorous plants in the Asian part of the Holarctic floral kingdom (Siberia). In addition to the seven European species, there is *Pinguicula algida*, which is endemic to Siberia. As might be expected, there are no known carnivorous plants in the temperate dry deserts of central Asia (the Takla-Makan and Gobi Deserts) or the winter-cold grass steppes of Kazakhstan and Mongolia.

As with the western continental margins, the far-eastern regions (China, Japan, and Korea) are also characterized by deciduous hardwood forests, with a transition to moist ever-green forests at their southern boundaries. These regions are home to many species that are found in Europe as fossils and that are now planted as decorative trees, such as magnolias, rhododendrons, azaleas, Chinese windmill palms (*Trachycarpus*), camphor trees (*Cinnamomum*), *Ginkgo*, *Hamamelis*, and oranges and lemons (*Citrus*). Carnivorous plants are relatively well represented (forty-two species, with seven endemic species, including *Pinguicula ramosa*, *Utricularia brachiata*, *U. dimorphantha*, *U. kumaonensis*, and *U. peranomala*).

By crossing the Asian boundary of the northern Holarctic floral kingdom, we arrive somewhat south of a line passing through Saudi Arabia, Iraq, the Himalayas, and Taiwan in the Paleotropical floral kingdom, which is subdivided into the Polynesian, Indo-Malaysian, and African floral subkingdoms (Fig. 26). With decreasing levels of precipitation—corresponding to their increasing continentality—these zonobiomes are typified by rain-green monsoon forests and dry forests or savannas. The monsoon and dry forests include the Dipterocarpaceae forests from India to Indochina, with decorative timbers such as *Shorea robusta* (Asian mahogany), *Tectona grandis* (teak, Verbenaceae), and *Terminalia* (Combretaceae). In all, there are about fifty different carnivorous species in the Indian and Indochina regions (mostly *Utricularia* and *Drosera*), fifteen of which are confined to India and Sri Lanka (*Nepenthes distillatoria*, *N. khasiana*, *Utricularia albocaerulea*, *U. arcuata*, *U. cecilii*, *U. furcellata*, *U. lazulina*, *U. malabarica*, *U. polygaloides*, *U. praeterita*, *U. reticulata*, *U. smithiana*, *U. subramanyamii*, and *U. wightiana*). There are still extensive areas of rainforest in the central zone of Paleotropical Asia, which includes Indonesia, Malaysia, Papua–New Guinea, and the Philippines. This zone is also home to the Asian pitcher plants (*Nepenthes*), with a total of 108 species. In addition, there are thirty-three other carnivorous plant species found here (especially *Utricularia*).

Africa

The Sahara Desert divides the African continent into two floral kingdoms. The northern margin, influenced by its Mediterranean climate, belongs to the Holarctic kingdom; the coastal areas of northern Morocco, together with Spain and Portugal, are home to the Portuguese sundew (*Drosophyllum lusitanicum*). By contrast, the southern part of the continent is part of the Paleotropical kingdom. In the extensive dry forests and savannas of the Sudano-Zambesian region (including the Sahel zone, Ethiopia, Kenya, Tanzania, and Zambia), there are relatively large numbers of carnivorous species: a total of forty-nine species, including seven species of *Genlisea*, twenty-two species of *Drosera*, and twenty species of *Utricularia*.

At special edaphic sites (such as bogs, inland waters, inselbergs) in the western and central African tropical rainforest of the Guinea-Congolian region, there are some forty-five native carnivorous plants (five species of *Genlisea*, twenty-seven species of *Utricularia*, and twelve species of *Drosera*). The presence of the hookleaf (*Triphyophyllum peltatum*) in the undergrowth of the rainforests of the Ivory Coast, Liberia, and Sierra Leone is also quite remarkable. This endemic plant is a vine that is carnivorous only in its juvenile stage.

Madagascar, which from a floristic perspective is closely aligned with the African continent, is home to around twenty-five carnivores: seventeen species of *Utricularia*, five species of *Drosera* (*D. burkeana*, *D. humbertii*, *D. indica*, *D. madagascariensis*, and *D. natalensis*), *Genlisea margaretae*, and two endemic *Nepenthes* species (*N. madagascariensis* and *N. masoalensis*).

The Cape region represents an independent floral kingdom (the Cape kingdom) in the southwest of South Africa and is typified by sclerophyllous vegetation. This smallest of the floral kingdoms, covering an area of about 93,000 square kilometers, features an extraordinarily large number of species (more than 8500), some 80 percent of which are endemic. In view of the Cape kingdom's small area, there are relatively many carnivorous plant species, twenty-one in all. These include five species of *Utricularia*, fourteen species of *Drosera* (such as *D. regia*), and two species of an endemic family, the Roridulaceae, *Roridula dentata* and *R. gorgonias*.

Australia

With its highly contrasting vegetation zones, Australia is especially rich in species, with about 140 carnivores, including one endemic genus (*Cephalotus*). *Bybis*, the rainbow plant, which is commonly also considered to be endemic to Australia, spreads into neighboring Indonesia with one species (*B. liniflora*).

Conspicuously large numbers of carnivorous plants grow in the winter-rain sclerophyllous vegetation in southwestern Australia. In the Perth region in particular, there are some eighty-six taxa, seventy-five of which are exclusive to this region. This is the only place where the West Australian pitcher plant (*Cephalotus follicularis*) grows naturally, and eleven *Utricularia* species are also endemic to the region. For example, the primitive, terrestrial bladderworts of the taxonomic section *Polypompholyx* are found only here. Sixty-three of the sixty-nine *Drosera* species that are found here, in particular the dwarf sundews, make up the largest proportion of the endemic species.

In the northwest, especially in the Kimberleys and in Arnhem Land, there are another twelve bladderwort species. Here in the north of the country, the genus *Byblis* is represented by four species. Only *B. gigantea* and *B. lamel-*

lata are restricted to the southwest (Perth region). There are another thirty carnivorous species in Queensland, in Australia's northeast. Here, in the dominant tropical rainforest, *Nepenthes mirabilis* and *N. tenax* have spread to Queensland from the Malaysian–Asian region, together with *Utricularia* (eighteen species), *Drosera* (ten species), and *Byblis liniflora*.

For further reading, Lowrie (1998a) gives a very good overview of the carnivorous plants of Australia.

The Americas

As in the Eurasian tundra and taiga, there are only a few carnivorous plant species to be found in North America's Artic-boreal zone (Canada), with eleven in total: *Pinguicula macroceras*, *P. villosa*, *Drosera anglica*, *D. intermedia*, *D. linearis*, *D. rotundifolia*, four species of *Utricularia*, and *Sarracenia purpurea*. Of these, all of which also grow in Eurasia, only *S. purpurea* was originally restricted to North America. Today, this species is also found in Europe, where it has become naturalized in Germany and Switzerland, for example.

The deciduous hardwood forests along the eastern coast of the United States, together with the extensive grassland prairies of the Midwest, are home to about nineteen carnivorous species (*Sarracenia*, *Drosera*, *Pinguicula*, and *Utricularia*).

The coastal lowlands bordering the Atlantic and the Gulf of Mexico (North Carolina, South Carolina, Georgia, Florida, Alabama, Louisiana, and Texas) have a much greater abundance of species. Thirty-three carnivorous species are found in this zone (all eight species of *Sarracenia*, ten species of *Drosera*, ten species of *Utricularia*, four species of *Pinguicula*, and *Dionaea muscipula*.)

The temperate coastal rainforests of Oregon and northern California, with their characteristic giant redwoods (*Sequoia sempervirens*), are home to *Darlingtonia californica* (the cobra lily), and another eight carnivorous species (*Drosera* and *Utricularia*).

To learn more about the carnivores in the United States and Canada, the excellent monograph by Schnell (2002) gives detailed descriptions and distributional ranges of the carnivorous plants of the region.

The Mexican highlands, with their typical sclerophyllous vegetation and open oak forests, are the center of diversity for species of *Pinguicula* (forty-five species, including forty-two endemics). In addition, there are seven more carnivores in this region, *Utricularia gibba*, the endemic *U. hintonii*, *U. livida*, *U. macrorhiza*, *U. perversa*, *U. petersoniae*, and *Genlisea filiformis*, spreading northward from South America.

There are about fifty-five carnivorous species distributed throughout the tropical rainforests of Central America and the islands of the Caribbean: three species of *Drosera* (*D. brevifolia*, *D. capillaris*, and *D. panamensis*), thirty-six species of *Utricularia*, one species of *Genlisea* (*G. filiformis*), and fourteen species of *Pinguicula*. Two of the *Pinguicula* species (*P. casabitoana* and *P. lignicola*) grow in Cuba and in the Dominican Republic as epiphytes on pine trees.

In the tropical evergreen lowland rainforests of South America (the Amazon) and on the neighboring Guiana plateau there are numerous carnivores on special edaphic sites (fifty-eight species, including four species of *Drosera*, thirty-seven species of *Utricularia*, and six species of *Genlisea*). The most remarkable of these are the South American pitcher plants (*Heliamphora*, represented by eleven species) with their pitfall traps, and *Brocchinia reducta* (Bromeliaceae), whose distribution is restricted to the *tepuis* and Gran Sabana.

There are far fewer carnivores in the Atlantic coastal rainforests, the Mata Atlantica, in southeastern Brazil. Here, twenty-eight species are divided among the genera *Genlisea* (eight

species), *Utricularia* (fourteen species), and *Drosera* (six species).

The central highlands of Brazil, with their dry forests (*campo rupestre*) and savannas (*caatinga*), are rich in carnivores, with fifty-six species (four species of *Genlisea*, twenty-two species of *Utricularia*, and thirty species of *Drosera*). Especially on the low-nutrient quartz sand areas in Minas Gerais, there are numerous endemic species to be found, including *Drosera chrysolepis*, *D. graminifolia*, *D. graomogolensis*, *D. hirtella*, *Utricularia biovularia*, *U. blanchetii*, *U. flaccida*, *U. huntii*, and *U. laciniata*.

In the mountain rainforests of the northern and central Andes, there are twenty-five additional species (three species of *Drosera*, five species of *Pinguicula*, and seventeen species of *Utricularia*). Along these cordilleras, *Pinguicula antarctica* extends into the forest-free grassland zone (*páramo*), right down to the southern tip of South America to Patagonia and Tierra del Fuego, areas that form part of the Antarctic floral kingdom.

Centers of Diversity of Carnivorous Plant Species

The diversity of vascular plants is very unevenly distributed across the globe. In general, biodiversity tends to increase from the poles to the equator and from the dry to moist and the cold to warm regions, respectively. The same phenomenon of increased species numbers is also apparent when sites with uniform environmental factors are compared with large areas that feature a wide diversity of biotopes and habitats. In a map of the global distribution of vascular plant diversity (Fig. 26; Barthlott et al. 2005), the five most species-rich regions are located in the mountainous areas within humid tropics (montane rainforests), from Costa Rica to Ecuador (Chocó), the tropical eastern slopes of the Andes, Bra-

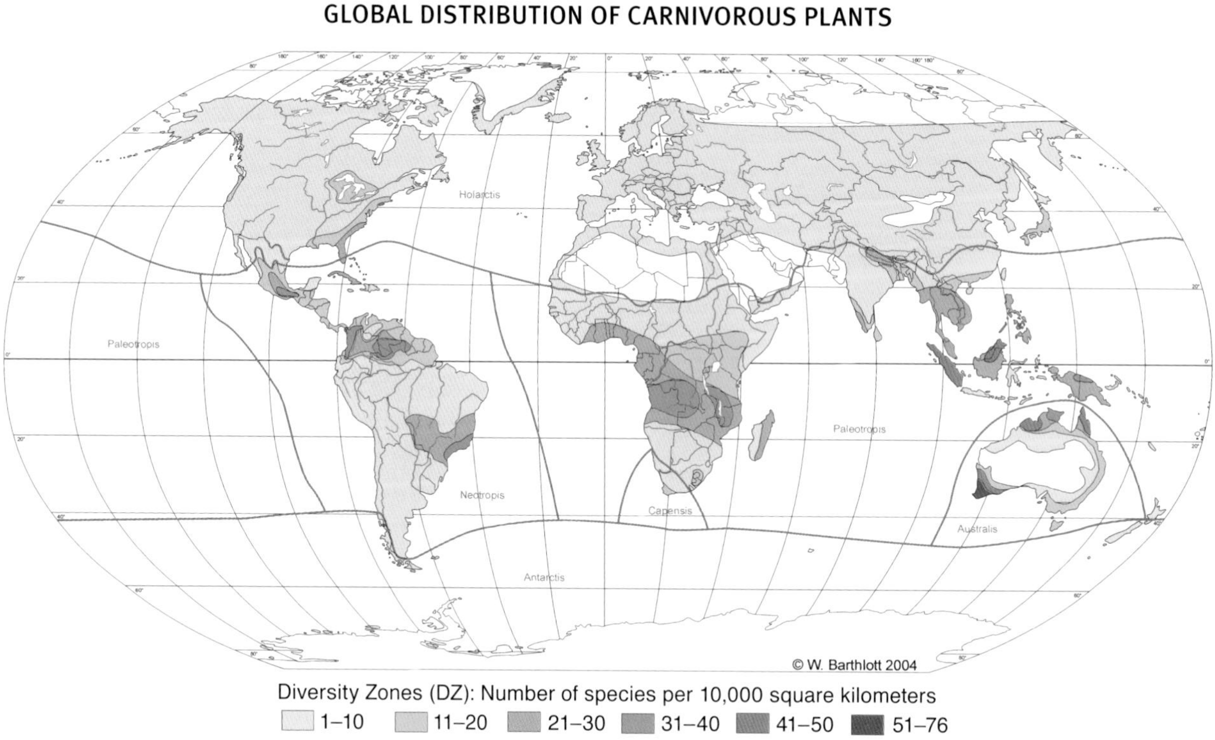

GLOBAL DISTRIBUTION OF CARNIVOROUS PLANTS

Diversity Zones (DZ): Number of species per 10,000 square kilometers

░ 1–10   ▒ 11–20   ▓ 21–30   ▓ 31–40   ▓ 41–50   ▓ 51–76

Fig. 27.
World map of
the diversity
of carnivorous
plants. W. Barthlott

zil's Mata Atlantica, northern Borneo, and New Guinea.

Often, the diversity of a region is expressed in terms of the number of species that are found there. The higher the total species number, including the number of endemic species, the greater the region's importance in terms of necessary nature conservation measures, such as demarcation of nature reserves.

This principle can be carried over to the value of plant groups. Among the carnivorous plants, in addition to families such as Droseraceae and Lentibulariaceae, which have a worldwide distribution, there are several families that have small areas of distribution, such as Cephalotaceae and Drosophyllaceae. A similar situation is found at the generic level: *Drosera* and *Utricularia* have wide distributions, for example, whereas *Dionaea* and *Heliamphora* have locally restricted distributions. At the level of the species, many fewer carnivores have a distribution that spans several continents as com-

pared to those that have a very narrow distribution. Among the carnivores, *Utricularia subulata* is the species with the widest distribution, occurring in the subtropical to tropical regions on all continents.

Carnivorous plants have a worldwide distribution (see Schlauer 2000). On the basis of available data, we have prepared a provisional world map showing the species numbers of carnivorous plants (Fig. 27). Regions of global significance for their richness of species and endemics are the Malaysian floral region (141 species), the southwestern Australian floral region (86 species), the Brazilian floral region (65 species), the Venezuelan-Guianian floral region (58 species), the Mexican floral region (54 species), the Indian floral region (50 species), the Sudano-Zambesian floral region (49 species), the southeastern North American floral region (33 species), the Cape floral kingdom (21 species), and the Mediterranean floral region (20 species).

Attracting and Trapping Mechanisms

Carnivorous plants have evolved often highly specialized traps with which to catch their prey. Before the actual trap mechanism can be effective, however, the prey must first be drawn near it. Carnivorous plants attract or lure their prey in many different ways. In addition to chemical attractants, the often-conspicuous trap coloration is an important means of attracting prey from a distance.

The trap coloration gives rise to the widely held misconception that the trapping organs of carnivorous plants are flowers. In fact, leaf organs alone are responsible for catching the prey. A little thought makes it clear that carnivorous flowers would not be very sensible. If the flowers were to trap and kill their visitors, the flowers themselves would not be pollinated, and the plant could not reproduce by seeding. There are indeed flowers in the plant kingdom that trap their visitors briefly, but the animals are released again after a certain time so that they can transfer the pollen to other plants and thus fulfill their role as pollinators.

Attracting Mechanisms

In carnivory, attracting mechanisms play a crucial role, luring potential prey animals into the danger zone, where they are caught in the trap systems. Carnivorous plants have developed a range of optical, tactile, and olfactory attracting strategies for this purpose. Nectar droplets are often secreted onto the traps and offered up to the potential prey, a strategy showing marked parallels to the mechanisms that plants employ for attracting pollinators.

This is a problem that has forced carnivorous plants to have their flowers on top of long stalks, as far away as possible from the deadly trap systems.

Attraction by Optical Signals

In a great many carnivorous plants, especially in many members of the American pitcher plant family (Sarraceniaceae), pitfall traps have conspicuous color patterns (see *Sarracenia leucophylla* in Fig. 153). The substances responsible for these colors include naphthochinons, flavonoids, and anthocyans, which to human eyes make the traps appear yellow, red, or purple, respectively. These attractive decoy "flowers" successfully lure large numbers of insects to the trap. Reddish-striped patterns lead the victim directly to what appears to be a source of nectar at the trap rim. Some *Sarracenia* and *Darlingtonia* species (Fig. 146) also have transparent, windowlike flecks (light windows or fenestrations) in the trap roof or lid that appear to show entrapped victims an escape route. After countless unsuccessful attempts at trying to escape through the impassable windows, the exhausted insects finally fall into the trap and drown, as, for example, in *Sarracenia flava* (Figs. 28–31). These deadly traps, which in their form, coloration, and even nectar production mimic the signaling mechanisms of flowers, invite comparison with the attack mimicry of certain tropical praying mantises that look like flowers (Barthlott 1992).

As with some flowers, the trap systems of many carnivorous plants exhibit ultraviolet

Figs. 28–31.
Attraction and
capture of a wasp
by *Sarracenia flava*.
Attracted by the
flowerlike appear-
ance and the pitfall
trap's nectar supply
(Fig. 28), the wasp
lands on the tubular
leaf (Fig. 29). Once
on the slick inner
side below the trap
rim (Fig. 30), the
victim loses its
footing and slides
down to its death
(Fig. 31). W. Barthlott

coloration patterns. Insects are able to perceive wavelengths that are in a short-wave
band, invisible to the human eye (Menzel
1979). Many insects, such as hymenopterans,
can therefore distinguish between three color
classes: yellow (500–650 nm), blue (410–480
nm), and ultraviolet (300–390 nm). Other insects, however, are unable to distinguish between these three colors and can differentiate
only between gradations of light and dark.
Different kinds of ultraviolet patterns in trap
systems also seem to attract different insects
(Joel et al. 1985; Glossner 1992). For example,
Drosophyllum lusitanicum attracts its prey with
a pronounced ultraviolet contrast effect. The
lower, died-off leaves further down the shoot
form a background that reflects ultraviolet
light, against which the live, gland-bearing
(glanduliferous) leaves appear dark, as if in

silhouette, since they absorb ultraviolet light.
The traps of the Venus flytrap (*Dionaea muscipula*) also have a marked ultraviolet pattern.
The peripheral margins of the two leaf halves
(between the leaf margin with its guard hairs
and the inner glandular zone) absorb ultraviolet light, and therefore appear darker than the
central digestive zone.

Attraction by Chemical Signals

Carnivorous plants also employ olfactory stimuli to attract insects. Whereas insects must
first learn reactions to optical signals, olfactory scents are targeted directly at the insects'
instinctive behavior. Because many insects
have a particularly well-developed sense of
smell, scents, rather than optical signals, are
employed for attracting insects from afar. In

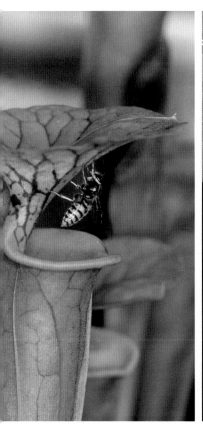
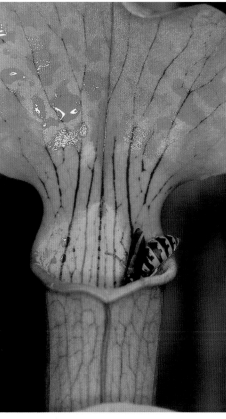
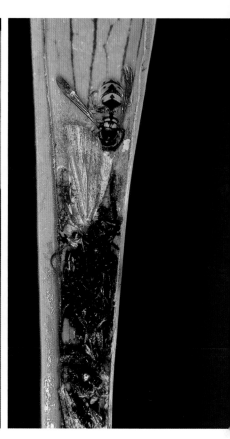

their search for nectar as a nutrient source, insects are attracted to a scent's source over very long distances.

The most common chemical signal for attracting prey animals is nectar, whose source is situated right next to the danger zone of the trap systems. For example, there are many nectar glands at the rims of the pitfall traps of *Nepenthes* that emit a sweet scent. The nectary density is much greater at the peristome (pitcher rim) of *Nepenthes* than in the trap interiors, which means that the animals are encouraged to linger exactly where it is most dangerous for them to be. *Heliamphora*, however, secretes nectar only on its spoonlike rudimentary lid projection.

Our own research on the attracting strategies of carnivorous plants with snare traps (*Genlisea*) and suction traps (*Utricularia*) has

indicated the presence of soluble attractants, which these plants use to attract unicellular animals (protozoans), particularly slipper animalcules (ciliates; see Figs. 36, 37).

Nepenthes albomarginata employs a combination of chemical and tactile signals in which a white ring consisting of protein-rich hairs beneath the pitcher rim attracts termites searching for food (Merbach et al. 2002).

Other Attracting Mechanisms

The filamentous, branched shoots and leaves of aquatic bladderworts are similar to algal threads and serve as a habitat for the growth of sessile microorganisms, such as diatoms and bacteria. In turn, these supposed algal threads attract small crustaceans, which feed on these sessile microorganisms in their search for nutrients. Thus, the crustaceans are systematically led to the entrance of the suction traps, a form of indirect attraction.

In addition, there are quite inconspicuous carnivorous plants whose color or morphology is adapted to match their surroundings (absence of attraction). Such an imitation of the surroundings is a special form of mimicry, called *mimesis*. In the Australian pitcher plant (*Cephalotus follicularis*), the traps are flush with the ground or often embedded in the substrate. Their color is virtually indistinguishable from the surrounding moss or herb layers, which means that only experienced observers can locate them. Small crawling insects, such as ants or beetles, blunder into the camouflaged traps and fall to their doom.

By definition, the capture of plant materials also does not involve any kind of attraction strategy, such as the accumulation of pollen on the sticky leaves of *Pinguicula* or the intake of algae in the bladders of aquatic bladderworts. In terms of its nutrient value, however, the importance of this vegetative material should not be underestimated. In *Pinguicula vulgaris*, for example, Harder and Zemlin (1968) demonstrated that more than 50 percent of the metabolized proteins originate from pollen grains. In *Utricularia australis*, Mette et al. (2000) observed a high proportion of trapped algae (more than 80 percent) in the prey spectrum.

Trapping Mechanisms

In all carnivorous plants, it is the leaf organs that are responsible for trapping the prey. The traps can be classified into five types according to their functional principle: pitfall traps, adhesive traps, snap traps, snare traps, and suction traps. In addition to this function-based classification, it is also possible to make a distinction between active and passive traps. Active traps are those in which there is an actual trapping movement in capturing the prey. Passive traps, by contrast, do not move at all. As their names imply, snap and suction traps are active traps, whereas pitfall and snare traps are passive. Adhesive traps include both active and passive forms.

Pitfall Traps

Pitfall traps are passive systems in which single leaves or leaf rosettes are transformed into tubular or pitcher-shaped traps. The attraction is mostly the result of the flowerlike appearance of the traps, in which the red, white, or yellow color of the trap leaf, particularly of the pitcher rim, accentuates the optical signal effect. The production of nectar at the pitcher rim makes the flower decoy perfect and sure to attract prey. Below the pitcher or pit rim on the inside of the trap, there is a very slick surface on which the prey animals lose their footing and slide down into the trap base. Escape from the pitcher, which is filled with digestive fluid, is impossible, because complex surface structures, such as microscopically small wax crystalloids and/or hairs that are directed downward into the trap interior, prevent this. This type of trap is found in the Nepenthaceae, Sarraceniaceae (*Heliamphora*, *Darlingtonia*, and *Sarracenia*), Cephalotaceae, and the Bromeliaceae (*Catopsis* and *Brocchinia*).

Adhesive Traps

Sundews (*Drosera*) and butterworts (*Pinguicula*) have adhesive traps, in which the leaf surfaces are covered with numerous stalked glands. The knobs of these glandular tips, which look like dewdrops glistening in the sunlight, are covered with sticky slime or muci lage. The glandular tips are always on the end of stalks, and the stalks may consist of either a single cell (*Byblis* and *Pinguicula*) or several cells (*Drosophyllum*, *Drosera*, and *Triphyophyllum*). Some sundews (*Drosera*) have especially long-stalked glands, known as *tentacles*.

The functional principle of these traps is very simple. Insects are attracted both by the optical stimulus of what appears to be a nectar droplet and by the sweet scent of the secretion. Smaller insects that land on the secreted drops of mucilage are immobilized immediately. In an attempt to escape, larger insects that are not immobilized immediately drag themselves past several secreted drops, becoming more and more entrapped in the process.

Among the adhesive traps, it is possible to distinguish between active types (stalked glands capable of motion) and passive types (immobile stalked glands). The former are capable of moving their glandular stalks or even the entire leaf surface—the glands actively bend toward the victim. In addition, the animal is rolled up by the entire leaf blade, so that it is ultimately completely enveloped in glandular knobs (Figs. 32–34). The killing of the prey insect is indirect: when its respiratory openings (spiracles) become blocked by the sticky mucilage, it suffocates. The chemical composition of the secreted mucilage is largely a watery solution of acidic polysaccharides: gluconic acids, galactose, xylose, and aribinose.

Adhesive traps are found in the Byblidaceae, Drosophyllaceae, Droseraceae (*Drosera*), Dioncophyllaceae (*Triphyophyllum*), Lentibulariaceae (*Pinguicula*), and Roridulaceae.

Snap Traps

In carnivorous plants that catch their prey with closing traps, the leaf blade (lamina) has been modified into a gin-trap that snaps shut over the midrib. Special morphological and physiological adaptations make the lightning-quick reaction of this closing mechanism possible. (For a detailed description of the closing mechanism, refer to p. 115. Each half of the lamina of these traps is equipped with trigger hairs that, upon contact, can convert mechanical stimuli into electrophysiological impulses. As in human nerve cells, the trap system reacts by initially establishing an action potential. In detailed examinations of the Venus flytrap (*Dionaea muscipula*), conductions of stimuli of about 17 cm/s were measured (Hodick and Sievers 1988). Once the prey has been captured, the numerous glands on the leaf upperside secrete a digestive fluid, and the animal protein is resorbed (Figs. 82, 83). The only representatives of this trap type are the Venus flytrap (*Dionaea muscipula*) and the waterwheel plant (*Aldrovanda vesiculosa*), both members of the sundew family (Droseraceae).

Snare Traps

Snare traps are found on the subterranean leaves of members of the genus *Genlisea* (Figs. 104–107). In contrast to the aerial, green leaf organs described above, these leaves contain no chlorophyll, which means that they are often mistaken for roots. The two free projections of the forked, Y-shaped leaves are twisted like a corkscrew and end in a bladderlike extension near the point of attachment to the leaf. For a long time, this trapping mechanism could not be explained. It was only a few years ago that it was possible to demonstrate that the fine tubes of the snare traps are specialized for catching unicellular soil organisms, which they attract by chemical means (Barthlott et al. 1998). Protozoans and ciliates enter the snare traps through the opening slits of the tubular projections. Unidirectional hairs obstruct the

Figs. 32–34.
Capture of a blowfly
by *Drosera capensis*.
The movement over
time of the ensnaring
tentacles of this
active trap is clearly
recognizable in this
picture sequence.

Fig. 32.
Ten minutes after
capture. W. Barthlott

way back, with the result that the prey animals are effectively directed along a one-way system toward the digestive bladder.

A combination of snare and pitfall traps is found in *Sarracenia psittacina*. Similar to other North American pitcher plants, prey are attracted by a sweet scent at the pitcher rim and the capture results from the animals losing their footing on the slick funnel entrance. The normally upright tubular leaves, however, lie horizontal and flat on the ground (decumbent) in *S. psittacina*. The entrance features a collar protruding inside the trap, thus creating a

lobster-pot effect (Schnell 2002). Inside the pitcher, unidirectional hairs force insects caught in the narrow tubular leaf along toward the far end, from which they can no longer escape.

Suction Traps

Suction traps are typical of bladderworts (*Utricularia*). This type of trap is a hollow, bladderlike structure, closed by a valvelike trapdoor that opens only inwardly. The negative hydrostatic pressure that is generated

causes the chamber walls to cave inward when the trap is set. If a prey animal in the water brushes against the bristles at the trap entrance, the door instantly swings inward. The caved-in bladder walls then relax and pop open again, creating a suction effect that flushes the victim with the water into the trap interior. The door then immediately returns to its original position and seals the trap shut again. In addition, glands secrete slime droplets to seal the opening.

The door opens and closes in less than $\frac{1}{500}$ of a second, which is one of the quickest move-ments known in the entire plant kingdom (Sydenham and Findlay 1973). To reset the trap so that it can trap prey again, water is excreted by osmosis from the trap interior to the outside. In this process, ion pumps build up a concentration gradient by the active transport of chloride ions, allowing the water passively to pass through the glands and the pavement epithelium at the trap margin (Sydenham and Findlay 1975; Sasago and Sibaoka 1985a, 1985b). Even today, the mechanism of these traps is not yet fully understood.

Fig. 33, left:
Three hours later.
W. Barthlott

Fig. 34, above:
About 24 hours later.
W. Barthlott

Digestion of Prey and Nutrient Uptake

After the prey has been caught, the nutrients contained in the prey animals must be converted into a usable form for the plant. Because these nutrients are generally present as large, complex molecules, they need to be digested, that is, broken down into smaller molecules that the plant can then absorb and use.

Nutritional Value of Prey

Plants need a range of nutrients and minerals for healthy growth, which is why fertilizers are regularly used in agriculture and private gardens alike to ensure that all the necessary minerals are available in the soil in sufficient quantities. As noted in the chapter on habitats, at least some of the required nutrients are lacking in sufficient quantities at the sites where carnivorous plants grow.

Animals, however, contain large quantities of most of the nutrients that plants need. The proportions of six of the most important nutrients in dried insects are 10.5 percent nitrogen, 3.2 percent potassium, 2.3 percent calcium, 0.6 percent phosphorous, 0.09 percent magnesium, and 0.02 percent iron (Reichle et al. 1969). The importance of these elements derived from the carnivorous plants' prey is well established (Adamec 1997) and will be examined in more detail in this chapter.

Carnivores never absorb from their prey all the nutrients that are available. Although the prey animals contain calcium, magnesium, and potassium, in addition to nitrogen and phosphorous, *Sarracenia* plants absorb only the latter two elements in significant quantities (Christensen 1976). Other studies have shown that *Utricularia* and *Triphyophyllum* resorb magnesium and potassium from their prey (Sorrenson and Jackson 1968; Green et al. 1979). Hanslin and Karlsson (1996) examined the uptake of the nitrogen in the prey at the carnivores' natural growth sites and found that *Drosera rotundifolia* uses 35 percent of the nitrogen content, *Pinguicula alpina* 29 percent, and *Pinguicula villosa* 30 percent; the corresponding figure for *Drosera erythrorhiza* is 76 percent (Dixon et al. 1980).

The proportion of nitrogen from prey animals found in carnivorous plants (expressed as a percentage of total nitrogen) very much depends on the species. Schulze et al. (1997) found approximately 60 percent of animal nitrogen in *Nepenthes mirabilis* and as much as 75 percent in *Darlingtonia californica*, but only 25 percent in *Cephalotus follicularis*. In different growth forms of *Drosera* species, Schulze et al. (1991) also found variable quantities of animal nitrogen as a proportion of the plant's total nitrogen content. In sundews with a rosette form, the proportion of nitrogen from the prey was about 20 percent, whereas in climbing or erect sundews the corresponding figure was about 50 percent. About 75 percent of the nitrogen in *Utricularia* comes from prey animals (Knight 1992).

In addition to mineral components, prey animals also contain chemically bonded energy. Animal predators depend on the caloric value of their prey for their metabolism and are therefore heterotrophic. As a rule, plants are autotrophic, meaning they obtain their energy from sunlight. Through photosynthesis, plants use the sunlight to produce carbohydrates as chemical energy carriers. What, then, is the relationship between heterotrophy and autotrophy in carnivorous plants, which both use their prey as an energy source and photosynthesize?

All carnivores contain chlorophyll, which is necessary for photosynthesis. Most carnivorous plants have large leaf areas that are devoted to this purpose. They need a brightly lit site in order to thrive, and their growth becomes stunted if they do not receive enough light. Thus, on first glance it appears that carnivores lead a "normal," energy-independent, autotrophic mode of life, as is typical for plants.

Among the bladderworts, however, there are terrestrial species that have only a very small green leaf area, with relatively large inflorescences and pale, underground shoot systems. This would seem to indicate that at least some of the energy supply comes from the caloric value of the animal prey. Cultivation trials with *Utricularia* on a carbohydrate-rich medium have shown definite growth even in complete darkness, along with an increase in

weight (Harder 1970). These results support the assumption that the plants are heterotrophic at least to a degree (see the chapter on the evolution of carnivory). Further research is currently proceeding on these aspects and will ultimately give us a better understanding of carnivorous plants in the years to come.

Digestive Enzymes

The prey of carnivorous plants is digested with the help of enzymes. Enzymes initiate a chemical reaction on other molecules, the substrate, without being altered themselves. In doing so, each enzyme can elicit only one particular reaction from one particular type of molecule; in other words, the enzyme is substrate-specific. Consequently, different enzymes are required for different substrates. Thus, for the digestion of prey by carnivorous plants, a large number of enzymes would be required to digest the prey completely. In reality, however, the plants generally produce only a few enzymes for digesting the most profitable nutrients.

The breakdown of nutrient substances has been demonstrated in the traps of all carnivores (Juniper et al. 1989). However, our knowledge of the plants' enzyme production is still unsatisfactory. Often, enzymes in the traps are also produced by other organisms that live on the plant, such as bacteria and fungi. The enzymes produced vary greatly from one genus to another, and, to a lesser extent, among the species of a genus. Table 1 gives an overview of the distribution of the most frequent enzymes across the carnivorous genera.

Table 1. Production of digestive enzymes in carnivorous plants.

(adapted from Juniper et al. 1989).

Enzyme	*Brocchinia*	*Byblis*	*Catopsis*	*Cephalotus*	*Darlingtonia*	*Dionaea*	*Drosera*	*Drosophyllum*	*Genlisea*	*Heliamphora*	*Nepenthes*	*Pinguicula*	*Roridula*	*Sarracenia*	*Triphyophyllum*	*Utricularia*
Amylase					+	+					+	+		+		
Chitinase						+	+				+					
Esterase				+		+	+	+	+		+	+		+	+	+
Lipase											+			+		
Peroxidase							+	+			+					
Phosphatase	+	+		+		+	+	+	+		+	+	+	+	+	+
Protease		+		+		+	+	+	+		+	+		+	+	+
Ribonuclease						+	+				+	+				

Digestive Glands

The enzymes of carnivorous plants are produced in special organs, the digestive glands. Depending on where they are located, these glands can be classified into three groups:

Stalked glands These are perched on top of a carrier structure, clearly above the trap surface. Stalked glands are found in the genera *Byblis*, *Drosera*, *Drosophyllum*, *Pinguicula*, and *Triphyophyllum*.

Sessile glands These are either flush with the trap surface or protrude above it only slightly. Sessile glands are found in the genera *Aldrovanda*, *Byblis*, *Dionaea*, *Drosophyllum*, *Genlisea*, *Nepenthes*, *Pinguicula*, *Triphyophyllum*, and *Utricularia*.

Sunken glands These are composed of glandular tissue embedded in the plant tissue beneath the trap epidermis. Sunken glands are found only in the genera *Cephalotus*, *Darlingtonia*, and *Sarracenia*.

The digestive glands not only produce enzymes, but are also the sites of sensory activity and nutrient uptake. Juniper et al. (1989) examined the enzyme-production, sensory, and nutrient-uptake functions of carnivores' digestive glands and reported the following requirements. For detection of a chemical stimulus, a receptor that can register an extremely small amount of the triggering substance is required for the uptake of the stimulus. For the receptor to be triggered quickly, the access to the receptor needs to be short and permeable. The production of digestive enzymes requires a large surface area that does not hinder the rapid discharge of enzymes, while preventing a backflow of the enzymes into the plant. The gland must produce the enzymes itself. It must be possible for the enzymes to be actively secreted against a concentration gradient, so that the required high enzyme concentration is attained in the external medium. The absorption of the dissolved nutrient components requires a large surface area and an active, selective transport mechanism. Finally, the nutrients must be transported away from the trap to prevent an excessive nutrient concentration in the interior of the uptake structure.

In spite of the many tasks of the digestive glands and their diversity of forms, certain structural characteristics are common to all of them. Regardless of the glands' size and complexity, they always consist of glandular tissue with an endodermal layer beneath. Usually, there is also a group of basal cells beneath the epidermis that support the glands' functions.

The glandular tissue is covered from the exterior to the interior with a thin, usually perforated cuticle that ensures a high permeability for water-soluble molecules. This permeability is important for the uptake of chemical stimuli and the transport of enzymes and digestive products. The glandular tissue synthesizes the digestive enzymes and can also absorb the digestive products. The secretory and absorbent surface of the glandular cells is often enlarged by inwardly growing protrusions of the cell wall. The cells of the glandular tissue have a pronounced endoplasmic reticulum for synthesizing the digestive enzymes. By contrast, the cells of the endodermal layer are characterized by water-impermeable cell-wall deposits that prevent the transport of water-soluble substances within the cell wall. The endodermal cells perform and control all transport processes between the glandular tissue and the cell layers beneath the epidermis.

Digestion Process

In all carnivores, the prey animals are digested in a fluid that Joel (1986) called a "digestive pool." The digestive fluid establishes a connection between the digestive glands and the prey, which allows the transport of digestive enzymes and products. It is possible to differentiate the following three digestive mechanisms.

Continuous digestion in a chamber The trap forms a closed digestive chamber and is constantly filled with digestive fluid. All the prey animals can be continuously digested in this "stomach." This type of digestion is found in pitfall traps (*Brocchinia*, *Catopsis*, *Cephalotus*, *Darlingtonia*, *Heliamphora*, *Nepenthes*, and *Sarracenia*), snare traps (*Genlisea*), and suction traps (*Utricularia*).

Cyclical digestion in a chamber The trap forms a closed digestive chamber only after successfully catching prey, which means that it is filled with digestive fluid only some of the time. In its quiescent state before and after digestion, the trap does not contain any digestive fluid. Cyclical digestion is employed in the closing traps of *Aldrovanda* and *Dionaea*.

Digestion at isolated points on the trap surface The digestive fluid is formed only in areas that are in immediate proximity to the prey. The drop of digestive fluid corresponds to the size of the victim and takes up only a part of the trap surface. Several prey animals can be broken down in parallel in separate digestive pools. Carnivorous plants with adhesive traps (*Byblis*, *Drosera*, *Drosophyllum*, *Pinguicula*, *Roridula*, and *Triphyophyllum*) use this method of digestion.

Carnivorous plants with pitfall traps secrete digestive enzymes continuously, and the enzyme production can be enhanced by a chemical stimulus (Hepburn et al. 1927; Zeeuw 1934). In species with cyclical digestion or digestion at isolated points on the trap surface, the production of digestive fluid is generally triggered by an external stimulus. This stimulus is generally a chemical one (ammonium ions, free amino acid groups, urea, and sodium ions); less commonly, a continual mechanical stimulus can also trigger the production of digestive fluid.

The time that elapses between the stimulation of the plant by the prey animal and the onset of enzymatic digestion varies from one species to another. *Pinguicula* exhibits initial enzymatic activity after only 1 hour (Heslop-Harrison and Knox 1971), whereas in *Dionaea* this takes 20 hours (Robins 1978). Similarly, the time taken for complete digestion of the prey varies greatly, and, of course, the size of the prey animal influences the duration of the digestive process. *Drosophyllum lusitanicum*, for example, can digest a mosquito within 24 hours (Quintanilha 1926). For the common butterwort, *Pinguicula vulgaris*, which usually catches very small prey animals, Darwin (1875) measured a digestive period of 2 days. The digestion of a victim in a *Nepenthes* pitcher requires about the same period (Lloyd 1942), whereas *Drosera anglica* can digest a whole fly within 4 days. The leaves of the Venus flytrap (*Dionaea muscipula*) remain closed for about 14 days after catching a fly; in the case of larger prey animals, however, digestion may take a lot longer than this (Darwin 1875).

Very large prey animals or too many victims may actually damage the traps. Watson et al. (1982) noted that *Drosera erythrorhiza* almost completely digests the springtails (Collembola) that it catches in its natural habitat. Springtails are small insects and not very powerful, whereas larger animals can generally escape the traps, because the slime is not viscous enough to hold them back. In feeding trials using *D. erythrorhiza* Dixon (1975) noted that fruit flies (*Drosophila melanogaster*) are not completely digested, because of their size. In cultivation, additional decomposition from bacteria often occurs in excessively large prey animals. This decomposition usually damages the leaf surface, and the leaf generally dies as a result.

Uptake of Digestive Products

In carnivores, the digestive glands absorb the small-molecular substances that are released during the digestive process. In *Nepenthes*, nutrient uptake occurs via the digestive glands at the base of the pitcher, and the role of digestive glands in the uptake of digested nutrients has been demonstrated in *Sarracenia* as well (Lüttge 1965; Panessa et al. 1976).

Among carnivores with adhesive traps, sundews (*Drosera*) absorb nutrients via their tentacles, as Darwin (1875) surmised. In *Pinguicula*, only the sessile digestive glands are responsible for nutrient uptake, whereas the stalked glands (tentacles) are responsible for secretion (Heslop-Harrison and Knox 1971).

The Venus flytrap also absorbs nutrients dissolved in the digestive fluid via its digestive glands (Lüttge 1965). In the tiny traps of *Utricularia*, the four-armed glandular hairs have been identified as the site of nutrient uptake (Fineran and Lee 1975).

Use of Nutrients in the Plant

The leaves responsible for uptake subsequently transport the absorbed nutrient components to other parts of the plant—reproductive organs, perennating organs, or young tissue that is still growing. As early as 1878, Francis Darwin (Charles Darwin's son) was able to show that *Drosera rotundifolia* plants fed insects produced more flowers and seeds than did unfed plants. Darwin conducted his experiments on potted plants; Thum (1988), however, showed that feeding the plants at their natural growth sites also resulted in increased growth, flowering, and fruiting. In *Cephalotus follicularis*, most of the nitrogen from the prey was found in the flowers (Schulze et al. 1997). Hanslin and Karlsson (1996) quantified the proportion of the nitrogen from prey animals that is later received by the reproductive organs; they found that *Pinguicula* invests 17–32 percent of this nitrogen in its reproductive organs and *Drosera* 17 percent.

By comparison, *Pinguicula* plants store 45–61 percent of the nitrogen in their winter buds. *Drosera* species may store as much as 71 percent of the nitrogen from the prey in their perennating bud. At the initiation of growth after fire, *Dionaea muscipula* receives 75 percent of the nitrogen from prey. When D. muscipula later becomes overgrown by the surrounding vegetation, so that only a few large insects can be trapped, the rate of insect derived nitrogen is reduced to 46 percent (Schulze et al. 2001). The sundew *Drosera erythrorhiza*, from the winter-rain regions of western Australia, survives the dry season with the aid of underground tubers. When it grows the main tuber, daughter tubers for vegetative reproduction appear as well. About 63 percent of the absorbed nitrogen is used for the development of the main tuber and 29 percent for the daughter tubers (Dixon et al. 1980).

Utricularia vulgaris transports nitrogen and phosphorous from the prey, which are supplied by the older active traps, into the young parts of the plant (Friday and Quarmby 1994). It is possible to identify the prey components in these parts of the plant after as little as 2 days. The younger leaves of *Nepenthes mirabilis*, which are still growing, have a high concentration of nitrogen, although they do not as yet catch any prey. Here, too, the nitrogen within the plant is transported from the traps to the growing areas (Schulze et al. 1997). Likewise, in *Aldrovanda vesiculosa*, nearly all the amino acids originating from the prey are transported into the growing tissue (Fabian-Galan and Salageanu 1968).

Costs and Benefits of Carnivory

Carnivorous plants go to comparatively great lengths to catch and digest their prey. These costs are offset by the often-proven benefits of greater vitality and seed production when prey is caught. The increased research on cost-benefit analysis in carnivorous plants now provides a clearer understanding of the evolution of carnivory (Adamec 2006; Anderson and Midgley 2003; Brewer 1999; Ellison 2006; Ellison and Farnsworth 2005; Guisande et al. 2000; Laakkonen et al. 2006; Manjarres-Hernandez et al. 2006; Mendez and Karlsson 1999, 2004, 2005; Ne'eman et al. 2006; Ridder and Dhondt 1992; Sorrenson and Jackson 1968; Thoren et al. 1996; Worley and Harder 1996).

Under costs, we must first consider the proportion of biomass of the trap organs. *Utricularia vulgaris* employs 50 percent of its biomass for trapping insects, whereas in *Utricularia macrorhiza* the corresponding figure is about 38–48 percent (Friday 1992; Knight and Frost 1991). The traps of *U. macrorhiza* have only about half the photosynthetic rate of the leaves (Knight 1992); the cost of carnivory in this case, then, is a loss of photosynthetic potential. The same probably applies to the traps of other carnivores. In an extreme case, the loss of photosynthesis can be 100 percent, when the traps are underground and contain no chlorophyll, as in terrestrial bladderworts and *Genlisea*.

In carnivores with adhesive traps, a further cost is associated with the secretion of mucilage, which in *Drosera* can account for about 4–6 percent of the carbohydrates gained from photosynthesis (Pate 1986). To a lesser extent, this also applies to the nectar production of the pitcher plants. The production of digestive enzymes is also a cost factor for the plant, especially if there is a danger that the valuable proteins will be washed out by rainfall.

The benefits of the absorbed nitrogen lie in increased carbon dioxide fixation during photosynthesis. Field and Mooney (1986) discovered that there is a linear relationship between carbon dioxide fixation and the nitrogen content of plants. Those with a higher nitrogen content can therefore use more carbon dioxide for their photosynthesis and thus produce more carbohydrates that can be used for growth. By applying these findings to *Utricularia macrorhiza*, it can be demonstrated that the plant's photosynthetic rate would not enable it to survive without the uptake of nitrogen from animal prey (Knight and Frost 1991).

It is still unclear just how much carnivorous plants can influence their cost-benefit relationship in order to adapt to a particular site. Green (1967) noted that *Nepenthes* develops only small traps under poor light conditions. This could be a direct reaction to excessive costs of trap production. He added that the traps may be absent altogether if the plant is growing on comparatively nutrient-rich soil.

Prey

Depending on the size and type of trap, the size of the captured prey animals can range from microscopic unicellular animals to vertebrates. The trap systems of most carnivorous plants are essentially specialized to catch small arthropods, particularly insects (Fig. 35), hence the popular designation "insectivorous" plants. The carnivores' prey consists of a wide variety of insects, including springtails (order Collembola); butterflies and moths (Lepidoptera); wasps, bees, and ants (Hymenoptera), termites (Isoptera); beetles (Coleoptera); and mosquitoes and flies (Diptera); as well as arachnids (such as mites and spiders) and small crustaceans (such as copepods).

The prey of carnivorous plants may include even the smallest animals. For example, the genus *Genlisea* is specialized to catch protozoans that live in the soil. These unicellular animals (mostly ciliates), which are about 200 μm long, crawl through the narrow, slit-shaped openings of the snare traps (Figs. 36, 37), attracted

Fig. 35.
Prey animals in a pitcher of *Nepenthes madagascariensis*, growing in its natural habitat in southeast Madagascar.
W. Barthlott

47

Figs. 36 and 37.
Attraction and
capture of slipper
animalcules by
Genlisea aurea.

Fig. 36.
The tiny, unicellular
prey animals swim
toward the trap
openings.
W. Barthlott

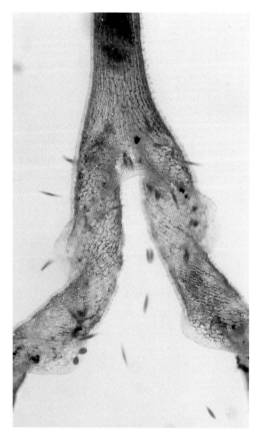

by an as-yet-unidentified chemical agent that
lures them to their doom (Barthlott et al.
1998). Meanwhile, the prey spectrum of many
terrestrial bladderworts (*Utricularia*) includes
protozoans and nematodes that live in the soil
(Seine et al. 2002). The suction traps of aquatic
bladderworts also catch rotifers, nematodes,
rhizopods, and water bears (*Tardigrada*; Friday
and Quarmby 1994; Harms and Johansson
2000), which become trapped while attempting to feed on the microflora growth of the
plants (Meyers and Strickler 1978, 1979; Mette
et al. 2000). Mention should also be made of
the bacterial microflora contained in the
pitcher plants, which is digested along with
the rest of the prey. Finally, predatory fungi,
which are present in almost every soil, specifically catch nematodes with their trap hyphae.

Larger prey animals are known from Asian
pitcher plants (*Nepenthes*), in which frogs, liz-
ards, and even rats have been found in the
pitchers, which may have a capacity of up to

Fig. 37.
A trapped slipper
animalcule inside a
snare trap (scanning
electron microscope
detail from Fig. 36).
W. Barthlott

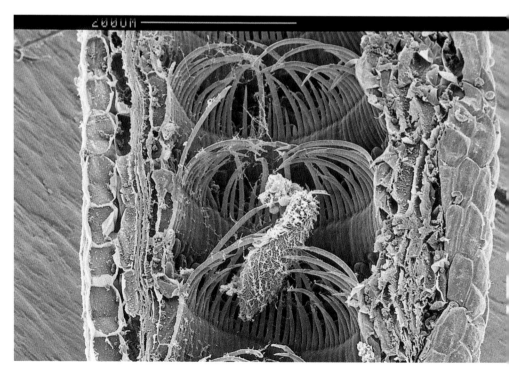

L (Clarke 1997; Cheek and Jebb 2001). Such captures are probably the result of accidents, however, in which the animals have fallen into the pitchers of the epiphytic or climbing *Nepenthes* while searching for drinking water, or, in the case of their young, have fallen out of their nests and into the traps. The capture of fish fry in *Utricularia* has also been reported (Grudger 1947; Englund and Harms 2001).

In addition to feeding on animals, some carnivores also feed on vegetative matter, including aquatic bladderwort species that consume green algae (Mette et al. 2000). Carnivorous plants with adhesive traps are also not averse to protein-rich pollen grains that may land on them. Harder and Zemlin (1968), for instance, examined the protein uptake from pollen grains in butterworts (*Pinguicula*), which can account for up to 70 percent of the plants' total nitrogen resorption.

The number of animals that one plant may be able to catch can be very great. For example, the pitfall traps of *Sarracenia* are typically functional over a period of several months, and they can become full to the brim with the decomposing remains of the prey animals (Fig. 31). In plants whose traps are functional over a shorter period, it is somewhat more difficult to measure the total volume of the trapped prey. During the growing season, for example, the long-leaved butterwort (*Pinguicula longifolia*) grows a new leaf about once a week, which means that a total trap surface of up to 400 square centimeters is formed over each growth period.

Francis W. Oliver (1944) once observed a truly apocalyptic feeding frenzy. He described a vast stand of *Drosera anglica* covering several hectares on the coast of Norfolk, England, in which huge numbers of butterflies had become entrapped. After a long flight over the North Sea, the butterflies—mainly small whites (*Pieris rapae*)—descended on the deadly meadow in exhaustion. Oliver found up to six butterflies caught on each sundew and estimated their total number at nearly 6 million.

Because carnivorous plants are so efficient at catching prey, some of them have been used for biological pest control. For example, orchid-growers often use *Pinguicula moranensis* to decimate populations of sciarid flies in greenhouses. Similarly, predatory fungi are now used in agriculture to combat nematodes, which damage the roots of crops. In the tropics, it has been shown that ponds with aquatic bladderworts contain fewer insect larvae than those without (Angerilli and Beirne 1980). Bladderworts have been used to help combat tropical diseases, for example, by targeting malaria or schistosomiasis carriers (Gibson and Warren 1970; Gordeev and Sibataev 1995).

The capture of prey is generally subject to seasonal fluctuations, especially in the carnivorous plants of temperate and subtropical climates. The plants do not grow any trapping organs during the dormancy period (dry or winter season), and the range of available prey species changes over the course of the year. The sliced-open pitcher of *Sarracenia flava* in Figure 31 shows the prey animals layered one on top of the other, their composition clearly changing during the course of a growing season. The bottom layer is mainly comprised of ants that are caught in spring, while in June and July bees and other hymenopterans make up the bulk of the prey. In late summer and autumn, it is mainly wasps and butterflies that are caught, and the plant's final course on the menu in October consists of moths.

Guests at the Carnivores' Table: The Commensals

Given their rich pickings, it is not really surprising that the traps of carnivorous plants attract thieves and other "guests." In their association with carnivorous plants, animals do not always have to play the role of prey. For example, insects that visit the flowers must be able to fulfill their role as pollinators without running the danger of ending up as a nutrient reserve. However, another group of animals can linger on carnivorous plants without any danger, even around the trap organs: the so-called commensals.

It was recognized early on that carnivorous plants often provide a habitat for other animals without actually using them as a nutrient source. In his *Natural History of Carolina*, Catesby (1754) noted that a variety of animals frequented the pitcher interiors of *Sarracenia* and used them as a safe haven from predators. Riley (1873) also noted such mutualistic relationships between plants and animals. He identified two of these colonists as a moth in the genera *Xanthoptera* and the blowfly *Sarcophaga sarraceniae*, "insects which brave the dangers of *Sarracenia*," as he wrote.

Commensalism is defined as an association between two organisms in which the commensal (such as the moth *Xanthoptera*) feeds on the nutrient surplus of the other (*Sarracenia*), without harming the host plant (Joel 1988). For these eating companions, the term *mutualism* is also used in this context. Mutualism is a relationship between different kinds of organisms that is generally necessary to maintain their existence, a form of symbiosis in a broader sense, to which there can also be transitional forms. For example, there are mutualistic relationships involved in the pollination of flowers by animals, the dispersal of seed by animals (such as ants: myrmecochory), and the interrelationships between ants and honeydew-producing aphids.

Commensals of Pitfall Trap Carnivores

There is a whole commensal network associated with Asian pitcher plants (*Nepenthes*), whose pitcher interiors provide a habitat for a large number of animals and microorganisms without using them as a nutrient source. As early as the eighteenth century, Rumphius

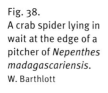

Fig. 38.
A crab spider lying in wait at the edge of a pitcher of *Nepenthes madagascariensis*.
W. Barthlott

held that there were live as well as dead animals in the pitchers of *Nepenthes*. Phillipps and Lamb (1996) identified nearly 150 animal species that are present in the pitcher fluid and gain their nutrition either from the animals caught in the pitcher or as predators feeding on other commensals. In addition, there are many bacteria, fungi, and unicellular animals that inhabit the pitchers; these are given the scientific designation *phytotelmata*. Complex interdependencies and food networks develop inside the traps, and Beaver (1985) described six different feeding habits in pitcher plants: detritus-feeders, filter-feeders, carrion-feeders, aquatic predators, terrestrial predators, and pupal parasitiods.

Most animal inhabitants of pitchers are mosquito and fly larvae that colonize older pitchers, whose digestive fluid is only weakly acidic. Such nonfunctional traps have also been known to contain live frogs, tadpoles, and even small crabs.

Fig. 39.
The crab spider *Misumenops nepenthicola* lurking above the digestive fluid in a pitcher of *Nepenthes rafflesiana*.
T. Carow

Of the nonaquatic predators, the crab spider *Misumenops nepenthicola* (Fig. 39) has been particularly well studied. This species lives on the edges of the pitchers of *Nepenthes gracilis*, *N. gymnamphora*, and *N. rafflesiana*. The spider catches its prey either directly at the pitcher rim or just after the prey has fallen into the digestive fluid. In case of danger, the spider can even move down into the fluid at the end of a thread and remain there submerged and hidden for several minutes. On Madagascar, another crab spider occupies the pitchers of *Nepenthes madagascariensis* (Fig. 38). The same ecological niche in *Darlingtonia* is occupied by an insect larva (*Metriocnemus edwardsi*) that blocks the pitcher opening beneath the peristome with a web, thus catching prey animals that fall in.

Nepenthes bicalcarata (Fig. 141), *N. gracilis*, and *N. rafflesiana* are often home to ants. *Nepenthes bicalcarata* has developed a particularly close relationship with a small ant species of the genus *Campanotus*. The plant develops a hollow space in its pitcher stalk that is occupied by about twenty ants, together with their eggs and pupae. *Campanotus schmitzi*, like other ants (such as *Crematogaster* species), is attracted by two large, nectar-secreting projections on the upper peristome margin (Merbach et al. 1999). Whereas most ant species lose their footing on the slick inner surface of the pitcher and drop into the digestive fluid, *C. schmitzi* is able to move safely on the pitfall traps. At first glance, the benefit to the pitcher plant of this special role of *Campanotus* is not clear. Clarke and Kitching (1993) speculated that the ants remove surplus prey from the pitcher, from which they then gain their nutrition. This, in turn, prevents rot from developing in the pitchers, and the plant is still able to resorb the nutrients through the ants' excretions. Merbach et al. (2001), however, saw the benefit to *Nepenthes* of the presence of *Campanotus* as a protection against small herbivorous

insects (such as aphids), which the ants conveniently remove from the plant.

In addition to *Nepenthes*, North American pitcher plants (*Sarracenia*) have a well-developed network of commensals. Yet here, too, there are crab spiders (*Misumena*) or praying mantises (Fig. 40) that, mimetically matched to the color of the pitcher rim, lie there in wait for their victims. Other commensals that live in the pitfall traps of *Sarracenia purpurea* and feed on the prey there include the larvae of mosquitoes (*Wyeomyia smithii*, *W. haynei*), sarcophagid flies (*Blaesoxipha fletcheri*) and midges (*Metriocnemus knabi*) (Bradshaw 1983, 1984; Bradshaw and Creelman 1984; Istock et al. 1983; Bergland et al. 2005; Ellison et al. 2003). Some noctuid moths (such as *Papaiperma appasionata*, *Exyra fax*) and wasps (such as *Isodontia philadelphicus*) utilize the pitcher traps of *Sarracenia* too, also as breeding stations, where their larvae feed on the trapped prey and pupate (Atwater et al. 2006). Dipteran larvae (such as *Megaselia ovestes*, *Aphanotrigonum darlingtoniae* [syn. *Botanobia darlingtoniae*], *Metriocnemus edwardsi*) or web-forming spiders of the genus *Eperigone* are found in the pitfall traps of the cobra lily (*Darlingtonia californica*) (Fashing 1981; Nielsen 1990).

Commensals of Adhesive Trap Carnivores

For carnivorous plants that catch their prey with adhesive traps, the typical commensals are true bugs (Heteroptera) of the family Miridae, subtribe Dicyphina, as found in *Roridula*, *Byblis*, and *Drosera*. Although *Roridula* does not produce any digestive enzymes of its own, the plants are nevertheless able to benefit from the trapped prey by means of a remarkable symbiosis with bugs (*Pamerica roridulae* and *P. marthlothi*) and spiders. These are highly spe-

Fig. 40, facing page: A feeding praying mantis, which previously caught the bumblebee at the trap rim of the pitfall trap of *Sarracenia leucophylla*.
T. Carow

cialized species that live on the sticky *Roridula* plants and live off the prey that the plants have caught (Dolling and Palmer 1991; Anderson and Midgley 2002). They also use the plants as a refuge. In return, the plants benefit from the excretions of the bugs and spiders, whose droppings serve as manure. In addition, the remains of the prey animals drop to the ground, where they contribute nutrients to the plants' immediate surroundings. Hence, it is ultimately still possible for the plant to use the nutrients contained in the prey animals.

The Australian rainbow plant (*Byblis gigantea*) provides an unusual habitat for another bug, *Setoceris bybliphilus*. This bug lives as a commensal on the plant and feeds on the prey animals caught on the mucilaginous glands. It can move freely on the surface of *B. gigantea* without becoming stuck to the mucilaginous secretions (Lloyd 1942; China and Carvalho 1951). Bugs of the genus *Setocoris* (Fig. 41), such as *S. droserae* and *S. russelli*, live on Australian species of *Drosera* in much the same fashion.

Noncarnivorous Animal-Trapping Plants

Many plants trap animals without actually using them as a nutrient source. With the exception of certain accidental events, this is associated with floral biology and protection from possible feeding animals. It is occasionally mistaken for carnivory, because certain characteristics of carnivory are present (such as attraction and capture) and sometimes the animals die as well.

Defense Against Feeding Animals

Many plants have developed sticky leaves as a defense against feeding insects (herbivores; Spomer 1999), such as tobacco (*Nicotiana*), red German catchfly (*Lychnis viscaria*), and passion flower (*Passiflora foetida*). Insects, such as aphids, are unable to move and remain firmly stuck to the plants; they suffocate beneath the adhesive glands or starve to death on the leaf surface. In this case, they are not digested, however, because these plants have no digestive enzymes.

Capture in Water-Filled Leaf Axils

Especially in the family Bromeliaceae, there are many plants that have water-filled leaf cisterns. As an important habitat for amphibians, such as poison-dart frogs, these epiphytic plants often form little aquatic biotopes. Of course, crawling insects occasionally fall into

the open cisterns as well and drown. In fact, two precarnivorous plants have developed within the Bromeliaceae, *Brocchinia reducta* and *Catopsis berteroniana*, which use these resources for their nutrient supply.

In addition, there are many plants that temporarily develop water reservoirs in their leaf axils. An example is the common teasel (*Dipsacus*), in which dead animals can be observed in the water-filled leaf axils. In this plant, the lower shoots in particular form a widened leaf stem, which means that two opposite leaves can form small cisterns that fill with rainwater. Small, flightless insects (such as ants), on their way to the tip of the shoot—and hence to the younger, juicier leaves—cannot overcome this obstacle and typically fall into the water cisterns and drown.

Animal-Trapping by Flowers

To force pollination and to take up the pollen that insects are carrying on their bodies from previous visits to other flowers, several plants have developed traps for their pollinators. In most cases, the pollinators are able to safely escape their prisons, freshly laden with new pollen. For instance, the common milkweed (*Asclepias* species) and other members of Asclepiadaceae have threadlike structures associated with their anthers, called *translators*, that become entangled around the legs of butterfly pollinators, temporarily trapping them. However, illegitimate pollinators that are too small, mainly bees, become permanently trapped

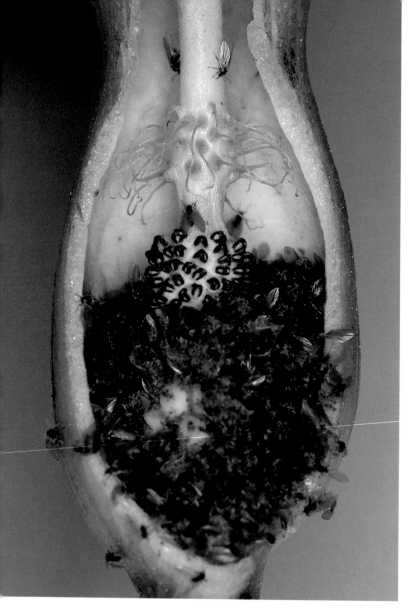

the higher temperatures inside the cavity compared with the ambient environment. At the base of the cavity there are female flowers, and one level up are the pollen-bearing male flowers. Pollinators (mosquitoes in *A. maculatum*, beetles in *A. triphyllum*) are unable to leave the cavity, however, because at its narrowest point the way out is blocked by trap hairs. New arrivals forcing their way in kill some of the insects lower down by the sheer virtue of their mass. After successful pollination, however, the trap hairs lose their turgidity, and the trapped insects can then leave their prison. A gigantic relation of *A. maculatum* from tropical Sumatra, the titan arum (*Amorphophallus titanum*), a huge foul-smelling flower some 3 m high, deals with its pollinators in a similar fashion (see Barthlott 1992).

Perhaps the most surprising and most beautiful of all flowers are those among certain blue-flowering waterlilies in southern Africa (such as *Nymphaea caerulea*). These large, vividly colored, and sweet-scented flowers attract insect pollinators, including hoverflies, beetles, and bees that land on the flowers in their search for pollen. Each night the waterlilies close, opening up again only the following morning, when the stamens offer up ripe pollen grains. This richly laid table only seems to be harmless for insects, however. On the first day of flowering (anthesis), when the stamens have not yet opened and the waterlily is undergoing its female phase, the stigma is coated with a liquid. In their search for pollen, insects fall into this fluid, which contains a wetting agent, and drown. When the flower closes during the night, the pollen that the dead insects have brought with them is flushed away. The next morning, the flower, now in its male phase, is completely safe for pollinators to enter.

Fig. 42.
In this lords-and-ladies (*Arum maculatum*), the inflorescence bract forms a cavity that is closed off by trap hairs and is filled with hundreds of *Psychoda* flies.
W. Barthlott

and die in the flowers. Brief detainments of pollinators can also be observed in some orchids (such as *Coryanthes*).

Similarly, carrion flowers and fungi-mimicking flowers are little prisons for their pollinators. Lords-and-ladies (*Arum maculatum*; Fig. 42), a plant native to central Europe, and the Jack-in-the-pulpit (*Arisaema triphyllum*) of North America have such pitfall flowers. During flowering early in spring, the pitfall flowers attract countless numbers of small insects with their pollen supply, as well as by

The Evolution of Carnivory

If we look back on everything to do with the distribution, trap types, and digestion processes of carnivorous plants, some questions inevitably come to mind. For instance, how did carnivory arise in the course of evolution? And how did these carnivorous plants derive from "normal," nitrogen-autotrophic plants?

To examine the origin of the carnivores, we largely have to revert to hypotheses, since there are few available fossils (Ellison et al. 2003). Fossil evidence is available only in the form of the seeds of hookleaf-like plants (related to *Triphyophyllum*) from the Eocene (Müller 1981). Müller also listed seed and pollen records of *Aldrovanda*, known in fossil form from England, dating as far back as the Lower Tertiary. Hence, we can assume that the complex trap mechanisms developed over a period of perhaps as much as 100 million years.

The ability to catch animals and then digest them arose completely independently (that is, convergent evolution) in five groups of flowering plants (Fig. 43): (1) the lineage including the families Droseraceae, Drosophyllaceae, Nepenthaceae, and Dioncophyllaceae, which belong to the Caryophyllales (carnivores and allies); (2) the Cephalotaceae, which are related to the wood sorrel family (Oxalidaceae); (3) the Roridulaceae and Sarraceniaceae, which are related to the tea family (Theaceae) and the Ericaceae, which includes the heathers; (4) the Lentibulariaceae and Byblidaceae, which belong to the figworts (Lamiales); and (5) certain bromeliads (*Brocchinia* and *Catopsis*), which are monocotyledons, have developed characteristics on their way to carnivory.

But how did carnivory arise? Some structures can be recognized as pre-adaptations

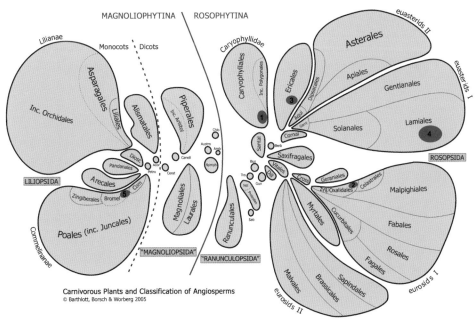

CARNIVOROUS PLANTS AND CLASSIFICATION OF ANGIOSPERMS

Carnivorous Plants and Classification of Angiosperms
© Barthlott, Borsch & Worberg 2005

Fig. 43.
Classification system of flowering plants. Carnivorous plants have arisen in five related groups:
(1) Caryophyllales: Dioncophyllaceae, Droseraceae, Nepenthaceae;
(2) Oxalidales: Cephalotaceae;
(3) Ericales: Roridulaceae, Sarraceniaceae;
(4) Lamiales: Byblidaceae, Lentibulariaceae; and (5) Poales: Bromeliaceae.
Barthlott, Borsch & Worberg 2005

that allowed the evolution of a carnivorous syndrome. These include the presence of tubular
leaves as precursors of pitchers and the presence of adhesive, enzymatically active glandular hairs.

Tubular leaves This leaf form is widespread
in the plant kingdom and can arise through
the simplest of mutational steps. For example,
there are mutants of the plantain (*Plantago*,
Fig. 44) that bear a striking resemblance to the
tubular leaves of *Heliamphora*. Water collects
in tubular leaves, and animals occasionally fall
into them.

We can postulate the possible evolution of
pitfall-trap carnivory taking the Sarraceniaceae as an example. The genus *Heliamphora*
has simple, conical leaves that fill with rainwater. There are no digestive enzymes, but
absorbing structures have arisen nevertheless.
From a morphological point of view, the closely
related North American *Sarracenia* species are
much more complex and have digestive enzymes to break down proteins. These evolutionary steps are clearly evident in the bromeliads. Many hundreds of species have
developed funnel rosettes in which rainwater
collects that is then absorbed by water-absorbing scales. Animals that fall into the funnels
can easily escape by crawling up the hairs on
the surface. However, at least two genera of
bromeliads (*Brocchinia* and *Catopsis*) prevent
this through their slick, waxy leaf surfaces and
nearly vertical leaves.

Adhesive glands Glandular hairs that secrete sticky mucilage are widespread throughout the plant kingdom. As a protection against
herbivores, the sticky substance immobilizes
attackers, rendering them harmless (Juniper
1986; Juniper et al. 1989). The mucilage blocks
the respiratory openings (spiracles) of small
flying insects, and most of the animals, who

Fig. 44.
A malformed, funnel-shaped leaf of the plantain
Plantago lanceolata, a species endemic to central
Europe. W. Barthlott

Table 2. Comparison of the trap characteristics of *Drosera* species and *Dionaea muscipula*

Characteristics	Typical *Drosera* leaf	Transitional form	*Dionaea* leaf
Petiole	rounded	flattened into a leaf form (*D. falconeri*)	flattened into a leaf form
Marginal tentacles	glanduliferous	without glands (*D. rosulata*)	without glands ("guard hairs")
Surface tentacles	glanduliferous	without glands	without glands
Digestive glands	sessile and stalked	sessile	sessile
Electric potentials	present	present	present
Leaf (lamina) form	lineate to rounded	rounded (several species, such as *D. falconeri*)	rounded
Leaf (lamina) in the bud	folded over the stalk	folded over the stalk	folded over the stalk

die of suffocation or exhaustion, remain stuck to the plant. This freely delivered protein-rich nutrient supply can be used by precarnivorous plants, whose glandular knobs also contain enzymes that can dissolve the proteins (Spomer 1999). But not all carnivores have such enzymes, or proteases. Members of the genus *Roridula*, for example, catch large numbers of insects on their extremely sticky leaf surfaces but are unable to digest them due to a lack of enzymes. Bugs and spiders come to their aid by feeding on the trapped animals, and their excretions then allow the plants to resorb the nutrients. It is possible that Australian trigger-plants (*Stylidium*) may also be carnivorous (Darnowski et al. 2006).

Within Droseraceae, the highly complex snare traps of *Dionaea* and *Aldrovanda* are found alongside the relatively simple adhesive traps of *Drosera*. Recent research has shown that *Drosera* is a sister group to *Dionaea* and *Aldrovanda* (Cameron et al. 2002), which means that both types of traps evolved from a common ancestor. It is reasonable to assume that this common ancestor probably featured simple adhesive traps similar to those of *Drosera*, instead of complex snap traps. The trigger hairs of *Dionaea* are homologous to the surface tentacles of *Drosera* (Williams 1976). The same homology can be demonstrated for the marginal bristles of *Dionaea* and the marginal tentacles of the sundews (Seine and Barthlott 1993). Several leaf characteristics found in

Dionaea and *Aldrovanda* can also be found in some *Drosera* species (Table 2). This illustrates the likely development leading from an ancestor probably similar to extant *Drosera* to the present-day snap traps in *Dionaea* and *Aldrovanda*. In addition, the plasticity of the organs supports such evolution.

The common ancestor of *Drosera*, *Dionaea*, and *Aldrovanda* probably had a rounded leaf with sessile glands as well as tentacles both at the margin and in the center of the blade. The petiole of the leaf was likely rounded. Because electrical potentials are found in all descending genera, the tentacles were probably already motile. The leaf blade of the ancestor most likely featured some form of motility to fold up, similar to today's sundews.

We can picture the evolutionary steps from the common ancestor to *Dionaea* as follows. The petiole of the leaf became flattened and wide such that it could partly take over photosynthesis. The marginal tentacles lost their glandular tissue and motility, forming the marginal bristles. Only a few surface tentacles were maintained on the leaf, losing their glandular function but retaining their electrical excitability. These then evolved into the trigger hairs, which release a potential that induces the closure of the *Dionaea* trap. The sessile glands probably experienced only slight changes during the Venus flytrap's evolution. The motility of the leaf lamina became concentrated along the midrib, and the leaf was able

to snap shut. The speed of the closing movement increased dramatically.

Many related families within the Lamiales and Solanales have adhesive glands as a defense against herbivores (such as tobacco, *Nicotiana*, Solanaceae). The Martyniaceae, for example, have sticky glandular heads, but they lack the necessary enzymes to digest animal proteins (*Ibicella lutea*, Fig. 45). In the related family Lentibulariaceae, however, this principle has been taken a step further in a most sophisticated fashion. The genera *Pinguicula*, *Genlisea*, and *Utricularia* have glandular heads with enzymes that, in the case of *Pinguicula*, are present on leaves with an entire margin and that have a sticky secretion. Using molecular techniques, Müller et al. (2000, 2004) and Jobson et al. (2003) elucidated the phylogeny of the Lentibulariaceae.

Within this set of relationships, the butterworts (*Pinguicula*) have mostly flat leaves that lie on the ground (decumbent), are gland bearing (glanduliferous), and can occasionally be tubular (*Pinguicula agnata*, Fig. 46). The snare traps of *Genlisea* could have developed in this way. The Mexican butterwort *P. utricularioides* has almost completely bladderlike, rolled-up (involute) leaves. By imagining the leaf traps sunken into the ground, we can envision the origin of the *Genlisea* snare traps and the *Utricularia* bladder traps. In the soil substrate, there are always many small prey animals available

Fig. 45.
The sticky leaves of *Ibicella lutea* (Martyniaceae), covered with flies. W. Barthlott

There are extreme cases in which insect-catching trap leaves no longer develop on older plants, such as in *Drosera caduca* from northern Australia. This phenomenon of temporary carnivory, in which the plant is carnivorous only during a particular phase of its life cycle, is extremely rare and is known only in *Triphyophyllum peltatum* and *Drosera caduca*.

rotifers, ciliates, and nematodes), which is a considerable advantage for underground traps as compared with aboveground traps. The trap mechanism of *Genlisea* can be explained by a corkscrew twisting and extension of the forward bladder tip (see Fig. 104), which in *Utricularia* is restricted to the bladder-shaped digestive chamber as a trapping structure (Figs. 122–124).

Two carnivorous plants, *Triphyophyllum peltatum* and *Drosera caduca*, exhibit carnivory only during the juvenile phase of their development and lose their ability to develop traps as they grow older. It is also notable that many carnivores already have intact traps as seedlings. For example, seedlings of *Nepenthes madagascariensis* produce miniature pitchers filled with digestive fluids only 4 weeks after seeding. Similarly, the Australian bladderwort *Utricularia multifida* develops traps particularly early in its development. Even before the two cotyledons have developed, quite apart from the remaining assimilating foliage leaves, 6-week-old seedlings already have completely functional traps.

In at least some carnivores, we could ask

whether the origin of carnivory can be considered in connection with the establishment of the seedlings, because fully functional traps at such an early developmental stage would benefit a seedling's natural establishment. In the tough competition of colonizing a low-nutrient site, the young carnivorous plant would then be able to derive its nutrition from a wider range of sources than its noncarnivorous competitors could. This would give a carnivore a considerable growth benefit in comparison with its more modest rivals that are attempting to colonize the same site.

It is possible to explain the evolution of lifelong carnivorous plants through the developmental model of neoteny, in which some immature characters are retained into adulthood. The zoologist Julius Kollmann described the phenomenon of neoteny in 1885, using the example that is still the best known today, namely the Mexican axolotl (*Ambystoma mexicanum*). Throughout its life, the axolotl retains its gills as respiratory organs, whereas most other amphibians have gills only as tadpoles, developing lungs in the adult stage.

Fig. 46.
Pinguicula agnata, as other members of the genus, can occasionally grow funnel-shaped leaves, an evolutionary precursor to snare traps.
W. Barthlott

Growing Carnivorous Plants

Carnivorous plants are truly bizarre organisms. Their mode of life turns the accepted relationship between the "innocent plant" and the "wild predator" on its head, which is undoubtedly the main reason for the fascination that carnivores elicit in us. In addition, carnivorous plants have an unusual ability to move. Children are fascinated by the quick snapping shut of a Venus flytrap, whereas they are generally unable to muster much enthusiasm for African violets. Once the quick reaction of the Venus flytrap has awakened our interest, it is only a matter of time before we become fascinated by the sticky leaves of a sundew or discover the beauty of pitcher plants. Soon, we find ourselves wanting to grow these unusual plants in our own home or garden.

Initial attempts at growing carnivorous plants often end in disaster, however. The Venus flytrap barely survives a few weeks. By winter, at the latest, the sundew no longer looks very attractive sitting on the heater, and it no longer catches flies. After such initial experiences, carnivorous plants then tend to acquire the reputation of being difficult. But many carnivores do not deserve this label and can be grown very successfully by amateur gardeners by following a few simple rules. Nevertheless, within the wide array of carnivorous plants, there are also species that are very difficult to grow because their site requirements are so extreme.

This chapter provides an introduction to growing carnivorous plants, giving basic principles with which most of the species can be successfully cultivated and propagated. Advice for growing particular genera can be found at the end of each family chapter, where we provide a list of species that are suitable for beginners or experienced gardeners.

Basic Requirements

The conditions for growing carnivorous plants should be oriented toward the environmental conditions that prevail in the plant's natural habitat. This does not mean it is necessary to create a truly identical environment; instead it is important to keep a few certain factors within appropriate limits. In particular, the five most important interacting factors for growth—temperature, light, air humidity, soil, and water—must meet the requirements of the plant. If, for example, a carnivorous plant originates from the ombrogenic bogs of central Europe's temperate latitudes, it does not require a miniature bog in a flowerpot to survive, but instead the following basic conditions: temperature kept warm in summer and cold in winter; bright to sunny light; high air humidity; a low-nutrient, water-retaining potting mixture with an acidic pH (peat); and a watering regime that keeps the plant moist or wet at all times.

Only a few carnivore enthusiasts have the time, space, and financial resources to provide appropriate conditions for carnivorous plants from different biotopes. Therefore, we recommend limiting the range of habitats to one or two basic types. Even with such a limitation, however, it is still possible to build up an interesting and varied carnivore collection.

Temperature

The temperature requirements of carnivorous plants vary greatly, depending on their natural habitat. The species can be grouped as those growing in temperate latitudes, the Mediterranean and subtropical regions, tropical lowlands, and tropical highlands.

Carnivorous species from temperate latitudes need warm summers and cold winters. In summer, a significant difference between day and night temperatures is generally beneficial. In winter, the plants undergo a dormancy period in which some of the aboveground organs may die off. For the plants to be overwintered outdoors, frost protection is generally required in the form of a covering or cold frame.

Carnivores from the Mediterranean and subtropical regions are best grown in a greenhouse. They need warm summers and cool winters. In summer, a drop in nighttime temperature is important. The winter temperatures should match the plant's region of origin, but a range of 8–15°C (46–59°F) can serve as a general rule of thumb.

Tropical lowland carnivores need warm temperatures year-round and should be grown in a hothouse within the temperature range of 20–30°C (68–86°F). A slight drop in temperature at night is also advisable for hothouses, although drastic temperature fluctuations should be avoided.

Carnivorous plants from tropical highland regions need warm daytime temperatures and cool nights year-round. They are best grown in a greenhouse. It is important to ensure that the temperatures during the day do not rise too high, and there must be a sufficient drop in temperature at night. Ideally, the nighttime temperature should be sufficiently low to permit dew formation.

Light

For most carnivorous species direct sunlight is desirable, at least in the morning. In regions that experience hot summers with low air humidity, shading is advisable to protect the leaves from the direct midday sun. Frost-resistant carnivores that can be grown outdoors year-round will generally also tolerate intense midday sun. Plants grown in aquariums, terrariums, or similar containers require an open lid if placed in direct sunlight.

If there is no suitable naturally lit site, carnivorous plants also can generally be grown in artificial light. As a rule, it is important to keep only a short distance between the plants and the light source so that enough energy reaches the plant. This distance should not be too small, however, because the plants may otherwise become overheated. If artificial light is used in closed containers such as aquariums or terrariums, it is important to ensure sufficient ventilation to avoid heat buildup.

Carnivores whose natural forest habitats provide more or less shaded conditions, such as *Triphyophyllum* or *Nepenthes*, should not be grown under conditions that are too dark. A shaded site in tropical habitats is subject to markedly higher light intensities than a shaded site in temperate latitudes. The glass planes in a window or greenhouse also reduce the intensity of the light falling on the plants.

Air Humidity

Many carnivorous plants prefer a fairly high air humidity, although a relative humidity between 50 and 70 percent is generally sufficient. A relative humidity of less than 40 percent over a longer period causes leaf damage in most carnivorous species.

In practice, this means that carnivores that

are kept indoors should not be grown near a heater. In winter, the air humidity at such a location can easily fall below 30 percent. By contrast, on wide windowsills without a heater, simply placing a water-filled saucer under the pot can provide sufficient moisture for many carnivorous plants. The air humidity can also be raised if the plants are grown in a partially covered terrarium, although it is important to provide sufficient ventilation to avoid overheating and mold growth.

In greenhouses, the air humidity is generally kept at the correct level by the water-filled growing tables. The evaporation from water-filled trays also helps prevent overheating. If it is necessary to strongly ventilate a greenhouse in summer to avoid overheating, the humidity can drop markedly. In such cases, it is advisable to spray the ground and greenhouse walls with water to increase the moisture level and lower the temperatures. An additional fan can also provide cooling. Humidifiers and water mist generators that automatically maintain the humidity at a set level require a greater outlay, but they make it easier to maintain the plants if the gardener is absent for long periods.

Growing Media

Potting mixtures and garden soil are unsuitable for carnivores, because most such media are excessively fertilized and contain too many mineral salts. For beginners, the use of special growing media for carnivorous plants is recommended. These can be bought as ready-made, low-nutrient mixtures in garden centers. Experienced carnivore enthusiasts typically mix their own growing media for their plants. Individual mixtures can be tailored to meet the requirements of a particular species, resulting in better growth. The most useful components for self-mixed carnivore growing media are

briefly presented below and are available either in normal garden centers or at specialist carnivore nurseries. Some growing media can also be bought at specialist orchid nurseries, as they are often used for growing orchids as well.

Sand

There are many different kinds of sand. Quartz (silicate) sand is required for growing carnivores; this is a low-nutrient medium that has an acidic pH value, but hardly any buffer capacity. Calcareous sands are unsuitable, because they are too rich in minerals and too alkaline (pH > 7). Due to their high mineral content, marine sands also are unsuitable as growing media. Commercially available bricklayers' sands are often nondescript mixtures and should be avoided. The water-storage capacity of sand is dependent on the grain size—the finer the sand, the more water it can hold. As a rule, coarser, rougher sands (grain size 1.5–3.0 mm) are used to loosen up and aerate the soil. Before use as a growing medium, sand should be thoroughly washed so that it no longer contains any soluble minerals that could negatively affect the carnivores' growth.

Growing Media for Epiphytes

Bark, the outermost, solid layer of tree trunks, is enjoying increasing popularity as a supplementary medium for growing plants. The bark of conifer trees, especially the giant redwood (*Sequoia sempervirens*), is used most often because it has a low pH value. Water retention of bark is relatively low, and it varies with the size of the bark pieces—small particles hold more water than large ones do. Bark is also very good for loosening up and aerating the soil, and it can also be used as an attractive decorative mulch. In the wood industry, bark arises as a waste product in considerable quantities, which makes it a renewable raw material that can be used without reservation.

As the name suggests, coconut fibers from coconut palms consist of long, brownish fibers that envelop the coconuts. Depending on the length of the fibers and the density with which they are present in the growing medium, their water-storage capacity is low to moderate. Coconut fibers are mainly used to loosen up the medium.

Polystyrene, which can be used to loosen up the soil in the form of small granules or chips, is a very resilient material that retains its material characteristics even over long periods.

Rock wool is a synthetic product that combines a good water-storage capacity with good aeration. It is therefore used for cultivating epiphytic orchids and can be used for growing epiphytic carnivores, especially *Nepenthes*. D'Amato (1998) recommended using rock wool for the root development of *Nepenthes* cuttings.

Charcoal

Charcoal is mainly used for loosening up the growing medium, particularly in media for epiphytes. When growing carnivores that occur naturally on sites that are subjected to fire, charcoal can also be used to promote seed germination. In addition, charcoal absorbs some toxic compounds.

Perlite and Vermiculite

The glasslike perlite and vermiculite are minerals of volcanic origin that have swollen as a result of exposure to great heat. These minerals have a moderate water-storage capacity and are useful for aerating the growing medium. Perlite, which is usually white and grainy, does not release any minerals into the soil and is generally preferred as a supplementary soil

material for growing carnivorous plants. By contrast, when the golden brown vermiculite comes into contact with water, it releases aluminum, magnesium, and iron cations. Both dioctaedric and trioctaedric vermiculite are used for carnivores that occur naturally on comparatively nutrient-rich soils (such as Mexican highland butterworts). These butterworts can also be grown easily on large, artificial insulating stones (Fig. 50).

Peat Moss

In a sense, *Sphagnum* moss is "living peat." It grows on continuously moist, low-nutrient sites and releases humic acids with which it acidifies its surroundings. *Sphagnum* moss is available as a green, dried moss that is not as decomposed as peat is. Like peat, it is low in nutrients, has good water-storage properties, and has a low pH value. Due to its branched growth, it has a loose structure that can improve soil aeration. Live *Sphagnum* moss can be used to grow *Heliamphora* and highland species of *Nepenthes*. It is particularly sensitive to high temperatures and desiccation, however, and does not tolerate any fertilizer or manure. Therefore, living, growing *Sphagnum* in pots of carnivores indicates the absence of toxic compounds. Because *Sphagnum* moss grows very slowly and must be collected in the wild, however, it should be used very sparingly. In most countries, the collection of peat moss from natural growth sites requires a permit, and *Sphagnum* should be purchased only from legally traded sources. Specialist nurseries are able to supply legally obtained peat moss. When buying moss for carnivorous plants, make sure to obtain *Sphagnum*. Florists' "sheet moss" is not suitable as a potting medium.

Peat

In bogs, peat originates from plant material (generally peat moss or *Sphagnum*) that, in the absence of oxygen, is only partially decomposed. Peat is low in nutrients and has a low pH value, which is beneficial for most carnivores. Thanks to its buffer effect, peat can regulate pH over long periods. Peat holds moisture extremely well and can store many times its own weight in water. However, it is a very slow-growing natural product and should be used only when absolutely essential. It is extracted from bogs in northern latitudes, and these bogs are generally destroyed as a result. Only unfertilized peat should ever be used for growing carnivores.

Water and Watering

The water for watering carnivorous plants should contain only a very small quantity of dissolved minerals. The best source of water for carnivorous plants is rainwater, which is both chemically soft and low in nutrients. When gathering rainwater, the collecting surface should be clean and not release any soluble substances into the water. The same applies to collecting containers; those made of synthetic materials are especially suitable.

Fresh tap water is generally unsuitable for carnivores; it can be used only when it is extremely soft and the added chlorine has been removed by boiling. If the carnivore collection's water requirement is so great that it cannot be met by rainwater alone, a water-preparing device is advisable. This can be achieved by distillation or by demineralization using ion exchangers. If using such a device is not feasible, commercially available demineralized water may be used instead. Mineral water should not be used under any circumstances, however, because, as the name implies, it has a high mineral content.

When watering carnivorous plants, particularly those with delicate adhesive traps, the water should not come into direct contact with the leaves. Instead, the plant pot is often placed in a deep saucer that contains 1–2 cm of water, which rises up into the pot by capillary action.

Fertilization

Carnivorous plants do not require regular fertilization. By definition, all carnivores fertilize themselves by catching prey and using the proteins that the prey contains to meet their nitrogen and phosphorous requirements. In the descriptions of the individual genera, we mention whether occasional fertilization is desirable. Beginners should avoid using fertilizer; they may be surprised to see how well these plants do without it.

Housing the Plants

The choice of where to grow the plants is closely linked to the conditions that they require for growth. The easiest solution is simply to grow the plants on a windowsill. Growing plants in a terrarium, outdoors, or in a greenhouse involves a greater outlay, which nevertheless also greatly increases the range of possibilities for growing a wide variety of species.

Even on a windowsill, it is possible to grow some of the more robust species. A windowsill in a heated room is suitable for growing carnivores that need warm temperatures year-round and can tolerate relatively low air humidity. In particular, these include several *Drosera*, *Sarracenia*, *Pinguicula*, and *Nepenthes* species. Lighting conditions can vary between natural and artificial lighting, depending on the plants' requirements. If there is a windowsill available in an unheated room, it is also possible to grow plants that undergo a dormancy period, such as the Venus flytrap (*Dionaea*).

A terrarium greatly extends the range of possibilities, because the air humidity can be much better controlled. Hence, plants that are more demanding in terms of air humidity, primarily those from tropical and subtropical regions, can be grown if the terrarium is placed in a room that is warm year-round. Of course, the size of the terrarium limits the size of the plants that can be grown in it. Large *Nepenthes* species, for example, are unsuitable for growing in a terrarium. Again, note that terrariums should not be closed completely, especially when placed in direct sunlight.

Carnivores' growth requirements can best be met in a greenhouse, where the temperature can be well regulated with the aid of ventilation and heating. The air humidity also can be tailored to the needs of the particular plants. The most important deciding factor for the choice of plants is the greenhouse temperature. Species that require cool conditions generally do not thrive in a hothouse. Plants that need additional warmth, however, can still be grown in a small, separate area of a cooler house if such an area can be individually heated.

Depending on their frost resistance, carnivorous plants of temperate latitudes can also be grown outdoors, both in pots and in specially prepared beds. Mulching in winter can be beneficial for more sensitive species. Carnivores that thrive outdoors in the summer but are not frost-tolerant can be overwintered in a frost-free cold frame. In such a frame, the temperatures drop far enough so as not to disturb the winter dormancy, while avoiding frost damage.

What to Consider When Buying Plants

These days, carnivorous plants are generally propagated horticulturally, with large-scale production of seed, seedlings, or tissue cultures. The range of reasonably priced plants from such cultures has grown steadily in recent years and comprises an impressive selection of species and cultivars that are suitable for beginners. (See the list of carnivorous plant sources at the end of the book.) When buying plants, it is important to consider the origin and condition of the plants, avoiding those with wilted or dried-up leaves.

Origin

Unfortunately, plants that have been collected from the wild still occasionally find their way into the trade (see the chapter on nature conservation). Such plants often fail to thrive in a cultivation environment and slowly die. In addition, the removal of plants from their natural growth sites endangers the long-term survival of the species in those areas. Before making a purchase, therefore, it is important to make sure that the plants for sale come from a recognized nursery or a responsible carnivore enthusiast. Serious traders are only too happy to provide information on the origins of their plants and will not take offense if their customers wish to be properly informed.

Plant Condition

When buying carnivorous plants, the same principles apply as for buying plants in general. It is important to choose only well-developed and undamaged specimens, check whether the dealer has been giving the plants sufficient water, and examine the plants for pests and diseases.

The plant should be well developed at the time of purchase. Very young plants are generally less expensive, but often cannot survive the stress associated with transportation and transplantation. Even when they may still look fit and healthy at the dealer's, they can often wilt and die very quickly for no apparent reason. Care is needed in the case of older specimens as well, because they can often no longer adapt to the new growing conditions.

Damaged leaves are an indication of improper handling during transport and should always be a reason to examine the plant particularly closely. One or two damaged leaves present no problem for an otherwise healthy plant, because they can be replaced by new growth. If the growing tip of the plant has also been damaged, however, it may be difficult to cultivate further.

The plants' water supply at the dealer's may also be a problem; in large gardening and home-improvement centers plants are often not given much attention. A brief sprinkling with tap water upon their arrival is sometimes the only care they receive before they are sold. Plants on dried-up growing medium or with dried-up tentacles or pitchers are signs of inadequate care and should be avoided.

The plants' leaves should be free of pests and algal or fungal films, which rob the plants of their vitality. Pests and algae or fungi also can be introduced into private plant collections and damage plants that had been healthy. If after purchasing a plant it is found to have some sort of infestation, it should be kept under quarantine at home.

As a rule, it is important not to be overly taken with the attractive appearance of a particularly well-cultivated specimen. A purchase is worthwhile only when the plant's requirements can also be met in a private garden or greenhouse.

Propagation

Plants can be propagated from seed (sexually) or cuttings (vegetatively). Both methods are used for carnivores.

Seeds are formed through sexual reproduction, whereby the hereditary substances of the parent plants are combined (Figs. 47–49). The subsequent generation is heterogeneous in its appearance and can be markedly different from the parents. Propagation from seed therefore maintains the genetic diversity of the population and yields a selection of plants with different characteristics.

Propagation from seed takes place after the ripe seeds have been harvested. In many species of cold-winter regions, a cold period (stratification) is also necessary to break the seed dormancy. For stratification, the seeds are sown in pots and the soil is moistened. The pots are then wrapped in plastic bags and stored in a refrigerator for several weeks. After this treatment, the pots with their seeds are treated in the same way as when sowing any other seed.

For some Australian species (such as those of *Byblis)* smoke water treatment, which is increasingly employed in agriculture, is utilized for successful seed germination (Dixon et al. 1995; Baker et al. 2005; Sparg et al. 2006). In this method, the seeds are placed on the surface of a pot and covered with dry grass. The grass is then burned so that a smoky fire develops. Shortly thereafter, the fire is extinguished with water. Alternatively, the seeds can be soaked in smoke water overnight.

When preparing a sowing medium, it is advisable to use the same medium that will also be used for growing the adult plants. In the case of coarse media, however, a finer grain size should be chosen, with the same composition. The temperatures, too, should be matched to those of the adult plants. To prevent the seeds or seedlings from drying out, the air hunidity must be high during germination and the early life of the plants. A transparent cover will keep the humidity high and allow enough light to reach the plants, and fungal growth can be avoided by regular ventilation. The young plants should be thinned and acclimatized to a somewhat lower humidity as soon as they are strong enough. For potting on, the same medium as for the adult plants can be used, adjusting the grain size if necessary.

Vegetative propagation utilizes the regenerative capacity of the plants and can be thought of as "division" of the plants in the broadest sense. The development of a complete plant from a small cutting, or, in the case of meristematic propagation, from a few cells, means that the daughter plants will have the same genetic characteristics as the parent plant. If a particularly beautiful color variant or disease-resistant plant is to be propagated, this is possible only by vegetative means. The most common forms of vegetative propagation are division, segregation of tubers or gemmae, propagation of cuttings, and meristematic culture.

Division is the easiest method of vegetative propagation, and it can be used for all species that have branched roots that bear shoots. These include, for example, terrestrial bladderworts, *Cephalotus*, some *Drosera* species, and all aquatic bladderworts and *Aldrovanda vesiculosa*. When dividing, a sufficiently large part of the plant with growing medium is simply removed and placed in a separate pot.

The segregation of tubers or gemmae is similar to that of division. This method is suitable only for species that actually form tubers, such as *Utricularia* or *Drosera*, or that reproduce with the aid of gemmae, such as pygmy sundew species. The tuber-forming species are taken from the growing medium during the dormancy period, and the tubers are planted

Fig. 47.
Horticultural breeding of *Dionaea muscipula*.
A. Sievers

69

Fig. 48.
Germination stage
of *Nepenthes
madagascariensis*.
The two cotyledons
(1 cm long) have
developed from a
dark brown seed
after a period of
about 3 weeks.
I. Theisen

follicularis). Healthy roots are removed from the mother plant, cut up into pieces about 4 cm long, and placed horizontally in pots with a light covering of growing medium. The pots should be kept moist and in bright light, and the temperature needs to be somewhat higher than that required for the parent plants. Young plants appear after several weeks and can be thinned after slow hardening and when they are large enough.

Shoot cuttings are shoot sections with leaves that are inserted directly into a plant medium. This method is suitable for species of *Nepenthes* and *Drosera* with elongated shoots. The root growth of the cuttings can be promoted using hormones. To keep evaporation to a minimum, it is important that the cuttings are kept in very high air humidity after being cut.

Leaf cuttings are leaves or leaf sections that form new plants on or in the growing medium. This method is often used for *Pinguicula* or *Drosera*, using leaves that are fully grown and still vigorous. The fresh cuttings are kept in bright light, but protected from direct sun, at high air humidity. As a rule, young plants should have developed on the cut surfaces within a few weeks. If the young plants are sufficiently vigorous, they can then be hardened off and separated.

In micropropagation or meristematic culture, a few cells are taken from the vegetative tissue or from fresh seedlings, grown on a sterile nutrient medium, and encouraged to divide. Larger clumps of cells are separated and grown on to ensure a continuous supply of material. As soon as a sufficient number of cells have developed, they are allowed to grow under sterile conditions and develop into young plants. Meristematic culture requires a considerable outlay and is therefore primarily employed in the commercial sector. Using meristematic culture, it is possible to produce a large number of genetically identical individu-

out separately. The gemmae of pygmy sundew species are harvested as soon as they can be removed easily from the mother plant and then simply placed on a moist growing medium. Gemmae grow into new plants within the next 6 months.

Propagation with cuttings can be performed using cuttings from roots, shoots, and leaves. Root cuttings are taken toward the end of the dormancy period from species that have a thick root, which generally serves as a storage organ (such as *Drosera binata* or *Cephalotus*

The low-growing flowering stem of the unusual sundew *Drosera prolifera* regularly develops several plantlets, contributing to both generative and vegetative reproduction.

als within a very short time. Many of the Droseraceae, *Pinguicula*, and *Nepenthes* species in the trade that are sold in large numbers and at a reasonable price have been propagated in this way.

Pests and Diseases

Although it may seem counterintuitive, carnivorous plants also can be subject to infestation by animal plant pests. Insect pests that typically attack carnivorous plants include aphids, pseudococcids, and scale insects, in addition to various insect larvae that feed on the leaves or roots. If such pests are found, they can be removed from the plant or killed with insecticides. Spider mites and snails can also do considerable damage to carnivores. While snails can easily be removed, red spider mites can be combated only by using chemical means or biological control (such as predatory mites).

The most common fungal infestation of carnivores is the gray mold *Botrytis*, which tends to grow under conditions of high air humidity and low light levels. *Botrytis* can very quickly wipe out an entire population of seedlings or young plants.

It is better to prevent pests and diseases by providing good ventilation and carefully examining the young plants than to have to resort to chemical means. Unfortunately, infestation can still occur despite all precautions. If this happens, it is best to act immediately before the harmful organisms spread any further and cause even greater damage. Specialist stores can advise on the right choice of pesticides. Some sprays are not tolerated well by all plants; if this is the case, information is usually given on the packaging. The application instructions should be strictly followed to avoid risks to the gardener's health. After applying chemical pesticides, any leftover material should be properly disposed of or stored.

Fig. 49.
Nepenthes madagascariensis seedlings about 10 weeks after sowing, with fully developed pitchers. The visible part of the pin is 2 cm long.
I. Theisen

Carnivorous Plants for Beginners

This section gives brief instructions for growing carnivores that are suitable for beginners. These plants provide a particularly good introduction to the hobby of growing carnivorous plants and can be grown both easily and successfully. The experience gained from growing one's first plants then gives a solid basis for expanding the collection further. The instructions given here will make it easier for beginners to care for their plants right after buying them, until they have had time to read the more detailed instructions in the chapters on the individual genera.

Dionaea muscipula
Venus flytrap

For growing indoors. In summer, Venus flytraps can be grown indoors or outdoors. In winter, temperatures of about 10°C (50°F) are suitable. *Dionaea* should be kept in a very brightly lit and sunny spot; harsh midday sun should be avoided in midsummer. In summer, the plant container should be kept in a tray containing about 1 cm of water. Before watering again, the water in the tray should be allowed to dry out for a short time. In winter, the plant should be kept constantly moist but should not be grown continuously in water. Some of the leaves may die during the dormancy period. Figs. 81–84

Drosera binata
fork leaf sundew

For growing indoors. In summer, temperatures of about 20°C (68°F) are suitable. If desired, the plants can also be grown outdoors. In winter, the fork leaf sundew undergoes a dormancy period and should be kept at temperatures of about 5°C (40°F). *Drosera binata* needs

a lot of light to thrive and should be grown on a site that is as bright and sunny as possible. In summer, however, the plants should be shaded from the midday sun. These should be grown preferably in a pot in an open terrarium with about 1 cm of water in the tray. In winter, during the dormancy period, the plants should be kept moist, not wet. *Drosera binata* needs a comparatively high air humidity. The aboveground leaves die during the dormancy period. Fig. 70

Drosera capensis
Cape sundew

For growing indoors. In summer, the plant can be kept indoors or outdoors; in winter, temperatures of 10–15°C (50–60°F) are required. The plants should be kept in a brightly lit spot but protected from direct midday sun. *Drosera capensis* can be grown in 1 cm of water in a tray. Before watering, the growing medium should be allowed to dry out briefly. Figs. 32–34

Drosera rotundifolia
round-leaved sundew

For growing outdoors. The round-leaved sundew should be kept outdoors in full sunlight, although newly purchased plants should be slowly acclimatized to the direct sun. *Drosera rotundifolia* does best in an artificial bog—a large plastic tub filled with acidic peat is sufficient—with the plants level with the waterline. Alternatively, the plants can be grown in pots with about 2 cm of water in the tray. The plant dies back in the fall, leaving only a winter bud. Fig. 65

Nepenthes hybrids
Asian pitcher plants

For growing indoors. Temperatures should be maintained at 20–25°C (68–77°F) year-round. *Nepenthes* hybrids prefer brightly lit sites but should be exposed to direct sunlight only in the morning. Water by placing the pots in about 1 cm of water in a tray.

Pinguicula moranensis
Mexican butterwort

For growing indoors. During the growing period from spring to fall, the plants may be kept indoors or outdoors. In winter, the temperature should be reduced to about 10°C (50°F). Mexican butterworts should be grown in bright light with some direct sun. From spring to fall, they should be kept in a tray with about 1 cm of water. The tray should be allowed to dry out before watering again. In winter, the soil should be kept moist, not wet. Fig. 99

Pinguicula vulgaris
common butterwort

For growing outdoors. The plant should be grown in a cool, north-facing site. This butterwort should receive plenty of light but be protected from harsh midday sun. The plants should be kept in a tray with 1–2 cm of water and wetted frequently with a mister.

Sarracenia flava
yellow pitcher plant

For growing outdoors. In winter, the plants should be kept under frost-free conditions in a winter garden. Choose a sunny site, and keep the plants continuously moist to wet. Figs. 151, 152

Sarracenia purpurea
purple pitcher plant

For growing outdoors. In winter, the plants should be covered with leaves to protect them from heavy frosts. The plants are best grown on a sunny site and should be kept continuously moist to wet. Fig. 155

Utricularia vulgaris
common bladderwort

For growing outdoors. In the open, the plants prefer sunny ponds, lakes, or watercourses in low-nutrient, acidic water, such as a garden pond with a peat-covered bottom. In the fall, the perennating organs (turions) sink to the substrate, and in spring the plant reappears by itself. Fig. 110

Nature Conservation

The continued survival of carnivorous plants in their natural environments is endangered by two important factors: habitat destruction and the collection of plants from the wild.

The rapid increase in human populations throughout the world is leading to an increased demand for land for residential settlement and other uses. Formerly natural or near-natural areas are being converted for agricultural or other purposes, leading to a loss in the area remaining for undisturbed natural vegetation. In central Europe and the southeastern United States, bogs have long been subject to drainage, leading to a corresponding loss of valuable carnivorous plant habitats. In both North America and northern and eastern Europe, there is still an ongoing loss of such habitats through peat-cutting. Today, the low-nutrient sites that carnivorous plants preferentially occupy can easily be converted into arable land by mineral fertilization. In particular, this is occurring over wide areas in the tropics and subtropics.

Human impacts can also gradually alter the habitats of carnivorous plants, however, both indirectly and over long distances. Nitrogen compounds, which act as fertilizers, can be carried over long distances via the atmosphere and watercourses to low-nutrient sites where carnivorous plants grow. The fertilization effect benefits the carnivores' noncarnivorous competitors and leads to a shift in the overall ecological balance. The same applies to the dispersal of toxins and to gradual climatic change.

The collection of plants from the wild has become an acute threat to some plant groups, particularly the Venus flytrap (*Dionaea*), Asian pitcher plants (*Nepenthes*), and North American pitcher plants (*Sarracenia*). At times, these plants have been dug up and sold in the thousands, and the demand for specimens of these genera has become so great that it can no longer be met by the natural populations alone. *Nepenthes rajah*, for example, has been almost entirely eradicated from its natural habitat as a result of unchecked collecting activity.

In most countries, there is national conservation legislation in place to prohibit the collection of rare plants. In the case of rare—and therefore expensive—species, however, there is a greater temptation to ignore this legislation and to poach. Especially in poorer countries, market prices paid in hard currency can be very lucrative for poachers. Yet even in industrialized nations, such as the United States, there are repeated reports of large-scale poaching. For this reason, targeting the international trade in plants from their natural habitats is a crucial component of nature conservation legislation.

The Convention on International Trade in Endangered Species of Wild Fauna and Flora (CITES), which was originally drafted in Washington, D.C., in 1973, is designed to combat the threat to species from international trade. Today, more than 150 contractual parties have agreed on a range of trade restrictions. Depending on the level of endangerment or need for protection, the endangered species have been classified into three lists, Appendices I, II, and III. Appendix I offers the greatest degree of protection, Appendix II a more moderate degree of protection, and Appendix III the lowest degree of protection. In all three categories, import and export requirements must be observed and permits obtained.

Appendix I includes species threatened with extinction that are or can be endangered by trade. The import or export of such plants requires advance written permission. An export permit is issued only if removal from the natural growth site is carried out legally and is not detrimental to the survival of the species, the shipment is associated with a minimal risk for the plants, and an import permit has already been issued. The import permit sets out appropriate conditions for cultivation at the plants' destination and stipulates that the imported plants are not to be used primarily for commercial purposes.

Appendix II includes species whose degree of protection generally permits a regulated commercial use under proper scientific supervision. An export permit must be obtained in advance and presented to the customs office prior to importation. The export permit is issued under similar conditions to those under Appendix I. The development of the population and the numbers of exported plants are monitored continuously; thus, fewer export permits are issued if the level of endangerment increases. Commercial use is permitted for plants listed in Appendix II.

Appendix III includes species that are protected in the territory of at least one of the contractual parties. An export permit is required and must be presented to the customs office prior to importation. The export permit requires proof of legal removal from the site and appropriate conditions for shipment.

With its provisions on trading wild fauna and flora, the European Union has been implementing CITES and the European Union guidelines since 1984 and 1997, respectively. These international regulations are supplemented by national legislation. Listing all the national laws relating to nature conservation, of course,

In 1979 the Australian pitcher plant *Cephalotus follicularis* was included in Appendix II of the Convention on International Trade in Endangered Species (CITES), but the species was removed again in 2000. However, European Union species protection regulations have listed *Cephalotus* since 1997.

is beyond the scope of this book. However, detailed information should be obtained from the government of any nation that you wish to collect in or exchange plants with.

A list of the carnivorous plants that are protected in international trade is given in the CITES checklist (Arx et al. 2002), and currently includes *Byblis*, *Cephalotus*, *Darlingtonia*, *Dionaea*, *Nepenthes*, and *Sarracenia*. Table 3 gives an overview of the protection status of carnivorous plant genera.

The protection status that is accorded an individual species is subject to change, depending on the development of the species in its natural habitat and based on an assessment of its level of endangerment, carried out by the organizations responsible. Because both national and international authorities and organizations are responsible for enforcing legislation, it is crucial that prospective traders be thoroughly informed before buying, importing, or exporting carnivorous plants.

A quick overview can be gained by consulting the CITES homepage (www.cites.org). The national CITES agencies can give expert information and advice in individual cases and are responsible for issuing the required import and export permits. In addition, these authorities are also informed about national conservation laws, which generally apply to an increasing range of species.

The growing interest of rare plant enthusi-

Table 3. Historical overview of the protection status of carnivorous plants

Genus	CITES Appendix (status)	Period listed	European Union species protection regulations First listed
Byblis	II	1979–2000	1997
Cephalotus	II	1979–2000	1997
Darlingtonia	II	1981–2000	1997
Dionaea	II	since 1992	1997
Nepenthes	II and I*	since 1981/1987*	1997
Sarracenia	II and I**	since 1981/1987**	1997

Updated February 2006

Nepenthes khasiana, N. rajah

**Sarracenia oreophila, S. rubra subsp. alabamensis, S. rubra subsp. jonesii*

asts by no means has only negative consequences, however. Well-informed amateur growers demand plants propagated horticulturally, creating an alternative to the plunder of population sites in the wild. Market demands can be met by the propagation of seedlings, cuttings, or tissue cultures, and in some cases even species protection projects can be supported in this way. Meanwhile, carnivorous plant societies promote an awareness of nature conservation among their members and draw attention to cases of poaching. (Contact information is provided for two such societies at the end of the book.)

The cultivation of carnivorous plants by botanical gardens and plant enthusiasts represents an active contribution to the survival of these fascinating plants. Carnivores are available to collectors through exchange and propagation, while regular exhibits in botanical gardens raise public awareness of and enthusiasm for them. The plants grown in collections have one great drawback, however; in general, they consist of genetically uniform material that is not representative of the total diversity of the wild populations. This is because only a few plants are collected in the wild, and these few plants subsequently form the basic stock for most collections through meristematic or vegetative propagation.

Without the retention of carnivorous plant habitats, therefore, it will not be possible to guarantee the continued existence of the various species in the long term. Habitat retention

Fig. 50.
Head gardener W. Höller of the University of Bonn Botanical Gardens views *Pinguicula gypsicola* growing on insulating stone.
I. Theisen

Fig. 51.
Cultivation of
Utricularia australis
in the University of
Bonn Botanical
Gardens. I. Theisen

is the task of both public and private nature re-serves. Scientific research is crucial for establishing worthwhile refuges, because an effective protection plan can be developed only for species whose mode of life and requirements are properly understood. Effective reserves take into account not only the present distribution of the species in an area, but also exchanges and interactions with neighboring populations and the influence of the surrounding areas on the protection zone.

On the whole, the protection status of carnivorous plants is encouraging. By far the greater majority of species are not considered endangered, and reserves have already been established for some of those species that are. The most important tasks for protecting carnivorous plants in the future will be to combat poaching and illegal trade and to ensure the conservation of sufficiently large areas of natural habitat.

Bromeliaceae: Pineapple Family (Bromeliads)

With the exception of *Pitcairnia feliciana* in western Africa, bromeliads are exclusively of New World origin, including more than 2600 species in 56 genera (Smith and Till 1998). Within the superorder Commelinanae, which includes the families of the grasses (Poaceae), sedges (Cyperaceae), palms (Arecaceae), gingerworts (Zingiberaceae), and bananas (Musaceae), the bromeliads make up the order Bromeliales. Their nearest relatives are the members of the herbaceous Rapateaceae, which also are largely native to South America, especially the Guiana highlands. Together with the aquatic order Alismatales and the superorder Lilianae, which includes the orchids and the relatives of tulips and asparagus, the Bromeliaceae are monocotyledons (Monocotyledoneae; Fig. 43).

Within the Bromeliaceae, two species are considered to be precarnivorous: *Brocchinia reducta* and *Catopsis berteroniana*. Because not all characteristics of the carnivorous syndrome are present in these plants, Juniper et al. (1989) questioned whether they should be included among the true carnivores. For example, neither *B. reducta* nor *C. berteroniana* secretes enzymes to digest the prey that become trapped in the plants' leaf cisterns, which form pitfall traps.

The Bromeliaceae colonize a very wide range of habitats. Both the terrestrial species and the epiphytic ones, which grow in tree canopies, occupy sites characterized by a paucity of mineral nutrients. Some botanists long suspected that what are sometimes called "cistern bromeliads" or "tank bromeliads," into whose water-filled leaf rosettes insects and other animals fall and drown, might be carnivorous. Picado (1913) presumed that some cistern bromeliads have proteolytic enzymes that assist in digesting insects that have fallen into the cisterns. Benzing (1980), however, held that the proteases in the cisterns originate from the bacteria that live there and are not released by the bromeliads.

Brocchinia Schultes f.

This genus, which is found in Brazil, Guiana, Colombia, and Venezuela, was named after the Italian naturalist Giambattista Brocchi (1772–1826). The eighteen known *Brocchinia* species were traditionally assigned to the subfamily Pitcairnioideae (Smith and Till 1998). However, based on molecular genetic analyses (Horres et al. 2000), *Brocchinia* and the genus *Ayensua*, which is known from only a single species (*A. uaipanensis*) from Uaipán Tepui in northeast Venezuela, are no longer in the Pitcairnioideae but are instead placed before this basal subfamily directly at the base of the family. The only precarnivorous species is *Brocchinia reducta* Baker (Fig. 52), which is described below.

Distribution and Habitat

Brocchinia reducta grows on low-nutrient, sandy-swampy, and open sites in southern Venezuela and neighboring Guiana. It forms a characteristic element of the white-sand savannas of Venezuela's Gran Sabana, at elevations between 500 and 2900 m above sea level

(Varadarajan 1986). In this region of the Precambrian Guiana upland plateau, *B. reducta* is also found on the *tepuis*, sandstone table mountains.

Features

Brocchinia reducta is a terrestrial, perennial, stemless, herbaceous plant that develops funnel-shaped rosettes, growing in groups about 30–50 cm high. The plant has only weakly developed roots. A few yellowish green, sessile leaves, which are directed almost vertically upward, form a tubular rosette (so-called cistern bromeliad). The leaf laminas have entire margins and are oblong-linear, while the plant's specific epithet *reducta* refers to the rounded, truncate leaf tips. The plant develops an erect, loosely branched inflorescence borne on a stalk up to 60 cm high. The relatively inconspicuous flowers, which are about 5 cm long and have short peduncles, are seated in the axils of bracts that are about 3 mm in length; the flowers consist of three oval sepals about 4 mm long, three white petals, and two rows of three stamens each that are fused to the corolla. Three carpels are fused to form a trilocular ovary. Numerous elongated seeds develop in the cylindrical capsular fruits.

Trapping Mechanism, Digestion, and Prey

Brocchinia reducta traps its prey with the aid of its leaf rosettes, which are developed as pitfall traps. Attracted by a weak scent that emanates from the cistern liquid (Givnish et al. 1984) and glands at the leaf base, numerous insects (almost exclusively ants and some flying insects) gather at the rim of the tubular leaf rosette. *Brocchinia reducta* is the only species of the genus that produces this scent. The leaf uppersides are coated with wax, which makes the

Fig. 52.
Brocchinia reducta growing in its natural habitat in Venezuela.
W. Barthlott

leaf surfaces very slick, with the result that insects lose their footing and slide down into the cistern liquid. The liquid at the base of the leaf rosette has an unusually low pH value of 2.8–3.0, but there are no digestive glands. In this precarnivorous *Brocchinia* species, digestion takes place by bacterial decomposition (Givnish et al. 1984).

Like the epiphytic bromeliads, *Brocchinia reducta* also has water-absorbing scales at the base of the foliage leaves. In contrast to most other bromeliads, however, the shield cells of the water-absorbing scales remain functional throughout their lives. The latter have a labyrinthine cell-wall structure that consists of a

Fig. 53.
Catopsis berteroniana growing in its natural habitat in Florida.
G. Zizka

dead insects that have fallen into the cisterns (Benzing et al. 1985; Owen et al. 1988).

Cultivation

Brocchinia reducta is difficult to grow and is suitable only for experienced carnivore enthusiasts. Plants should be grown in a temperate to warm greenhouse, where they require high air humidity and a very brightly lit site. Excessive temperatures (over 28°C, 82°F) should be avoided, especially during the summer months. In winter, the plants can be kept at cooler temperatures (16–20°C, 61–68°F). They should be watered regularly, and the cisterns should always be filled with water. Live peat moss (*Sphagnum*) or a mixture of peat moss and noncalciferous sand are the best growing media. Regular fertilization promotes the plants' growth. Dead plant parts should be removed to prevent fungal disease and putrefactive bacteria.

The plants can be propagated vegetatively by scions. The plant dies after flowering, but plant buds (known as "pups") then appear. When 3–10 cm long, these buds can be separated from the dying base and potted on.

Catopsis Grisebach

The genus *Catopsis* (subfamily Tillandsioideae) comprises seventeen species (Smith and Till 1998; Horres et al. 2000), whose area of distribution extends from the southern United States through Central America and as far south as Peru and Brazil. The only precarnivorous species is *Catopsis berteroniana* (Schult. f.) Mez (Fig. 53), which is described below.

Distribution and Habitat

Catopsis berteroniana is found from southern Florida (where it grows as an epiphyte in the

network of finely branched channels. The resorption of proteins and amino acids (including leucine) from the cistern liquid probably takes place via these channels. Using autoradiographic methods, it was shown that *B. reducta* resorbs nutrients via the water-absorbing scales; the nutrients are released from

crowns of pine trees) to the Caribbean and Central America and as far south as eastern Brazil, growing at elevations from 0 to 1300 m above sea level. This species prefers open parts of the tree crown that are well exposed to the sun.

Features

Catopsis berteroniana is an obligatory epiphyte, perennial, and a stemless plant that develops a funnel-shaped rosette. The plant develops a few very fleshy, fingerlike roots with which it remains firmly attached to the substrate. The yellowish green leaves, which are directed almost vertically upward, form a funnel-shaped rosette about 40–90 cm high (so-called cistern bromeliad); the leaf laminas have entire margins and are covered in a whitish gray waxy layer. The plant develops an upright inflorescence, borne on a stalk 80–100 cm high, that towers far above the leaf rosette. Pollinating insects are therefore kept well away from the pitfall traps and are in no danger of falling in. *Catopsis berteroniana* develops small, white flowers, each with three free sepals and petals, two rows of three free stamens each, and a trilocular ovary. In addition, there are purely functional female flowers in which the stamens have been transformed into staminoids. The capsules contain relatively few seeds, each with a tuft of hair.

Trapping Mechanism, Digestion, and Prey

According to Givnish et al. (1984), *Catopsis berteroniana* is a precarnivorous species, because not all the characteristic features of true carnivores, such as the synthesis of digestive enzymes, are present. The trapping mechanism and digestion corresponds to that of *Brocchinia reducta* (see above); the prey spectrum is similar as well.

Cultivation

Like *Brocchinia reducta*, this species is difficult to grow and thus unsuitable for beginners. It is best grown in a hothouse. *Catopsis berteroniana* prefers high temperatures (25–30°C, 77–86°F), but it is important that the temperature drops to about 15°C (60°F) at night. Plants can grow as epiphytes, although *C. berteroniana* can also be grown terrestrially, on a peat-based medium. The leaf cisterns should always be filled with water.

Propagation is mainly by scions or less commonly by seed. The plant dies after flowering, but plant buds then appear. When they are 3–10 cm long, separate the buds from the dying base and pot on.

Byblidaceae: Rainbow Plant Family

The family Byblidaceae, which is native to Australia and neighboring New Guinea, comprises a single genus with six species, the rainbow plants (*Byblis*). These annual or perennial herbs catch their prey using passive adhesive traps.

The Byblidaceae are related to the figwort family (Scrophulariaceae) and thus also to the carnivorous bladderworts (Lentibulariaceae; Albert et al. 1992; Müller et al. 2000, 2004). Previously, the rainbow plants were taxonomically associated with the South African bug plants, Roridulaceae (such as Drude 1891), but recent molecular genetic analyses revealed them to be broadly related to the heather family (Ericaceae; Albert et al. 1992; Conran and Dowd 1993).

Byblis Salisbury
rainbow plant

The genus *Byblis* was described in 1808 by the English botanist Richard Anthony Salisbury (1761–1829), who initially classified *Byblis liniflora* among the sundews (Droseraceae). In 1848 Jules Emile Planchon (1823–1888) assigned the genus, which by then included three species, to the Pittosporaceae. Only in 1922 did Karel Domin (1882–1953) establish a separate family for the rainbow plants, after Lang (1901) had assigned them to the bladderworts (Lentibulariaceae). The most recent taxonomic analyses of the genus (Lowrie and Conran 1998; Conran et al. 2002) were concerned with the classification of the northern Australian species, among other things, and have yielded three new additions: *B. aquatica*, *B. lamellata*, and *B. rorida*.

The generic name is a reference to a figure of Greek mythology, Byblis, the daughter of Miletus, who was the son of Apollo. Unhappy in love, she shed many tears, which—like the drops of mucilage on the leaves of the rainbow plant—glistened in all the spectral colors in the sunlight.

In 1875, Charles Darwin mentioned the trapping of insects by *Byblis* in his seminal work *Insectivorous Plants*. In contrast to what he had done with the sundew and Venus flytrap, however, Darwin was unable to carry out experiments on live plants and had to rely on herbarium specimens alone.

Distribution and Habitat

Byblis gigantea (Fig. 54) and *B. lamellata* are restricted to the winter-rain region in the southwestern part of Western Australia and are concentrated in the area around Perth, Badgingarra, and Eneabba. The other four species colonize sometimes-extensive areas in northern Australia, with *B. liniflora* also found in neighboring Indonesia, in the south of Irian Jaya (island of New Guinea; Steenis 1971). *Byblis aquatica* has the smallest area of distribution and is found only near the city of Darwin. With the exception of *B. aquatica*, rainbow plants mostly colonize sandy soils in swamps and on riverbanks. They avoid the moistest or most waterlogged habitats, however, and instead prefer more elevated or marginal sites. *Byblis aquatica*, on the other hand, thrives on sites that are flooded at least during the rainy season, and this species often grows in shallow water. During the dry season, the sites that *B. gigantea* occupy are subject to the influence of

Fig. 54, facing page:
Byblis gigantea
W. Barthlott

bush fires. The rootstock is completely adapted to fire and generally withstands the bush fires without damage. It seems that fire promotes seed germination, as is the case in many fire-adapted plants in Australia (De Buhr 1976). All six species of the genus *Byblis* are protected in Australia.

Features

Byblis gigantea and *B. lamellata* are the only perennial species, and they develop thick, woody stem bases from which the plants grow as subshrubs, reaching a height of 60 cm. The other four species are annuals and generally remain much smaller. The shoots are densely covered with glandular hairs. *Byblis* species form well-developed fibrous roots. *Byblis gigantea* and *B. lamellata* also have thick, fleshy, and deep rootstocks. The linear to filiform, alternate leaves have numerous glandular hairs, especially on the leaf undersides. In bud, the leaves of all the species are rolled up in an inverse circinate fashion, or toward the outside. This feature of young leaves is extremely rare, and it is also found in *Drosophyllum lusitanicum*. The flowers develop individually in the leaf axils in late spring. They each consist of five sepals, petals, and stamens and two carpels. The small sepals are covered with glandular hairs; the petals are fused at the base, are purple to lilac, and have rounded free tips. A white form is known in *B. gigantea*; the yellow stamens of this form have anthers that lie close to one another. The anthers of *B. gigantea* do not normally release pollen by themselves. Instead, when flying toward the flowers, pollinating insects produce a certain sound frequency that causes the pollen to be released (De Buhr 1976). The carpels ripen to yield a bilocular capsule that opens along two seams and contains several elongated seeds.

Trapping Mechanism, Digestion, and Prey

The leaf surfaces of *Byblis*, which are densely covered with glandular hairs, are passive adhesive traps. There are two types of glands: stalked glands, with a head that secretes mucilage, and sessile glands that secrete digestive enzymes. The stalked glands are immobile. The stalk, which consists of a single cell, can roll up in a spiral if it dries out (Darwin 1875). The glandular knob usually consists of thirty-two radially aligned cells. The sessile glands feature a basal cell that bears a head consisting of four or eight cells.

As with all carnivores that have adhesive traps, the prey consists of flying insects (such as bees, wasps, flies) that are attracted by the glistening drops of mucilage and become caught on the plant after landing on it. The insects then suffocate or starve. The proteins of the insects are broken down with the aid of proteases that are secreted by the sessile glands. The exact uptake path of the digestive products into the plant has not yet been elucidated, but it is presumed that the sessile glands are mainly responsible for resorption.

Byblis gigantea provides an unusual habitat for *Setocoris bybliphilus* (Miridae). This bug lives as a commensal on the plants and feeds on the prey animals that are stuck to the glands. The bug is able to move freely over the surface of *B. gigantea* without touching the glandular hairs (Lloyd 1942; China and Carvalho 1951).

Overview of Species

Byblis aquatica Lowrie & Conran
Distribution and habitat: Northern Australia (Northern Territory), from Darwin to Berry Springs; growing on slightly flooded to water-

logged, sandy soils near watercourses and ponds. *Byblis aquatica* has the smallest area of distribution of all *Byblis* species. Features: Annual herb. Erect shoot (up to 5 cm high) or creeping or floating in water (up to 45 cm long). The inflorescence is the same length as the leaves or shorter (about 2–4 cm). Purplish red flowers; sepals 3–4 mm long, with short-stalked glands only; anthers shorter than the filaments. Seeds 1.0–1.3 mm long, smooth, without a transverse groove.

Byblis filifolia Planch.

Distribution and habitat: Northern Australia (Western Australia, Northern Territory, and Queensland); found on moist, sandy soils near watercourses. This species has the largest area of distribution of all *Byblis* species, found from Port Hedland on the west coast to the Kimberleys, Arnhemland, and near Cairns on the east coast. Features: Annual herb. Erect shoot, 20–60 cm high. Leaves up to 9 cm long. Pedicels shorter than the leaves. In comparison with *B. liniflora*, many simultaneously opened flowers; flowers pink to lilac, with yellowish white to light pink undersides; sepals 4.5–6.5 mm long, with short stalked glands only; petals half as long as the sepals; anthers longer than the filaments. Seeds 0.5–0.6 mm long, warty, with a deep transverse groove. Fig. 55

Byblis gigantea Lindl.

Distribution and habitat: Southwestern Australia (Western Australia), in the region around Perth; found on sandy, moderately moist heathland soils. Features: Perennial herb. Shoot erect, up to 45 cm high, with a thick, fleshy rootstock. Pedicels as long as or shorter than the leaves. Flower color different shades of pink (from dark violet to light purplish red), rarely white to cream-colored; sepals 4.5–6.5 mm long, covered with short

Fig. 55.
Byblis filifolia
W. Barthlott

stalked glands only; anthers longer than the filaments. Seeds 0.6–1.5 mm long, warty, with a deep transverse groove. Fig. 54

Byblis lamellata Conran & Lowrie

Distribution and habitat: Southwestern Australia (Western Australia); in open heathland environments from the Arrowsmith River south to Cataby (Geraldton Sandplains and Swan Coastal Plain bioregions); on moderately moist silicate sandy soils. Features: Perennial herb. Shoot erect, up to 60 cm high. Like *B. gigantea* (in which *B. lamellata* was formerly integrated as *B. gigantea* 'Eneabba'), this species has a thick, fleshy rootstock. In terms of its inflorescence, flower form, and flower color, *B. lamellata* is indistinguishable from *B. gigantea*. The only difference is in the seed morphology: the numerous winged ribs along the longitudinal axes of the seeds, which are about 1.0–1.8 cm long, differ from the warty seeds of *B. gigantea*.

Byblis liniflora Salisb.

Distribution and habitat: Northern Australia (Western Australia, Northern Territory, and Queensland), from near Kununurra on the west coast to Cairns and Kennedy on the east coast, and in southeastern New Guinea (Indonesia: state of Irian Jaya) near the city of Merauke; found on sandy, waterlogged soils of seasonally flooded grassland savannas or in open *Eucalyptus-Acacia* forests. Features: Annual, bushy herb attaining a height of 5–15 cm. Leaves 4–8 cm long, as long as or shorter than the pedicels (up to 10 cm long at the fruit ripening stage). Compared with *B. filifolia*, only a few simultaneously opened flowers. Flower color pink to lilac; sepals 3.0–5.5 mm long, only a little shorter than the petals, and with short glands; anthers shorter than the filaments. Seeds 0.6–0.8 mm long, with longitudinal and transverse grooves.

Byblis rorida Lowrie & Conran

Distribution and habitat: Scattered distribution in northwestern Australia in the Kimberleys (Western Australia); found on waterlogged, sandy, or laterite soils in the vicinity of seasonally flooded lakes and streams. Features: Annual herb, 6–30 cm high. Unlike the similar *B. filifolia* and *B. liniflora*, the leaves are only 2.5 cm long. The flowers are concentrated at the shoot apex; flower color light violet, sepals bear both sessile and stalked glands (the latter up to 1.5 cm long). Anthers longer than the filaments. Seeds 0.7–0.8 mm long, similar to those of *B. liniflora*.

Cultivation

Byblis species are unsuitable for growing indoors; all of them prefer a very bright to sunny place in a greenhouse. The annual species from northern Australian (*B. aquatica, B. filifolia, B. liniflora, B. rorida*) are relatively easy to grow; they require daytime temperatures of 25–30°C (77–86°F) and a continuously moist growing medium; the temperatures at night should not fall below 15°C (60°F). By contrast, the perennial *B. gigantea* does not need such high temperatures, and in summer the plant can be grown outdoors. The temperatures in winter should not fall below 5°C (40°F), however. In addition, stagnant water should be avoided, especially in winter during the plant's dormancy period. *Byblis gigantea* can survive even longer dry periods; the aboveground parts will die under these circumstances, but new shoots will develop from the rootstock. Perlite-sand or a peat-sand mixtures are suitable as growing media.

Propagation is by seed. The seeds of the fire-adapted *B. gigantea* are more likely to germinate if they are treated with "smoke water" after sowing. Smoke water can be made by simply pouring water over the hot ashes of a wood or grass fire. The chemical components dissolved in the water appear to induce germination, as bush fires do in the wild. This species can also be propagated by shoot cuttings, which are then grown at high humidity under glass.

Cephalotaceae: Australian Pitcher Plant Family

The Australian pitcher plant family (Cephalotaceae) contains just one species, the Australian pitcher plant, *Cephalotus follicularis* Labill. Cephalotaceae is related to the wood sorrel family (Oxalidaceae), and, in a broader sense, the roses (Rosaceae). *Cephalotus* has a very small area of distribution in southwestern Australia, and it catches prey with the aid of pitfall traps.

region of the extreme southwest of Australia. It is restricted to areas near the coast, from Augusta in the west to Cape Riche northwest of Albany. Moss cushions on moist sites with a constant water supply are its preferred habitat (Fig. 56).

The soil on these sites is peaty or sandy and generally moist year-round, but not waterlogged. The plants can survive occasional dry-

Fig. 56.
The Australian pitcher plant, *Cephalotus follicularis*, growing in its natural habitat in Western Australia.
R. Seine

Cephalotus Labillardière
Australian pitcher plant

The Australian pitcher plant was first described in 1806 by the French naturalist Jacques Julien Houtton de Labillardière (1755–1834). Between 1791 and 1803, several European expeditions visited the southern Australian coast, including a British expedition headed by Captain Flinders, with the botanist Robert Brown (1773–1858) on board. Upon visiting the plants' natural habitat in December 1800, Brown observed that *Cephalotus* caught insects. Live specimens were first brought to Kew Gardens in 1823. Although the plants were initially assigned to the rose family (Rosaceae), in 1829 Barthélemy Charles Dumortier (1797–1878) established the monotypic family of the Cephalotaceae. The generic name, which is a reference to the spherical anthers, is derived from the Greek term *kephalotus*, meaning "headed."

Distribution and Habitat

Cephalotus follicularis has a very small area of distribution in the Mediterranean winter-rain

Fig. 57.
Red projections around the pitcher rim of *Cephalotus follicularis*.
W. Barthlott

have a glossy surface and bear numerous nectar glands. The trap leaves consist of a petiole and the pitcher-shaped lamina. The petiole is attached to the rear of the upper trap rim. This feature distinguishes *Cephalotus* from all other pitcher plants, in which the petiole always forms the base of the pitcher. The pitcher has a lid with conspicuous translucent grooves. It remains closed while the leaf is still developing, opening only once the leaf is fully grown. The upper rim of the pitcher bears toothlike projections that resemble the peristome of *Nepenthes*. Beneath the row of projections, the inside of the pitcher is smooth and funnel-shaped, with an overhanging collar that constricts the free trap space. There are three wing ribs on the outside of the trap. The most prominent of these is T-shaped in cross-section and runs along the front of the pitcher from top to bottom. Its free edges are densely pubescent. The other two wings are on both sides of the trap and are also pubescent. The pitchers are 2–5 cm high. The inflorescence is borne on scapes up to 60 cm long that are formed individually or in small numbers in the center of the leaf rosette, the inconspicuous flowers are borne on short, headlike panicles. The individual flowers are about 8 mm in diameter and white. They have six petals, twelve stamens, and six free carpels. The bases of the flowers bear nectar glands, and the flowers produce a heavy, sweet scent. Each carpel contains one ovule. Each of the free carpels develops into a follicular fruit at maturity. According to Lowrie (1998a), the seeds will germinate only if they remain in the ripened carpel.

ing out by means of their underground organs. The accompanying vegetation can consist of pure moss or be interspersed with other plants, especially species of the grasslike Restionaceae.

Features

The Australian pitcher plant is a perennial, herbaceous rosette plant with a very short shoot that can attain a height of about 10 cm during the vegetative growth phase. The plant develops a thick, branched rootstock. In addition to the normal, flat foliage leaves, the plant has pitcher-shaped trap leaves (Figs. 57, 58). Both leaf forms, of which there are also intermediate forms, grow in a seasonal alternation. The color of the leaves is dependent on the incoming sunlight: on shady sites, they remain green, while on sunny sites they take on a vivid red to brownish red coloration. The foliage leaves are oval, stalked (petiolate), thick, and fleshy, and attain a length of up to 15 cm. They

Trapping Mechanism, Digestion, and Prey

The pitcher-shaped leaves serve as a trapping device. As with all pitfall traps, there is an attraction zone, a slip zone, and a digestive zone.

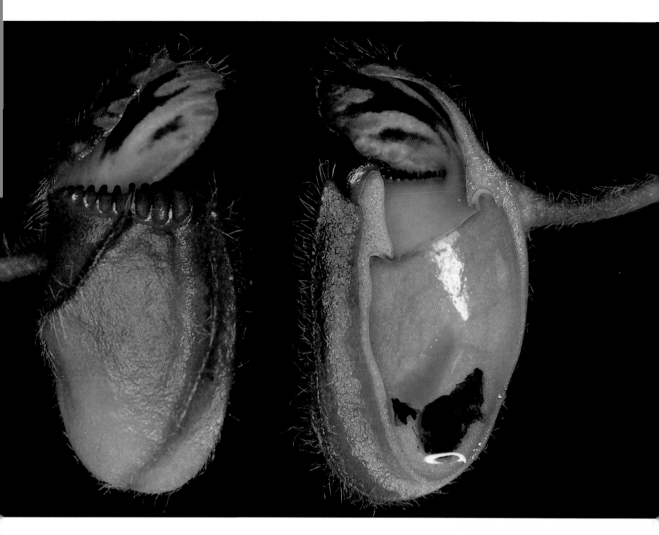

In *Cephalotus*, the transition from slip zone to digestive zone is not sharply defined.

The attraction zone comprises the lid and the pitcher rim. There are nectar glands on both sides of the lid, as well as on and between the toothlike projections. The pitcher-shaped interior of the trap beneath the projections also bears numerous nectar glands. In addition, the vivid red to brownish red coloration of the lid is also regarded as an attracting mechanism. The underside of the lid is covered in short hairs that are directed toward the trap opening. It is likely that not all the Australian pitcher plant's victims are actually attracted to it. The traps are often sunk into the surrounding moss, so that the pitcher rim is level with the moss surface. In such cases, passers-by will also occasionally fall into the traps.

The slip zone comprises the funnel-shaped zone of the trap interior beneath the row of projections. This zone is covered with short, downward-pointing, scalelike hairs (Fig. 59). Between the hairs, there are nectar glands that encourage the prey to climb over the edge of the pitcher and onto the slick funnel zone. From here, the victims fall into the trap, which is filled with liquid. Because the trap opening is constricted by the collar, the prey find a considerable obstacle to climbing back out again.

The slip zone leads into the digestive zone beneath the funnel. The trap wall is covered

Fig. 58.
Longitudinal section through the pitfall traps of *Cephalotus follicularis*.
W. Barthlott

Fig. 59.
Scanning electron micrograph of the slip zone of *Cephalotus follicularis* with short, downward-pointing hairs. W. Barthlott

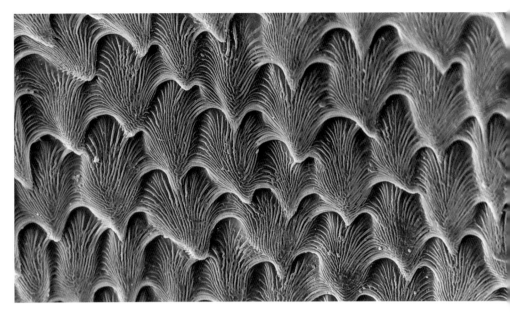

with digestive glands, which are especially dense in the two purplish brown, kidney-shaped areas on the lateral walls near the bottom of the pitcher. The digestive zone is partially filled with liquid, in which the prey animals drown. Ants make up the greater part of the prey of the Australian pitcher plant, together with flying insects, although detailed studies of the prey composition have yet to be conducted.

Cephalotus produces esterases, phosphatases, proteases, ribonucleases, and amylases, which are used to digest the soft body parts of the victims. However, Australian pitcher plants do not produce any enzymes to break down the chitin that makes up the outer shell, or exoskeleton, of insects and spiders. Opened traps typically feature a bacterial flora in the trap liquid that is apparently also involved with the digestion. Young, still-closed traps do not yet contain any digestive fluid. Froebe and Bauer (1988) conducted a detailed study on

the development of the pitcher leaves in *C. follicularis*.

Cultivation

The Australian pitcher plant is not suitable for beginners. It is best grown in a greenhouse or cold frame. *Cephalotus* prefers a brightly lit site that is cool in both summer (20–28°C, 68–80°F) and winter (5–15°C, 40–59°F). Properly hardened plants can even survive mild frosts. Peat is suitable as a growing medium, with sand or bark added to improve drainage. The soil should be kept moist, but it must never become waterlogged. The plant pots should be kept in a shallow tray with a little water that is allowed to dry out in between watering. Plastic and clay pots are suitable, the latter permitting cooler soil temperatures in summer.

Cephalotus is most easily propagated by dividing up older specimens or by leaf cuttings from the flat foliage leaves.

Dioncophyllaceae: Hookleaf Family

The Dioncophyllaceae (hookleaf family), which is native to the moist and hot lowland rainforests of western Africa (Sierra Leone, Liberia, Ivory Coast, and Gabon), comprises three monotypic genera, *Dioncophyllum*, *Habropetalum*, and *Triphyophyllum*. These are very large lianas characterized by hooked leaves with two backwardly directed hooks at the tips, which the plants use to climb up through the branches of the surrounding trees into the forest canopy (Porembski and Barthlott 2002).

Within the Dioncophyllaceae, concrete evidence of carnivory has to date been found only for *Triphyophyllum peltatum* (Hutch. & Dalz.) Airy Shaw. Although Schmid (1964), in his morphological discussion of the family, noted a distinct resemblance to carnivorous genera, he did not specifically associate this characteristic with *Triphyophyllum*. Marburger (1979), in his detailed study of *Triphyophyllum* glands, suspected the carnivorous nature of the genus. However, it was Green et al. (1979), using field studies and subsequent laboratory analysis, who were first able to demonstrate that *T. peltatum* is a carnivorous plant. As its molecular and biochemical features indicate, the hookleaf family belongs to a group of related taxa (the order Nepenthales) that, together with the Droseraceae and Nepenthaceae, includes other carnivorous families. Apparently, there is a particularly close kinship between the Dioncophyllaceae and the Portuguese sundew, *Drosophyllum lusitanicum*. Research is currently proceeding on the question of whether the sundews and pitcher plants evolved from the Dioncophyllaceae, with some members of the hookleaf family, which are rainforest lianas, having

secondarily lost the trait of carnivory. In biochemical terms, the Dioncophyllaceae are distinguished by the presence of naphthochinon compounds (including plumbagin) and naphthylisochinolin alkaloids (such as dioncophyllin), indicating a close kinship with the Ancistrocladaceae (Bringmann and Pokorny 1995). Based on morphological and anatomical features, Airy Shaw (1951) and Metcalfe (1951) suspected a kinship between the Dioncophyllaceae and the Ancistrocladaceae and Droseraceae (in particular *Drosophyllum*). The most recent molecular genetic data (Meimberg et al. 2000) indicate that *Triphyophyllum* represents a link between the carnivorous members of the Droseraceae-Nepenthaceae group that has recently been assigned to the Caryophyllidae, which are also related to the carnations and the cacti.

Triphyophyllum (Hutchinson & Dalziell) Airy Shaw
hookleaf

The generic name of this plant, which was coined by the British botanist H. K. Airy Shaw (1951), refers to the most conspicuous feature of this liana: *Triphyophyllum peltatum* has three different kinds of foliage leaves that assume different functions. The Latin specific epithet *peltatum* refers to the discus-shaped seeds.

Distribution and Habitat

This species is distributed in western Africa from the southwest of the Ivory Coast to Libe-

has well-developed roots. The alternate leaves occur in three variations: juvenile plants (up to 1 m high) develop narrow lanceolate leaves, up to 30 cm long, for photosynthesis. Hooked leaves develop on the climbing stem axes of older plants, with two hooks at the tips that the plant uses for climbing. The third type is filamentous, glandular leaves up to 25 cm long (Figs. 60, 61), the tips of which—like the Portuguese sundew—are rolled up in an inverse circinate fashion (toward the outside). According to current knowledge, these are found almost exclusively in juvenile plants that are undergoing the transition to the adult form. However, glandular leaves can also develop on lateral shoots if older specimens are cut back. Observations from cultivation have shown that glandular leaves are not necessarily found in the juvenile stage, but rather that hooked leaves can immediately develop in the transition to the climbing habit. *Triphyophyllum*, therefore, can be regarded as a temporary carnivore. If we exclude the incidence of seasonal carnivory due to winter dormancy (such as in *Pinguicula*), this phenomenon is known only from *Triphyophyllum* and *Drosera caduca,*. The flowers develop on loosely arranged panicles. The small, white, weakly scented flowers have a superior ovary that opens in a valvate fashion, even in the unripe phase. The pendulous seeds, which are at the end of a 5-cm stalk, are discus-shaped and are surrounded by a membranous margin. They are tinged reddish, attain a diameter of 5–8 cm, and are wind-dispersed.

Trapping Mechanism, Digestion, and Prey

On the insect-trapping leaves of the transitional phase between the juvenile and adult stages, there are two types of glands (stalked and unstalked), which were first studied by Marburger (1979). The multicellular glandular

Fig. 60.
A juvenile hookleaf, *Triphyophyllum peltatum*, growing in its natural habitat in Ivory Coast. The two sticky glandular leaves are clearly recognizable.
S. Porembski

ria and Sierra Leone. *Triphyophyllum peltatum* grows in both primary rainforests and secondary forest communities.

Features

This perennial liana develops a shoot that can attain a length of 70 m in older plants, and it forms a rosette in the juvenile stage. The plant

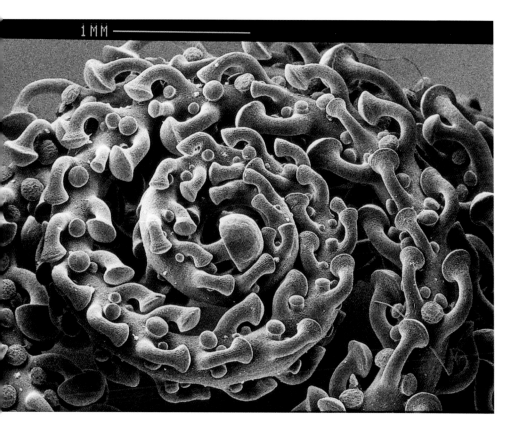

1 MM

Fig. 61.
Detail of a scanning
electron micrograph
of a young glandular
leaf of *Triphyophyl-
lum peltatum*, rolled
up in an inverse
circinate fashion.
W. Barthlott

heads are reddish and connected to the vascular tissue (phloem). They exude a sticky secretion that contains several digestive enzymes, proteases, peroxidase, and esterase. The presence of prey animals stimulates the glands to intensify their secretions. The prey consists mainly of flies and beetles, but ants and butterflies are also caught.

Cultivation

As a rule, *Triphyophyllum* is extremely difficult to grow, and its cultivation is essentially re-stricted to botanical gardens. Because of its origins, the hookleaf needs hothouse conditions with a semishaded growth site and a constantly high air humidity and regular watering. The temperatures must never fall below 18°C (64°F). The growing medium should be water-permeable and contain humus. The cultivation of hookleaf plants in pure expanded clay has occasionally also been successful.

Propagation is by seed only, as successful propagation through the use of cuttings is apparently not possible.

Droseraceae: Sundew Family

The family Droseraceae comprises three genera, with some 162 carnivorous species: *Aldrovanda* (waterwheel plant), *Dionaea* (Venus flytrap), and *Drosera* (sundew). The family has a nearly global distribution, which is primarily due to the widespread distribution of *Drosera*. The three genera are markedly different from one another: *Drosera* has active adhesive traps, while both *Dionaea* and *Aldrovanda* catch their prey with active closing traps. The leaves of both *Dionaea* and *Aldrovanda* resemble a steel trap (or gin trap), like those used to trap bears and wolves. How the relatively simple adhesive traps evolved into complex closing traps was examined in detail in the chapter on evolution.

Until very recently, the genus *Drosophyllum* (Portuguese sundew) was also included in the sundew family, but it has now been assigned to its own family, Drosophyllaceae. The sundew family and its affiliated group the Drosophyllaceae belong to the order Nepenthales, which mainly includes carnivorous plants (Meimberg et al. 2000). The nearest relatives of the Droseraceae include the Old World pitcher plants (*Nepenthes*) and the African hookleaf family (Dioncophyllaceae). Together, these families are related to the carnation-like plants (Caryophyllidae; Kubitzki 2002a, 2002c). The genus *Drosera* occupies a basal position within the Droseraceae, with *Dionaea* and *Aldrovanda* representing more advanced taxa, as supported by both morphological and molecular genetic research (Seine and Barthlott 1993; Cameron et al. 2002; Rivadavia et al. 2003).

Drosera Linnaeus
sundew

The genus *Drosera* comprises about 160 species, most of which are herbaceous perennials. The generic name is derived from the Greek word *droseros* (meaning "dew-covered") and refers to the leaves of the plant, which are covered in mucilaginous drops. The plants catch their prey with these active adhesive traps.

The central European sundew species were known in the late Middle Ages and were illustrated in herbal books, such as the *Cruydeboeck*, by the Dutchman R. Dodoens (1554). *Drosera rotundifolia*, the round-leaved sundew, was the most important study object for Charles Darwin (1875), who was the first to demonstrate strong evidence of carnivory in the plant kingdom.

The relationships among the sundew species and their systematic classification have not yet been fully elucidated. Diels (1906) published the last monograph on the genus, and, as might be expected, his classification does not accord with state-of-the-art research. Rivadavia et al. (2003) published a comprehensive molecular genetic examination of the genus that gives a better understanding of its anatomical and morphological features.

The genus *Drosera* has been divided into three subgenera and eleven sections (Seine and Barthlott 1994), with the subgenus *Drosera* containing the herbaceous species that do not develop tubers. The tuber-forming species

are contained in the subgenus *Ergaleium*, and the subgenus *Regiae* contains just one species, the unusual *Drosera regia* from South Africa.

The subgenus *Drosera* comprises eight sections (*Drosera, Bryastrum, Coelophylla, Lasiocephala, Meristocaules, Phycopsis, Ptycnostigma,* and *Thelocalyx*), which will not be discussed in detail here; for a detailed description of these sections, see Seine and Barthlott (1994). The section *Drosera* includes all the Northern Hemisphere species of the genus. The Australian dwarf sundew species, or pygmy sundews (Fig. 62), make up the section *Bryastrum. Drosera binata* is the sole member of the section *Phycopsis*, while the section *Ptycnostigma* includes the large-flowered sundew species of South Africa that develop storage roots.

The subgenus *Ergaleium* (syn. *Sondera*) is nearly exclusive to Australia and comprises three sections: *Ergaleium, Erythrorhizae,* and *Stoloniferae*. The section *Ergaleium* includes the species with long shoots and peltate leaves. These include the Australian climbing species, but also *Drosera gigantea* and *D. peltata*. The section *Erythrorhizae* includes the rosette-forming, tuber-forming species, while the section *Stoloniferae* includes the erect, tuber-forming species whose leaves are not peltate.

The subgenus *Regiae* was established for *Drosera regia* (Figs. 63, 64), because this species has a subshrub habit and a pollen form that is quite different than that of the rest of the genus. These differences are not great enough to justify establishing a separate genus, however. Chrtek and Slavikova (1996) named the species *Freatulina regia*, a name that is now considered invalid.

European sundew species have been used in folk medicine since the Middle Ages, as remedies for coughs and respiratory ailments. More

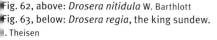

Fig. 62, above: *Drosera nitidula* W. Barthlott
Fig. 63, below: *Drosera regia*, the king sundew.
I. Theisen

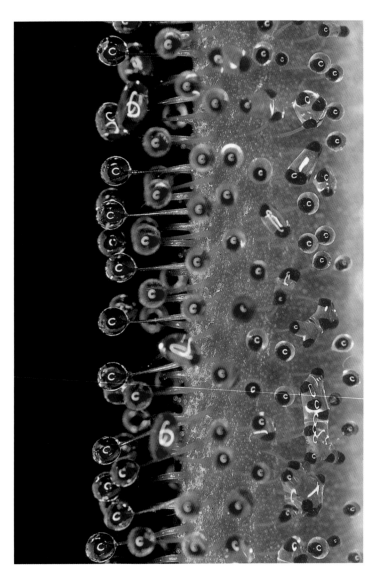

Fig. 64.
Detail of the glandular leaf of *Drosera regia*.
W. Barthlott

the name "red ink sundew" for *Drosera erythrorhiza* would seem to indicate a corresponding use. The most important economic use today is for the ornamental plants trade. *Drosera* species are a standard item of larger florists, and they are also frequently sold as curiosities in home-improvement and garden centers.

Distribution and Habitat

The genus *Drosera* has a nearly global distribution, although there are large gaps in the desert and rainforest regions of the world. In the far north, *D. rotundifolia* (Fig. 65) colonizes the entire boreal zone, and in Canada the species extends as far north as the Arctic Circle. In the Southern Hemisphere, too, sundew species extend far down toward the pole: *D. stenophylla* is found south of latitude 50°S on the Auckland Islands, and *D. uniflora* grows south of latitude 60°S on Clarence Island off the Antarctic Peninsula. The sundew species that grows at the highest elevation is *D. meristocaulis*, which occurs at an elevation of 3014 m above sea level on the summit of Neblina Tepui, Brazil's highest mountain.

The center of diversity of the genus *Drosera* is located in Australia, where there are some seventy species in the southwest of the continent, in the environs around the city of Perth. A second center of diversity is in the southwest of South Africa, around the Cape of Good Hope and Table Mountain. In both regions, the individual species generally have very small areas of distribution. These are endemic species that are sometimes found on only a very few sites. By contrast, the very few sundew species of the Northern Hemisphere have vast distributions.

As might be expected in such a large and widespread genus, sundews occupy a wide range of habitats. The bogs and swamps that the Northern Hemisphere *Drosera* species

recently, dried material of species from other regions (*Drosera madagascariensis*, *D. peltata*, and *D. ramentacea*) has also been used. Alcohol extracts containing *Drosera* are believed to strengthen the heart. The aphrodisiacal effect ascribed to the sundew has led to the production of liqueurs containing *Drosera*, such as the Italian "Rosoglio." Reports on the use of mucilage to treat sunburn and freckles are more likely to be anecdotal than anything else.

The Australian Aborigines use the plant tubers as a source of nutrition. Confectioners used the red pigment as a food coloring, and

ccupy are relatively atypical for the genus as
whole. In fact, the overwhelming majority
of the species prefer seasonally moist sandy
reas. With the aid of various perennating or-
ans (storage roots and hibernation buds), the
plants survive dry periods in a state of vegeta-
ive dormancy.

In Australia, *Drosera* grows mainly in heath
ommunities (Fig. 12), on sandy soils that fea-
ure herbal and low, open, small-scrub commu-
ities. The same applies to South Africa, where
he physiognomically similar *fynbos* represents
he main habitat for sundew species. By devel-
ping underground perennating organs, both
South African and Australian sundews are
ble to withstand the regular bush fires that
occur in their respective habitats. Indeed,
many species profit from these fires, because
he fires keep the surrounding shrub growth
rom becoming too dense and nutrients from
he ashes become available in the soil. In North
and South America, numerous *Drosera* species
colonize moist sandy soils during the rainy
season.

On rocky sites, sundews often grow on fine,
gravelly, weakly developed soils that are sub-
ect to runoff water flows during the wet season but dry out during the dry season. Such
conditions are found, for example, on inselbergs (Fig. 17) and on sandstone formations
in northern Australia (Seine et al. 1995).

Some species colonize forest sites, which is
unusual for carnivores; for example, there are
tuber-forming *Drosera* species in Australia
that thrive in the undergrowth of open eucalyptus forests. Shady rainforests in the northeast of Australia provide a habitat for *D. adelae*, *D. prolifera*, and *D. schizandra*.

Features

Most *Drosera* species are perennial herbs; a
few species are annual herbs or dwarf shrubs.

Fig. 65.
The central European
native *Drosera rotun-
difolia*, the round-
leaved sundew, on
a site immediately
adjacent to Cologne/
Bonn Airport.
W. Barthlott

In addition to rosette plants and erect herbs,
there are also climbing plants that reach a
length up to 3 m. The majority of species survive unfavorable weather periods with the aid
of perennating buds, storage roots, or tubers.

Tuber-forming sundew species may also
have underground lateral shoots (stolons).
Small daughter tubers develop at the end of
these stolons, which the plant then uses for
vegetative reproduction. This means that genetically identical individuals, or clones, can
be produced. A few sundew species, such as
Drosera hamiltonii, have flat, creeping, under-

nodes generally have self-supporting stems (such as *Drosera indica*). Some tuber-forming sundew species grow as climbing plants, with shoots that are both wiry and elastic (such as *D. pallida*, Fig. 66). The leaves serve as climbing organs (see below). These plants have a regular branching pattern in which a short shoot, located in a leaf axil on a long shoot, bears two leaves. *Drosera gigantea* often produces many branches, forming a little bush in each new growth season.

The roots are mostly only weakly developed. The primary roots die off quickly and are replaced by only a few adventive roots. An exception is *Drosera regia*, which has numerous, thick adventive roots. Some South African species, such as *D. cistiflora*, have greatly thickened adventive roots that serve as storage organs for the dry season.

The leaves are arranged alternately on the shoot, with most *Drosera* species producing a short shoot supporting a leaf rosette (Figs. 67, 68). The leaves are the trapping organs of the plant, and they are used for photosynthesis as well. The leaf form is highly variable within the genus: there are linear, spatulate, elliptical, rounded, reniform, and peltate leaves. Perhaps the most extreme leaf form is that of *D. binata*, with its bifurcate or multifurcate leaves (Fig. 70). The size of the leaf, too, can vary greatly from one species to another. *Drosera regia* has leaves that are up to 70 cm long, while the leaves of the smallest species are only a few millimeters long. In the bud, the leaves of *Drosera* are rolled up facing inward, like a fern frond. As the leaves mature, they open until they are ultimately spread out flat.

The structure of the *Drosera* leaf corresponds to that of a normal foliage leaf and consists of a base, a stalk (petiole), and a blade (lamina). The leaf base generally bears a membranous, papery-thin appendage (median stipule) on the upperside that can be regarded as

Fig. 66.
Drosera pallida, a climbing sundew, in its natural environment in Western Australia (with Dr. Seine for scale).
R. Seine

ground shoots (rhizomes). They bear a leaf rosette at the tip of each lateral shoot, serving both the plant's dispersal and the storage of nutrients.

Sundew species produce few or no branches. Species with longer shoots and larger inter-

In many Australian species, the shoot develops an underground tuber each year. This helps the plant survive the extremely hot and dry Australian summer. At the beginning of the rainy season, the aboveground parts of the plant then regenerate from the tuber. Meanwhile, a new tuber begins to develop immediately adjacent to, or even within, the old one. By examining the papery remains of old tubers in the sheaths of *Drosera erythrorhiza* tubers (Fig. 71), it has been demonstrated that this plant can reach an age of more than 50 years.

Fig. 67.
Drosera lowriei
R. Seine

Fig. 68, left:
Drosera erythrorhiza
subsp. *squamosa*
W. Barthlott

Fig. 69, right:
Drosera gigantea
leaf with tentacles
arranged in a
pincushion fashion.
P. Pretscher

the product of fused stipules. This feature is absent in all tuber-forming sundews. The median stipules play a major role in the formation of the perennating buds of the rosette-forming species. This bud helps the species of temperate and cold climates to overwinter and the species of subtropical climates to survive through to the next rainy season. The median stipules, which develop long before the rest of the leaf, lie close together, and the space between them is filled with air. Due to the inclusion of this air, the bud often appears white

 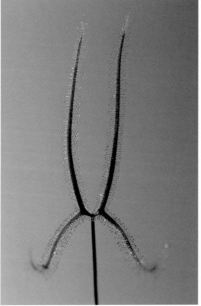 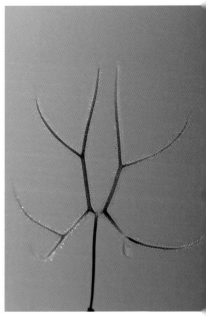

Fig. 70.
Three different leaf forms in *Drosera binata*. W. Barthlott

and reflects sunlight well, while water is virtually unable to penetrate into the bud.

The petiole connects the leaf base with the lamina, which is covered with tentacles. In many rosette-forming species, the petiole represents only a short and inconspicuous transition zone. By contrast, in many dwarf species and in *Drosera falconeri*, it is very well developed in comparison with the leaf lamina and probably assumes much of the photosynthetic function. As part of the climbing organ, the petiole of the Australian climbing, tuber-forming sundews is equipped with a strong reinforcing tissue with which the petiole can withstand the mechanical stress from the plant's weight and additional movements in the wind.

In *Drosera*, the leaf lamina serves as an active adhesive trap, although the form of the lamina varies greatly within the genus. In all species, the leaf upperside bears small sessile glands and tentacles, which consist of a stalk and a glandular knob or head. The glandular knob secretes the mucilage for catching prey. As a rule, the tentacles are short in the middle of the lamina and longer toward the margins. The glandular knobs of the tentacles on the

lamina are always rounded, whereas those on the leaf margins exhibit a great diversity of form, which can also be used as a basis for systematic classification of the genus (Seine and Barthlott 1994). In addition to simple marginal tentacles that are similar to the central tentacles, there are also flattened tentacles that bear glandular tissue only on their uppersides. *Drosera glanduligera* has a particularly unusual form of flattened tentacle: the glandular portion is separated from a flat portion that has no glands. Marginal tentacles of this kind are able to move particularly quickly. On the plants' natural growth sites in Australia, the marginal tentacles able to bend toward the middle of the leaf within about one second. By contrast, *Drosera rosulata* develops marginal tentacles without glandular knobs. Its marginal tentacles very strongly resemble those of the Venus flytrap, *Dionaea muscipula*, in which they are known as "marginal bristles" (Seine and Barthlott 1992).

The dwarf species, which are mainly found in Australia, exhibit a marked leaf dimorphism, that is, they have two different leaf types. In addition to normal foliage leaves, reproductive leaves (gemmae) are formed that serve vegetative reproduction. In general, the gemmae begin to develop at the beginning of the wet season. In place of the normal leaf blade, the gemmae develop compact tissue that bears a young plant. The first gemmae develop inside the perennating bud, which then opens as the gemmae grow and expand. After some time, the gemmae are fully ripe and can easily be detached from the petiole. They are then knocked off the petiole by raindrops and dispersed by the rainwater in the vicinity of the mother plant. In this way, dwarf sundew species can very quickly form a large population of genetically identical individuals at the beginning of the rainy season.

The climbing Australian tuber-forming sundews generally use the leaf of the main shoot as a holdfast to anchor themselves to the surrounding vegetation. In the axil of this leaf, two more leaves grow on a short shoot. These are used primarily for catching prey and have a much shorter petiole than that of the leaf of the main shoot. Some climbing or erect tuber-forming *Drosera* species have a basal rosette in addition to aerial leaves. The leaves of this rosette often have a different form than that of the upper leaves.

There are extreme cases in which the insect-trapping leaf blades are no longer formed in older plants, such as in *Drosera caduca* from northern Australia. This phenomenon of temporary carnivory, in which the plant is carnivorous for only part of its life cycle, is extremely rare and is known only in this species and *Triphyophyllum peltatum*.

The inflorescence is usually a raceme (scor-

Fig. 71, above: *Drosera erythrorhiza* subsp. *erythrorhiza*, a tuber-forming sundew, on its natural habitat in western Australia. R. Seine

Fig. 72, below: *Drosera burmannii*, with conspicuous, fast-moving tentacles on the leaf margin. W. Barthlott

Figs. 73–78.
The diversity of
flowers in sundew
species.

Fig. 73.
Drosera menziesii
W. Barthlott

pioid cyme) that is rolled up (involute) on one
side. The flowers generally open one by one
from the bottom to the top, which results in
a long overall flowering time, even though the
individual flowers are short-lived. The flowers
are generally short-lived, opening for only one
or a few days (Figs. 73–78). Most species have
modestly sized white or pinkish flowers. Exceptions include the poppylike flower of the red
form of *Drosera cistiflora* (Fig. 76) and the yellow flowers of *D. zigzagia* (Fig. 77).

The inflorescence of *Drosera graniticola* produces a grand display, thanks to the large number of flowers that open simultaneously. The
flowers generally have five green fused sepals,
five free petals, five stamens, and three fused
carpels. The pollen develops and is released in
tetrads. The stigmata can be either simple and
button-shaped or deeply forked (furcate). To
date, there has been little research on the polli-

Fig. 74.
Drosera microphylla
W. Barthlott

Figs. 75 and 76.
White- and red-
flowered forms of
Drosera cistiflora.
W. Barthlott

Fig. 77, left:
Drosera zigzagia
I. Theisen

Fig. 78, right:
Drosera callistos
I. Theisen

nators of *Drosera*, although the flowers have an entomophilic (insect-pollinated) character.

Most sundew species are self-fertilizing and self-pollinating, which means that the seeds develop without the aid of pollinators. These then ripen in a capsule. The size and shape of the seeds vary from one species to another: some are fine and dustlike, whereas others can be as large as sesame seeds.

Trapping Mechanism, Digestion, and Prey

Sundews have active adhesive traps, with the trapping device consisting of the leaves and their tentacles and sessile glands. The stalks of the tentacles consist of an outer cell layer (epidermis), a few cell layers lying beneath it, and a central string of tracheids that conduct water. The glandular head is more or less egg-shaped. In its center, there are a group of short tracheids that form an extension of the conductive tissue from the stalk. Above and to the sides, the tracheids are enveloped in a bell-shaped endodermis. The endodermis is a layer of cells that acts as a seal between the water-conducting tissue and the glandular tissue, and it controls the transport of water. The two outer cell rows of the tentacle knob consist of glandular cells that produce mucilage and secrete it externally.

The sessile glands are much simpler, typically consisting of several glandular cells that lie above a few endodermal cells. There is almost no connection to the conductive tissue. Because they do not secrete any mucilage, the sessile glands are involved in digestion but not in the trapping of the prey.

The sundews' prey are attracted with the aid of optical signals. The reflection of light in the dewdrops and the usually conspicuous reddish color of the tentacles attract a very wide range of prey animals. These get stuck to the mucilage drops on the tentacles, becoming increasingly more covered in mucilage in their attempts to escape. In addition, the mechanically stimulated tentacles surrounding the trapped victim bend inward toward the middle of the leaf, making it more difficult for the victim to escape to the leaf edge. The prey animal ultimately dies in a large drop of mucilage, which makes breathing impossible. Small prey animals, such as ants, typically lie motionless on the leaf after as little as 15 minutes, while larger victims are generally not covered in mucilage so quickly. The mucilage is acidic and contains polysaccharides; for instance, *Drosera capensis* secretes a 4 percent solution of these polysaccharides with a pH value of 5. In addition, the mucilage contains calcium, magnesium, potassium, and sodium ions. Before digestion takes place, the mucilage does not contain any proteins.

The mechanical stimulus caused by the prey triggers the glandular knob of the tentacle. The physical contact elicits a change in the electrical potential of the knob, or a receptor potential. If the contact is vigorous enough or repeated several times, the receptor potential increases accordingly. Above a certain threshold value, the potential of the tentacle head triggers a series of electrical signals, or action potentials, that are carried from the tentacle stalk to the leaf surface. This causes the stimulated tentacles to curl up. The entire excitation process is similar to that of the conduction of stimuli and information in animal neural tracts. The tentacle movement that the action potentials trigger lasts up to 30 minutes and is known as the "rapid trapping movement." In addition to the tentacle movement triggered by mechanical stimuli, there are also slow trapping movements, which are triggered mainly by chemical stimuli. Those tentacles that have not been mechanically stimulated and the entire leaf lamina slowly curl toward the trapped prey animal. As a result of this movement, a hollow cavity develops around the victim or the leaf may envelope it completely. This slow movement appears to be triggered by an increased production of growth hormones.

The digestion of the prey animals by *Drosera* begins as soon as they have become trapped. The slow trapping movement overlaps in time with the production and secretion of digestive enzymes. Sessile glands and tentacles that receive chemical stimuli release digestive enzymes into the mucilage that surrounds the prey animal. The other leaf glands remain inactive. While the enzymes are released, the pH value may also fall by as much as two units, although this does not always occur.

The sundews produce esterases, phosphatases, proteases, and aminopeptidases for digestion. There is also evidence of chitinase in the trapping mucilage, although it cannot be ruled out that this is the result of microbial activity. The soft parts of the victims are digested very quickly, and the chitin exoskeletons are emptied after several days. Darwin (1875) found that *Drosera rotundifolia* was able to break down a 1.25-cm cube of egg white completely after 50 hours. The dissolved nutrient components are resorbed by the plant's tentacle knobs and the sessile glands.

Articulates, particularly insects, make up the bulk of the prey animals of *Drosera*. The prey spectrum within the insects is wide, with hardly any specialization observed with respect to species of prey animal. Ninety percent of the prey of the European species *D. anglica*, *D. intermedia*, and *D. rotundifolia* consists of winged insects. In contrast, wingless springtails (collembolans) make up more than 70 percent of the prey of the Australian sundew *D. erythrorhiza*.

The prey of a particular plant frequently varies during the growth period, because some insect species are present in large numbers for only brief periods and are then replaced by others. Similarly, different prey spectra have been identified in the species *Drosera intermedia* and *D. rotundifolia*, which regularly occur together. However, these two species prefer different areas along a moisture gradient that represent different habitats for the prey animals. Hence, the prey spectrum is primarily dependent on the animals that are present in the habitat at a small scale. In addition, the leaf shape and size also influence the size of the prey animals that can be caught. *Drosera regia* can catch large flies on its broad and long leaves, for example, whereas dwarf species can catch only much smaller prey.

Selected Species

Drosera binata Labill.
fork leaf sundew

Distribution and habitat: New Zealand, eastern Australia, and Tasmania; on sandy to peaty soils in grassland and heathland vegetation. (Specimens found on newly discovered sites in Western Australia may have been introduced.) Features: Perennial herb with fleshy storage roots. Leaves arranged in a rosette and up to 30 cm long; they die off at the end of the growth period and appear again at the beginning of the next season. Leaves bifurcate or multifurcate, that is, the leaves resemble deer antlers. White flowers about 1 cm across are present in inflorescences of several flowers each. The considerable variability in this species means that there are many cultivars available in the horticultural trade. Fig. 70

Drosera capensis L.
Cape sundew

Distribution and habitat: South Africa (Cape region); on sandy soils in *fynbos* and on fallow land. Features: Perennial, evergreen herb with a shoot that can be several centimeters long in older plants. Leaves in the form of a rosette or tuft near the tip of the shoot, linear-lanceolate, about 10 cm long; leaf stalk slightly flattened. Inflorescences up to 20 cm long, with small, pinkish flowers that each last only 1 day. Due to the large number of flowers that appear sequentially, however, the plant has a long flowering time. With this species' variable leaf coloration and growth form, numerous cultivars are available. Figs. 32–34

Drosera erythrorhiza Lindl.

Distribution and habitat: Australia (southwestern Western Australia; Fig. 68); on sand, laterite, loam, and peat in heathland vegetation and eucalyptus forests. Features: Tuber-forming sundew with annual leaf rosette. The tubers are enclosed in vivid red sheaths. Underground daughter tubers serve reproduction. Leaves fleshy, with a very short petiole that merges into the leaf lamina, elliptical to broadly ovate, up to 6 cm long and 4 cm wide. Inflorescence short, with up to thirty small white flowers. Several different subspecies with isolated areas of distribution and habitats have been described. Figs. 68, 71

Drosera pulchella Lehm.

Distribution and habitat: Australia (southwestern Western Australia); on sand, peat, laterite, or loam on watercourse margins in open vegetation or open forests. Features: Mostly evergreen dwarf sundew with leaves arranged in a rosette. Leaves about 1.5 cm long, with a flat wide petiole and rounded leaf lamina, with widely projecting marginal tentacles. Gemmae develop in the rosette center at the beginning of the growth period. Flowers 1 cm in diameter, in small numbers on short inflorescences; color mostly pink, although white- and orange-flowered forms are also known. Fig. 79

Drosera regia Stephens
king sundew

Distribution and habitat: South Africa, Cape region; on sandy-peaty soil in short grasslands. Features: Subshrub with fleshy storage roots. On the tips of the shoots there are tufts with linear leaves up to 70 cm long. Leaves with a short petiole that merges into the leaf lamina, which is 1 cm wide. Inflorescences tall, with a few pinkish or white flowers 3 cm across. This species is extremely rare in the wild, and is threatened with extinction. Figs. 63, 64

Drosera rotundifolia L.
round-leaved sundew

Distribution and habitat: Temperate and cool regions of North America, Europe, and Asia; on peaty soils. Features: Perennial herb with annual basal leaf rosette. Overwinters with a perennating bud. Leaves up to 8 cm long, with a long flat petiole and rounded leaf lamina. Flowers small and white, arranged on a long inflorescence. This is the quintessential sundew; it was once studied by Charles Darwin (1875) and is the most widely distributed species. Fig. 65

Cultivation

The genus *Drosera* offers rewarding plants and demanding challenges for all growers, from beginners to experienced specialists. Useful information regarding the cultivation of the individual species may be gained from the climatic conditions at their natural habitats, especially as far as temperatures and any dormancy periods are concerned. (For the natural distributions of all *Drosera* species, see the appendix.) There are sundews that are suitable for growing outdoors, indoors, and in greenhouses.

Sundews need a brightly lit to sunny site. In summer, some shade is required as protection from the midday sun. As rainforest natives, *Drosera adelae*, *D. prolifera*, and *D. schizandra* prefer a moderately lit site without direct sun. Cultivars with red pigmentation generally turn a more vivid color if they receive plenty of light. Northern Hemisphere species that are grown in the open year-round should be planted in a sunny site.

Drosera thrives best in a mixture of peat and sand; smaller admixtures of fine-grained charcoal or perlite may also be beneficial. Species of temperate and cool latitudes should be grown on a mixture containing more than 50 percent peat, while tropical and subtropical species, especially those that require a strict dormancy period, prefer a mixture containing about 75 percent sand. When growing dwarf sundews, the sand should not be too coarsely grained. *Sphagnum* is often used for mulching species from the Northern Hemisphere. Dwarf and tuber-forming sundews thrive especially well if the growing medium is covered with sand. Fertilization is not necessary if the plants are able to catch insects occasionally.

Sundews are best watered by using a tray underneath the main growing container with a water level of 1–2 cm. The water then rises into the main container by capillary action. Except when growing species that must survive a dry period in the wild, the soil should not be allowed to dry out. The soil should never be completely waterlogged. Dwarf species can generally be grown on only slightly moist soils, without the need for a strict dormancy period. The above method of watering is then applied during the growth period. The tuber-forming species and South African species with storage roots require a strict dormancy period of several months, which falls in the northern summer. The dormancy period begins when the leaves begin to wilt. During this time, the plant should be watered less and

the plant subsequently kept completely dry. In autumn, the plant can be watered again slowly, and, as soon as the first leaves appear, the method of watering using a tray is applied again. Rainwater or demineralized water is suitable for watering. All *Drosera* species prefer high air humidity during their growth period. Still air should be avoided, however, to avoid the spread of fungal infections. Dormant, tuber-forming sundews should not be kept in extremely humid conditions.

During the growth period, the temperature for all sundew species should be maintained within the range of 15–25°C (60–77°F). A moderate drop in temperature at night is beneficial, although tropical species will also thrive at temperatures that are constantly above 20°C (68°F). During their dormancy period in the winter, species of temperate and cool climatic zones should be kept at just above the freezing point. However, some species can survive frosts in the open without any problems. Subtropical species (such as Australian tuber-forming and dwarf sundews) that require a strict winter dormancy in northern latitudes (southern summer) should be kept at 20–35°C (68–95°F) during the dormancy period and at 5–20°C (40–68°F) during the growth period.

There are several possible propagation methods: sowing seed and growing cuttings, gemmae, and daughter tubers. Numerous sundew species are also highly suitable for tissue culture. Many species easily develop seeds and are therefore best propagated by sowing. The seeds are sown on a somewhat finer growing medium with the watering method as described above and without mulching. The most suitable time for sowing seed is in late winter or early spring, whereas tuber-forming species should be sown in early fall. In the case of the Australian species, if the seeds do not germinate, it is advisable to spray them with

Fig. 79.
The detached
gemmae of *Drosera
pulchella* can be
used for vegetative
propagation. R. Seine

water that has been allowed to run over natural charcoal. The residues from burning that are dissolved in the water are beneficial for the seeds' germination.

In addition, many *Drosera* species can be propagated by leaf cuttings. (*Drosera regia*, tuber-forming sundews, and annual species are unsuitable for this, however.) The leaves should be cut off above the petioles at the beginning of the growth period, with the leaf undersides placed on a moist sand-peat mixture and gently pressed in. Long leaves can be cut into sections about 4 cm long. When covered and placed in bright, indirect light, young plants will sprout after several weeks.

Root cuttings can be taken from species with thickened storage roots. At the beginning of the growth season, healthy roots are cut off from the mother plant and divided up into sections 4 cm long. These are then laid horizontally on the growing medium and covered with 0.5 cm of potting mixture. The pots should be kept moist, covered, and placed in bright light. After several weeks, leaves will appear. The covering should then be removed and the plants given light as appropriate to the species.

Dwarf species are easiest to propagate by their gemmae (Figs. 79, 80). Ripe gemmae are easily detached from the mother plant by gently pulling them off. They are then simply sown in a pot and treated like normal seedlings. Tuber-forming sundews often develop daughter tubers that are easily recognizable by the additional plants growing in the pot. If the groups become too dense, the tubers can be separated during the dry season and put into separate pots.

Dionaea Solander ex J. Ellis
Venus flytrap

The genus *Dionaea* includes one species, the Venus flytrap, *Dionaea muscipula* J. Ellis. This is undoubtedly the best known of all carnivorous plants (Figs. 81–84). Charles Darwin (1875) called it "one of the most wonderful plants in the world," and Carl Linnaeus spoke of a *miraculum naturae*.

John Ellis (1710–1776) first described the Venus flytrap in a letter to the editor of the *St. James's Chronicle* in 1768. Rumors of a touch-sensitive plant had already reached England from the colony of North Carolina about a decade earlier, and many botanists and gardening enthusiasts had subsequently attempted to import live specimens to England. William Young was the first to successfully transport the plants across the Atlantic in 1768. Nelson

(1990) described the Venus flytrap's exciting discovery and research history, one that is littered with famous names.

The scientific designation *Dionaea muscipula* derives from the goddess Dione, mother of Aphrodite, and the specific epithet *muscipula* from the housefly or the house mouse. Even in the original description of the species, Ellis allowed both interpretations (see the introduction for more on the naming of the Venus flytrap).

Nothing is known of a traditional use of the Venus flytrap in its native region. In alternative medicine, *Dionaea* is sometimes used as a remedy for cancer, although in orthodox medicine does not recognize the plant's efficacy in this respect. The species' greatest present economic importance is horticultural, with large numbers of propagated plants offered for sale in the trade as curiosities. Due to strict conser-

Fig. 80.
Numerous gemmae appear in the center of the leaf rosette of *Drosera nitidula*.
R. Seine

109

Fig. 81.
Dionaea muscipula,
the Venus flytrap.
W. Barthlott

ing ever smaller. Suppression of bush fires also has a negative impact on the plants' survival, as they are unable to receive enough light under the increasingly dense grassland vegetation that then develops.

Features

The Venus flytrap is a relatively small rosette plant that is mostly dormant during the winter and produces shoots in the spring. The plant attains a diameter of about 10–20 cm and has an underground, horizontally growing rhizome in the soil. This rhizome is typically unbranched and bears a leaf rosette at its tip. The primary root dies early, following germination. A few fibrous, adventive roots then supply the plant with water.

The fully grown leaves, which are approximately 5–15 cm long, are rolled up (involute) in the bud form; the leaf lamina is folded over the petiole. In addition, the lamina is folded closed along the midrib and bent inward at the margins. The leaves do not bear any stipules, such as those found in *Drosera*. The petiole is greatly flattened and makes up half to three-quarters of the leaf length. There are stomata on the upper- and underside of the petiole, which is completely green and mainly serves photosynthesis. The basal, narrower part of the petiole also serves as a storage organ for starch. This part, which mostly lies embedded in the soil or in a moss cushion, withstands cold periods better and serves as an energy reserve for the new growth in spring. At the tip of the petiole is the leaf lamina, the Venus flytrap's trapping organ. The lamina is reminiscent of a steel trap. The midrib is clearly recognizable and the two leaf lobes are usually bent slightly upward. Stomata are present only on the leaf underside, while the leaf margins have marginal bristles, or teeth. Each leaf lobe usually has three trigger hairs (sometimes more)

vation legislation and optimized propagation methods, plants collected in the wild are generally not sold commercially.

Distribution and Habitat

The Venus flytrap has a very limited area of distribution on the coastal plains of North and South Carolina. There it thrives in open grassland vegetation between swamp pines and grasses, on continually moist sandy soils. Near water bodies and watercourses, the plants are mostly found in areas that are flooded only seldom or not at all. In its natural habitat, *Dionaea muscipula* receives precipitation year-round, with temperatures varying from –10°C (14°F) in brief frost periods to over 40°C (104°F) during the long, hot summers. The plants withstand the naturally occurring bush fires with the aid of underground rhizomes, which are deep enough in the soil to escape the heat of the fire.

Due to the broad-scale use of fertilizer for agriculture, drainage of wetlands, and continuing demand for land for residential housing, the Venus flytrap's remaining habitat is becom-

and a large number of digestive glands. The exact structure and function of the trap is described in detail below.

The inflorescence is an involute cyme (Fig. 84). The flowers appear in late spring and early summer, in small numbers at the end of the inflorescences, which are borne on tall scapes up to 30 cm tall. This spatial arrangement of flowers and traps ensures that pollinators are not likely to be caught by the traps. The individual flowers are about 1 cm in diameter and have five free sepals and five free, white, mostly nervate petals. There are between ten and twenty stamens, and the pollen is released in tetrads. The ovaries consist of five fused carpels with fused styles. After pollination, the flower ripens into a capsule with numerous black seeds.

Trapping Mechanism, Digestion, and Prey

The fast-moving trapping leaves of the Venus flytrap are active closing traps, or snap traps (Figs. 82, 83), that have kept researchers occupied for more than 200 years. As a result, the

Venus flytrap features probably the best-studied traps of all carnivorous plants, even though not every detail of their function is fully understood. Early notions that the trigger hairs stabbed the victims proved wrong, and

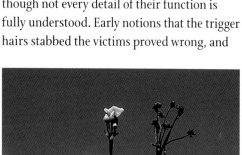

Fig. 82, above left: The six trigger hairs can be seen on the two halves of the closing traps, which are ready to capture prey. W. Barthlott

Fig. 83, above right: The snap trap before and after capture of prey. The leaf cut open in cross-section contains a fly that has been trapped. W. Barthlott

Fig. 84. *Dionaea muscipula* in flower, with the very tall scape bearing the flowers high above the leaf rosette. W. Barthlott

our present-day understanding confirms Linnaeus's estimation of the plant as a "miracle of nature."

The trap itself is the leaf lamina, which has a distinct midrib and two symmetrical lobes. As mentioned above, each lobe has bristles on its margins and digestive glands and several trigger hairs on its inner surface. In the leaf's fully grown state, the marginal bristles are straight, rigid structures that are incapable of movement. The marginal bristles of one leaf lobe correspond to the spaces between those marginal bristles of the opposite lobe, so that the bristles intermesh when the trap closes.

At the base of the marginal bristles there is a narrow, generally green zone that contains embedded glands. These glands secrete nectar to attract prey animals. This part of the trap absorbs ultraviolet light; thus, to insects, it appears in contrast to the rest of the trap. This contrast also presumably serves to attract prey animals.

The remaining inner surface of the trap is covered in sessile digestive glands that are usually a vivid red color. These digestive glands are visible even to the unaided eye. They do not produce any secretions when the trap is open, however.

Between the digestive glands on each half of the leaf lamina, there are three trigger hairs. These form a triangle whose base runs parallel to the leaf midrib. Each trigger hair has a thickening at the base that acts as a joint. The joint contains a special cell layer known as the endodermis. The upper part of the trigger hair is stiff and cannot be bent by prey animals.

If a prey animal lands on the leaf lamina, it can move around there freely; the nectar glands near the leaf margins entice it to stay longer. In moving around the leaf lamina, however, the animal inevitably brushes against one or more of the trigger hairs, which then bend at the basal joint. The endodermal cells perceive the stimulus and produce an electrical receptor potential that triggers an action potential in the cells beneath the joint (Buchen et al. 1983; Hodick and Sievers 1989). This action potential is transmitted over the entire leaf lamina at a velocity of about 17 cm/sec. The trap closes only if, within about 0.5 minute, two action potentials are triggered at one or two trigger hairs (Hodick and Sievers 1989). If the intervals between the stimuli are longer, more stimuli are necessary before the trap will close. The ecological benefit of this mechanism is clear: the trap closes only if there is a high likelihood that it contains prey. This is particularly important, because the trap leaf can close and open again only a few times before it dies.

The rapid closing action of the Venus flytrap causes the marginal bristles to come together and intermesh, although there are still gaps left between them. This movement is probably caused by a rapid change in the inner cell pressure of individual cell layers of the trap. In addition, there is also an elastic distortion of the trap (Forterre et al. 2005). A subsequent, slow closing action presses the trap margins together, sealing off the trap interior. This slow movement occurs only if the trigger hairs in the trap interior continue to be stimulated mechanically, or if urea or sodium or ammonium ions generate a chemical stimulus. In other words, the trap closes completely only if a prey animal is caught inside, struggling, and in its panic excretes feces that contain the abovementioned substances. Smaller prey that are not worth catching can then escape through the gaps between the marginal bristles, and the trap is saved the energy of closing completely. The prey is digested in the completely closed trap.

Due to the activity of the digestive glands, the fully closed trap then fills with liquid. This digestive fluid has a pH between 2.5 and 3.5, and this acidity supports enzymatic activity.

Dionaea produces esterases, phosphatases, proteases, and nucleases. Chitinases, which can break down insects' hard exoskeletons, also have been identified in Venus flytraps. Nevertheless, the chitinous exoskeletons still remain in the trap, undigested, at the end of the digestive process. The digestive glands of the Venus flytrap produce enzymes and simultaneously absorb the dissolved nutrients, which are then distributed within the plant.

The length of the digestive phase varies considerably and very much depends on the size of the prey animal. The digestion of a fly can take from 5 to 35 days, and sometimes the leaves will no longer open after digestion is complete. The catabolic products released during the digestive process maintain the chemical stimulus that is required to keep the trap closed. Only when the plant has resorbed all the digestive products is this stimulus no longer present, and the trap opens again. Before this can happen, all the digestive fluid must be resorbed, and the empty shell of the prey animal then remains on the surface of the opening leaf. The freshly opened trap cannot be stimulated for several days, which means that wind or rain can remove the exoskeleton without the trap closing again.

The nature of the prey varies from site to site and throughout the year. Venus flytraps mainly catch insects, including wasps, ants, flies, grasshoppers, springtails, beetles, and butterflies, as well as various spiders. In the plant's natural habitat, the average length of a prey animal is 9 mm.

Cultivation

The Venus flytrap is not as difficult to grow as is commonly assumed. It can be successfully grown on a sunny windowsill in an unheated, cool room. In climatically favorable regions—areas with cool winters that do not experience long, hard frosts—it can even be grown outdoors year-round, as long as it is covered with some brushwood or twigs during winter. Tap water and heated air, as well as constant stimulation of the leaves to make them close, are usually to blame for the premature death of a plant.

Venus flytraps should be grown on a sunny site, although a little shade in summer prevents overheating and scorching of the leaves. Plenty of light also promotes good leaf coloration, while high air humidity prevents damage to the leaves. Poor ventilation can easily lead to fungal infections. An equal mixture of sand and peat is suitable as a growing medium; often, peat alone is used. The plants should be watered by setting the main container into a tray filled with water, with a low water level, to allow the water to rise into the main container by capillary action. The growing medium should not be allowed to dry out, nor should it be totally waterlogged. If a plant does happen to dry out, it will often regenerate from the rhizome, as long as it has remained unaffected. The temperature should be within the range of 20–35°C (68–95°F) during the growth period. Care should be taken to ensure sufficiently high air humidity at high temperatures. In central Europe, the plant can also be grown successfully outdoors. In winter, the temperatures range should be 4–10°C (39–50°F). The plants will tolerate light frost, but will then lose all their leaves and must regenerate from the rhizome.

Venus flytraps can be propagated either by seed or vegetative methods. As soon as they are ripe, the seeds should be placed, widely spaced, on a fine-grained growing medium in a brightly lit spot with high air humidity. The seedlings should be separated out only at the beginning of the second year. Plants with branched rhizomes and several rosettes can be separated in the spring by carefully cutting through the rhizome, but each piece must have both roots and leaves. In fact, it is simpler to propagate the plant by leaf cuttings. Entire leaves, including the leaf bases, are separated from the rhizome by peeling back in spring and then placed in a fine growing medium. The leaf base should be slightly covered with growing medium, and the plants placed in a brightly lit place with high air humidity. Young plants will develop within several weeks, and after a year they can be potted separately.

Aldrovanda Linnaeus
waterwheel plant

This genus includes only one species, *Aldrovanda vesiculosa* L., the waterwheel plant. This is a small, free-floating, freshwater plant that, like the Venus flytrap, catches its prey using leaves that have been modified to become snap traps.

Although this inconspicuous plant is actually native to Europe and grows in Asia, Africa, and Australia, it was discovered only toward the end of the seventeenth century, in India. It was then brought to England, where Leonard Plukenet (1642–1706) kept it in the exotic plant collections of Queen Mary II, describing it in his three-volume work *Almagesti Botanici Mantissa* as "*lenticula palustris indica*." In 1747, Gaetano Lorenzo Monti (1712–1797) also found specimens of the waterwheel plant in lakes near Bologna, Italy. He dedicated the generic name to the Italian naturalist and physician Ulisse Aldrovandi (1522–1605), who established Bologna's botanical garden. The genus was originally called "Aldrovandia," but this was changed to "Aldrovanda," presumably through a spelling mistake, and was adopted as such by Linnaeus in 1753 (Lloyd 1942).

Distribution and Habitat

Aldrovanda has a wide distribution in Europe, Africa, Asia, and Australia. The species occurs only sporadically throughout this area, however. The distribution extends from France in the west to eastern Europe, Asia, and Australia. The waterwheel plant is found as far north as Lithuania, and in the south it reaches the Tropic of Capricorn in Africa and Australia.

Most of the European stands are currently to be found in Belorussia, Poland, Romania, Hungary, and the Ukraine. In central Europe, only a few colonies have been reported in Italy (Po River plain), Switzerland (Zurich, St. Gallen, and Aargau cantons), Austria (Bregenz), and Germany (Schwedt and Luckenwalde in Brandenburg, on Lake Constance; Akeret 1993; BUWAL 1999). According to Adamec (1995), most of the central European populations are extinct, although the colony in the Zurich, Sankt Gallen, and Aargau cantons is confirmed to be thriving.

Aldrovanda appears to be primarily dispersed by waterfowl that carry plant fragments or seeds from one site to another. The transport of vegetative plant parts is probably of particular importance in the north of its range, where the plant flowers only rarely because of the low temperatures.

The habitats of *Aldrovanda* are stagnant or very slowly flowing watercourses. The nutrient content of the water does not appear to be very important. Akeret (1993) reported a site with low-nutrient water, while Carow and Fürst (1990) listed rice paddies as a habitat. A feature common to all the sites is that the water warms up quickly and is largely free of algae, which means that plenty of sunlight can reach the plant. Adamec (1995) described the high carbon dioxide content of the water as a beneficial factor. *Aldrovanda* is also found growing in association with water soldiers (*Stratiodes aloides*), salvinias (*Salvinia*), bladderworts (*Utricularia*), and reeds (*Phragmites communis*).

Features

Aldrovanda is a herbaceous floating aquatic plant that seldom grows longer than 30 cm (Fig. 85). Typical plants are pale green, but some Australian forms become an attractive red color if exposed to direct sunlight. The fully grown plant is rootless; the seedling has a root, but this soon dies off. The shoot is about 0.6–0.7 mm thick and contains large, gas-filled intercellular spaces or air ducts (Cohn 1850). It grows continuously from the tip during the growth season and dies from the end. Branching is common. Through the death of the shoot, the branches separate from the main stem, resulting in vegetative propagation. In winter-cold regions, dense leaf whorls (turions) develop at the tip of the shoot toward the end of the growth season, serving as a perennating unit. These turions sink to the bottom of the lake or watercourse and rise to the surface again in the following spring, when they resume normal growth.

The leaves on the shoot are arranged in whorls, each consisting of five to nine leaves that are fused at the base (Fig. 86). The leaves are similar to those of the Venus flytrap, but are much smaller, with a length of about 1 cm. The leaf has a wide, wedge-shaped petiole that narrows toward the leaf base. At the tip, the petiole bears the leaf lamina in the middle, and at the edges it tapers off into four to eight bristles that extend beyond the lamina. The petiole is green and serves as an assimilation organ. The leaf lamina is more or less circular and folded along the midrib, yielding two semi-circular lobes that are adjacent to one another. Along the midrib, the leaf lamina is twisted 100° to the left in relation to the petiole, so that the trap opening is directed toward the left, not upward as in the Venus flytrap. The edge of the leaf lamina bears unicellular epidermal hairs, sometimes known as "spikes," and there are four-armed hairs, glands, and sensory bristles on the leaf lamina surface. The

Fig. 85. *Aldrovanda vesiculosa*, the waterwheel plant. W. Barthlott

exact location and function of these structures is discussed in the chapter on trapping mechanisms.

Flowers are on short scapes that are borne slightly above the water surface. The literature contains no reports on pollinators, and Diels (1906) mentioned cleistogamy. The flower is about 8 mm wide and consists of five sepals that are fused at the base, four white petals, five stamens, and a fused superior ovary consisting of five carpels. A seed capsule develops and ripens underwater.

Trapping Mechanism, Digestion, and Prey

Aldrovanda catches its prey with snap traps that close with a quick movement. The trap corresponds to the leaf lamina and consists of two zones. The marginal zone, from the edge to the middle of each leaf half, consists of only two cell layers and is extremely thin. The central part of the trap, from the midrib to the middle of each leaf half, consists of two thin epidermises and a layer of tissue between them, with a row of large cells.

In addition to the epidermal spikes at the leaf margin, the marginal zone has four-armed hairs on the inside of the trap. Toward both the margin and the central zone, the zone with the four-armed hairs alternates with a hairless zone. The central zone has sessile digestive glands on the inner surface and about twenty trigger hairs per leaf half. There are two-armed hairs on the outside of the leaf.

When the trap is open, the two trap halves are at an angle of a little over 90° to one another. If a trigger hair is bent, the traps snap shut so the spiked margins come into contact with one another. In young leaves, it is generally sufficient to stimulate a single trigger hair, while in older leaves it may be necessary to apply several stimuli, one after the other, until the trap closes. The mechanical stimulus of a bent trigger hair produces an electrical impulse (action potential) in the hair. The action potential is transmitted across the trap with a velocity of 10 cm/s (Sibaoka 1966). When the action potential reaches the cells responsible for movement, the trap closes.

The closing movement occurs primarily in the central zone of the trap, on both sides of the midrib. This is a turgor movement that is caused by a loss of pressure in the epidermal cells on the inner side of the trap (Ashida 1934). This change in the internal cell pressure (turgor) is caused by a transport of potassium ions out of the cells (Iijima and Sibaoka 1985). The closed trap still allows the prey animal some freedom of movement inside the relatively large trap cavity. Over a period of several minutes, the trap closes completely, that is, the marginal zones are closely appressed together. As a result, the hollow cavity of the trap becomes much smaller, and in the fully closed trap is restricted to the central zone of the two leaf lobes. According to one hypothesis, the four-armed hairs are associated with the transport of water out of the closed trap (Joel 1986).

The resulting negative pressure in the trap then results in a sealed-off space in which digestion can take place.

The prey is digested in the closed trap. Fermi and Buscaglione (1899) demonstrated the breakdown of gelatin in the traps, an indication of proteolytic enzymes.

Akeret (1993) studied the prey of *Aldrovanda* at a site in Switzerland. He found mainly small crustaceans (water fleas, ostracodes, and copepods), insect larvae (mosquitoes and mayflies), and snails, although only 11 percent of the traps contained prey.

Cultivation

Aldrovanda is a very difficult plant to grow and can therefore be recommended only to experienced carnivore gardeners. Depending on the origin of the material, the plant may be grown either in outdoor ponds or in an aquarium. While plants grown outdoors undergo a dormancy period, those grown in aquariums will grow year-round.

The plants need plenty of sun. The water temperature should be 20–30°C (68–86°F) during the growth period, as higher temperatures will impede growth. During the dormancy period, the water temperature may be allowed to drop to just above freezing, but the turions must not be allowed to freeze. When growing *Aldrovanda*, it is essential to suppress algal growth. The water should therefore be low in nutrients and have a slightly acidic pH of about 6. This can be achieved with the aid of peat, *Sphagnum*, or other acidic plant material at the base of the container. Live reeds and rushes in the growing container are also beneficial. If major algal growth develops, the water should be exchanged immediately. Fertilizers should not be added, because these will promote algal growth. The occasional addition of water fleas as feed animals is sufficient to keep the plants adequately supplied with nutrients. More detailed information on the cultivation of *Aldrovanda* was compiled by Adamec (1999).

Aldrovanda can be propagated by separating shoot segments, particularly lateral shoots. Because *Aldrovanda* flowers only very rarely, propagation by seed is not practical.

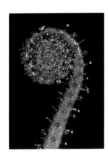

Drosophyllaceae: Portuguese Sundew Family

The family Drosophyllaceae contains only one species, *Drosophyllum lusitanicum* (L.) Link, the Portuguese sundew. This species, which is native to Spain, Portugal, and Morocco, catches its prey with the aid of passive adhesive traps.

Until recently, the Portuguese sundew was classified among the sundew family (Droseraceae). On the basis of the arrangement of the vascular tissue in the petals and morphological data, however, Chrtek et al. (1989) raised the status of the genus to that of a separate family. Subsequent molecular genetic research (Williams et al. 1994; Meimberg et al. 2000) has justified this special status of the plant as an immediate relative of the Droseraceae (Kubitzki 2002b). In addition, the research demonstrated a close kinship with the Asian pitcher plants (Nepenthaceae), hookleaf family (Dioncophyllaceae), and the Ancistrocladaceae.

Drosophyllum Link
Portuguese sundew

The Portuguese sundew, *Drosophyllum lusitanicum* (L.) Link, has been known since the seventeenth century. Linnaeus (1753) first described it as a sundew (*Drosera lusitanica*); however, Link separated the genus *Drosophyllum* from the other sundew species in 1806. The scientific name *Drosophyllum* is derived from the plant's leaves, which bear mucilaginous glands, and can be translated literally as "dew leaf" (Greek *drosos*, dew; *phyllon*, leaf). Darwin (1875) reported that, in Portuguese homes, the plant was hung from the ceiling to catch flies.

Drosophyllum played an important role in research on general cell structures. While studying the mucilaginous glands, Schnepf (1960) elucidated the function of the Golgi apparatus. This cell organelle, which was discovered in human nerve cells and described by the Italian pathologist Camillo Golgi in 1898, is found in both animal and plant cells. This organelle primarily has a synthesizing function; in *Drosophyllum* the Golgi apparatus is also responsible for the production of mucilage for the adhesive traps.

Distribution and Habitat

Drosophyllum is restricted to the western parts of the Iberian Peninsula and Morocco. It is found from Oporto in Portugal along the coast as far as Cape Sao Vincente. In addition to growth sites along the coast, *Drosophyllum* also grows further inland, extending as far as the Portuguese–Spanish border. There is a gap in the distribution around the Gulf of Cadiz. The remaining sites are concentrated on both sides of the Straits of Gibraltar: in Spain from Cape Trafalgar to Estepona and in Morocco from Tangier to Tetouan. Hence, in both Spain and Morocco, the species is found on the Atlantic and Mediterranean coasts alike. In a map of its distribution, Ortega-Olivencia et al. (1995) also indicated two isolated sites in the Spanish hinterland, between Ciudad Real and Cordoba.

In its natural environment, *Drosophyllum lusitanicum* is increasingly threatened by habitat destruction through the expansion of arable land and urban settlement, so that today only about 20 percent of the historically documented stands are still extant (Correia and Freitas 2002).

The habitat of *Drosophyllum* differs markedly from what is usual for carnivorous plants. The plant grows on stony or sandy hills or on slopes facing the ocean, whose water-permeable, low-nutrient, and acidic soils dry out considerably during the summer. The Portuguese sundew colonizes open habitats that are partly or completely free of vegetation as a result of fire or human activities, and it is found in open pine or oak stands. When the heathlike Mediterranean hard scrub (*macchia, maquis*) vegetation on the site becomes too dense, however, the plants tend to die out and are unable to reestablish. The Portuguese sundew is not fire-resistant, and bush fires can kill the plants. The seeds, however, are able to germinate after fire and establish new populations on the now open terrain. Müller and Deil (2001) ascribed a pioneer character to the Portuguese sundew in the colonization of fire-scorched areas. Most of the growth sites of *Drosophyllum* are subject to the influence of coastal fog, and some scientists hold that this plays an important role in the plants' water supply during the dry summer months (Mazrimas 1972; Juniper et al. 1989). However, there is no real evidence to support this hypothesis.

Features

Drosophyllum is a subshrub with a woody base that generally attains a height of less than 1 m (Fig. 87), but can occasionally grow to 1.6 m high. The mostly unbranched shoot has a diameter up to 15 mm. By counting the annual rings of stems of this diameter, Juniper et al. (1989) calculated an age of about 6–7 years. The roots of the plant are very well developed and consist of a taproot and numerous fine lateral roots. Despite the arid summer conditions, there is no evidence of water-storing organs. The linear-lanceolate leaves are astipulate and sessile. The upperside of the leaves is grooved. The leaves are spirally arranged on the shoot and are not shed when they grow old, but in-

stead remain on the plant. During their development, the leaves are rolled up in an inverse circinate fashion, that is, the leaf is rolled up spirally toward the outside (Fig. 88).

This form of prefoliation sets *Drosophyllum* apart from the sundew family (Droseraceae), while linking it to *Triphyophyllum* (Dioncophyllaceae). The leaves bear two kinds of glands: sessile digestive glands on the leaf uppersides and undersides and stalked mucilaginous glands (or tentacles) on the leaf undersides

Fig. 87. *Drosophyllum lusitanicum*, the Portuguese sundew. W. Barthlott

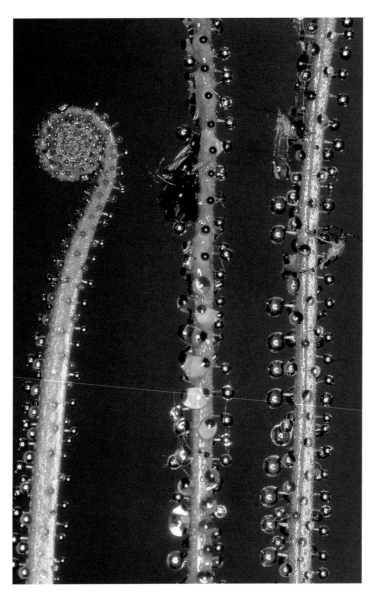

Fig. 88.
Older leaves with glands and a younger leaf of *Drosophyllum lusitanicum*, rolled up in an inverse circinate fashion. W. Barthlott

stamens in two rings, and five fused carpels forming a superior ovary. The pollinated flower ripens to form a capsule with a basal placenta and numerous oval seeds about 2.5 mm in diameter. Ortega-Olivencia et al. (1995) classified self-fertilization as an important component of the reproduction strategy of *Drosophyllum lusitanicum*. They were able to demonstrate wild bees (*Panurgus*), beetles (*Homalopia*), hoverflies (*Eristalis*), and other insects as pollinators.

Trapping Mechanism, Digestion, and Prey

The leaves of the Portuguese sundew act as passive adhesive traps. Neither the stalked glands (tentacles) nor the leaves have the ability to roll up and envelop a prey animal. Prey are attracted by the glistening mucilage drops, the strongly ultraviolet-reflecting dead leaves, and a honeylike scent. The prey are caught with the aid of the mucilage drops that are secreted by the tentacles' glandular heads. The stalk consists of a woody core (xylem) surrounded by the phloem and two outer layers of bark cells. The glandular head has two layers of glandular tissue on the outside, with a dome-shaped endodermis beneath. In their lattempts to escape, the prey animals become covered with the sticky secretions and die. The mucilage of *Drosophyllum* is easily dislodged from the glandular head and remains stuck to the prey animals when they try to move.

and margins. The mucilaginous glands produce a red pigment in the glandular knobs. In contrast to *Drosera*, the passive tentacles and leaves do not show any rolling-up movement when they come into contact with prey or are stimulated mechanically.

A few flowers form a nearly unbranched inflorescence that, like the leaves, is densely covered with glands. The stalked, sulfur yellow, radially symmetrical flowers have a diameter of about 2.5 cm. They consist of five sepals that are covered in glands and fused at the base, five free petals that are twisted in the bud, ten

The digestion of the trapped victims is largely the task of the sessile glands, which begin to secrete digestive fluids after the prey has been caught. When the tentacles are stimulated mechanically or chemically, they in turn stimulate the sessile digestive glands (Fenner 1904; Quintanilha 1926). Digestion is quickest when the prey and the mucilage come into contact with both types of gland; a mosquito can then be digested within 24 hours. The mucilage secreted by the stalked glands has a pH of 2.5–3.0 (Heslop-Harrison 1975), thus providing the acidic environment that is necessary for digestion. *Drosophyllum* produces esterases, acidic phosphatases, proteases, leucinaminopeptidase, and peroxidase (Juniper et al. 1989). Because it does not produce chitinase, however, the chitin exoskeletons of the prey are not digested. The prey animals of the Portuguese sundew are mainly flying insects. A more detailed study of the prey spectrum has yet to be performed.

Cultivation

Portuguese sundews are unsuitable for growing by beginners. The main problem is watering: the plants react very sensitively to both waterlogging and desiccation. In addition, they need a great deal of sunlight to thrive. With a little practice and skill, however, these problems can be overcome, and *Drosophyllum lusitanicum*, with its attractive flowers, unusual growth form, and honey fragrance can be a beautiful addition to any carnivore collection.

These exceptionally lime-intolerant (calciphobous) plants should be grown in clay pots. An equal mixture of peat and sand or of sand, vermiculite, and perlite is recommended as a growing medium. An admixture of fine gravel can also be beneficial. A constant and even soil moisture can be attained by sinking the pot into a larger pot filled with peat or sphagnum moss. The watered substrate in the large pot then transfers moisture to the inner pot. The plants should be watered from above and not sprayed.

In summer, the plants require daytime temperatures within the range of 20–30°C (68–86°F), although warmer periods are also tolerated. A marked drop in temperature during the night is desirable. In winter, the plants should be kept within the range of 10–15°C (50–60°F).

Propagation of *Drosophyllum* is possible only by seed. Because the plants are very sensitive to any disturbance to the roots, the seeds should be sown in what will be the final growing container.

Lentibulariaceae: Bladderwort Family

The bladderwort family includes three genera: *Pinguicula*, *Genlisea*, and *Utricularia*. Lentibulariaceae contains about 338 species, which makes it the most species-rich of all the carnivore families. As annual or perennial plants, the distribution of these species is nearly cosmopolitan. The family's scientific name derives from the lens- or lentil-shaped form (Latin *lens*, genitive *lentis*, meaning "lens" or "lentil") of the trapping bladders of the bladderworts (*Utricularia*), whose former, now invalid name was *Lentibularia*. However, each of the three genera is characterized by its own trap type: *Genlisea* has snare traps, *Pinguicula* has adhesive traps, and *Utricularia* has bladder suction traps (Fischer et al. 2004).

Members of the Lentibulariaceae are relatives of the figwort family (Scrophulariaceae; for example, *Digitalis*, foxglove) and the labiates (Lamiaceae; for example, *Salvia*, sage), whose common characteristics include zygomorphic, two-lipped (bilabiate) flowers. Molecular genetic studies have shown that *Pinguicula* represents an independent evolutionary line, while *Genlisea* and *Utricularia* are closely related to one another and possess the smallest genome of angiosperms, with chromosomes of bacterial size (Müller et al. 2000, 2004; 2006; Müller and Borsch 2005; Jobson et al. 2003; Greilhuber et al. 2006).

Pinguicula Linnaeus
butterwort

With about eighty-eight species (plus eleven subspecies and varieties), the genus *Pinguicula* is mainly native to the Northern Hemisphere.

Vitus Auslasser mentioned the butterwort as early as 1479 in his manuscript *Macer de Herbarium*, calling it "Smalz chrawt" (similar to the German name for butterwort, *Fettkraut*). The name *Pinguicula*, first used in 1561 by Konrad Gessner in his herbal, was adopted in 1753 by Carl Linnaeus in his seminal nomenclatural work *Species Plantarum*. The name *Pinguicula* is derived from the Latin *pinguis* (meaning "fat" or "thick") and refers to the particularly thick and fleshy, greasy-looking leaves of the butterwort.

Linnaeus described only four species of butterwort, but today there are nearly 570 known specific epithets, about 85 percent of which are synonyms. In his 1966 monograph of the genus, Jost S. Casper listed only forty-six species. Hence, nearly half of all the butterwort species known today have been discovered and described during the past 40 years. Many of these new species are from Mexico, where more than two dozen new species have been described over the past two decades (in particular, see Speta and Fuchs 1982, 1989; Zamudio and Rzedowski 1986, 1991; Zamudio 1988, 2005). In his review article, Laurent Legendre (2000), another leading expert on the genus, accepted only seventy-four species names as valid.

In the classification of the genus by Casper (1966), which was primarily based on the morphological features of the leaves and flowers, a distinction was made between three subgenera (*Isoloba*, *Pinguicula*, and *Temnoceras*), fifteen sections, and another fourteen subsections. (Luhrs 1993; Gluch 1995, 1997). Subgenera *Isoloba* (sections *Agnata*, *Cardiophyllum*, *Discoradix*, *Heterophyllum*, *Isoloba*) is characterized by more or less equal sized petals; subgenera *Pinguicula* (sections *Crassifolia*, *Homophyllum*, *Longitubus*,

Nana, Orcheosanthus, Orchioides, Pinguicula) shows distinct two-lipped (bilabiate) flowers with whole, undivided petals; whereas members of subgenera *Temnoceras* (sections *Ampullipalatum, Micranthus, Microphyllum, Temnoceras*) possess two-lipped flowers with divided or emarginated petal lobes. Ongoing molecular genetic research (Cieslack et al. 2005), however, indicated that most of the infrageneric units are unnatural. Thus, interdisciplinary research should yield a new classification in the coming years.

Distribution and Habitat

The butterworts' area of distribution extends over several continents and climatic zones. They are found in the subarctic, alpine, temperate, and subtropical regions, mainly in the Northern Hemisphere. The distribution limits in Europe extend as far south as the Mediterranean (for instance, *Pinguicula corsica* on Corsica and *P. crystallina* on Cyprus) and even onto the

African continent, with *P. lusitanica* found in Morocco and Algeria. Species such as *P. albida*, *P. filifolia*, *P. lilacina*, and *P. mesophytica* are native to tropical Central America and the Caribbean. *Pinguicula antarctica*, *P. calyptrata*, and *P. chilensis* are from South America, where they are found along the length of the Andes in higher and cooler alpine regions, scattered as far south as Tierra del Fuego. The center of diversity is Mexico, however, with some forty-seven species.

Fig. 89, left: *Pinguicula alpina*, the alpine butterwort. W. Barthlott

Fig. 90, center: *Pinguicula grandiflora* in its natural habitat in southern France. E. Groß

Fig. 91, right: *Pinguicula moctezumae* I. Theisen

Fig. 92, below: *Pinguicula cyclosecta* I. Theisen

Fig. 93.
Pinguicula lignicola, a Cuban epiphytic butterwort, growing on a pine branch.
H. Dietrich

Fig. 94.
As with most butterworts, very few roots develop in *Pinguicula ehlersiae*.
I. Theisen

Fig. 95. *Pinguicula gracilis* I. Theisen

Most butterwort species prefer moist to very wet soils on open sites. Although *Pinguicula calyptrata*, *P. lusitanica*, and *P. vulgaris* show a preference for acidic bog soils, most *Pinguicula* species grow on neutral to alkaline substrates. Sites that are moist from seepage on vertical rock faces are also colonized, for example, by *P. vallisneriifolia*.

Features

With a few exceptions, butterworts are perennial, terrestrial, herbaceous rosette plants. Only *Pinguicula pumila*, *P. sharpii*, and *P. takakii* are annual herbs. Two species are epiphytes: the Dominican *P. casabitoana* and the Cuban *P. lignicola* (Fig. 93), which grows on pine trees. In nearly all *Pinguicula* species, a compact leaf rosette sits atop a short shoot, which lies flat on the ground. The entire root system is much reduced (Fig. 94). In the epiphytic species, the roots have become flattened into holdfast organs. The usually narrow, lanceolate leaves are either erect (*P. filifolia* and *P. gypsicola*) or pendulous (*P. vallisneriifolia*). The length of the rosette leaves ranges from 1 cm (*P. gracilis*, Fig. 95) to as much as 30 cm (*P. vallisneriifolia*). Generally, the leaves as well as the shoots have a soft waxy consistency and a greasy sheen. In particular, the species in the winter-dry areas of Mexico have conspicuously fleshy, succulent

Fig. 96.
Pinguicula laueana
W. Barthlott

leaves. Species such as *P. heterophylla* develop small adventive buds at the leaf tips, with which it is very easy to propagate the plants vegetatively. All the aboveground organs are densely covered with glandular heads during the growing season and are a striking light green.

The flowers are mostly single and more or less unambiguously zygomorphic. Most species bear pink, violet, white, or blue flowers or less commonly red (*Pinguicula laueana*, Fig. 96) or partially yellow (*P. primuliflora*, Fig. 97). The calyx is made up of five fused sepals. The diameter of the corolla, which is also made up of five petals, ranges from 0.8 cm (*P. villosa*) to 6 cm (*P. moranensis*). The abaxial petal forms a spur 0.5–4 cm long. The capsules, which are bivalved, contain numerous seeds.

In line with their occurrence in temperate or tropical climates, butterworts have two different growth forms. The growth form of the temperate Eurasian zones (Casper 1966) is distinguished by the development of winter buds (hibernacula), which are absent in the tropical growth form. In both growth forms, the flowers appear during the development of the spring or summer rosette. At the end of the growing season in the fall, the plant often develops leaves that look quite different, producing the fall or winter rosette.

In *Pinguicula* species of temperate climates, the shoot development ends with the growth of small, fleshy basal leaves that form the winter bud. Similarly, winter buds can also develop in the leaf axils. After the foliage leaves and roots of the fall rosette die, these winter buds can overwinter below ground. Because they have no roots, the wind and rain generally transport winter buds to other sites, ensuring good dispersal. The new rosette leaves then grow from the winter bud during the following spring. The roots develop at the same time, so that the plant is once again anchored in the soil.

In the representatives of the tropical growth form, there are marked differences between

Fig. 97.
*Pinguicula
primuliflora*
W. Barthlott

leaves in the summer and winter rosettes have "heterophyllous foliage." Because both summer and winter rosettes can develop flowers, most butterworts have two flowering times (October–November and January–March).

Trapping Mechanism, Digestion, and Prey

The summer rosette leaves have two different types of glands: long-stalked glandular heads, which produce sticky mucilage and render the prey immobile, and sessile glands, which produce digestive enzymes (amylases, phosphatases, and proteases). The prey animals are mainly attracted by optical signals, in which ultraviolet patterns evidently play a role (Joel et al. 1985). However, pollen grains that are rich in protein are also trapped as a source of nutrition.

The trapping movement of the adhesive traps of *Pinguicula* initially went unnoticed; Charles Darwin (1875) did not mention that the traps are, in fact, active ones. Once the prey animal has fallen victim to the sticky mucilaginous secretions, the leaf surface beneath it sinks a little, due to a change in turgor. This small hollow becomes filled with digestive enzymes, forming a temporary stomach. In the extremely rare Mexican butterwort *P. utricularioides*, which is only known as herbarium specimens from the type locality, the describers of this species observed spoon-shaped (cochleate) leaves that resembled the bladderlike suction traps of the related genus *Utricularia*. The butterworts' prey consists mainly of flying insects, especially fungus gnats and sciarid flies.

Selected Species

Pinguicula alpina L.
alpine butterwort
Distribution and habitat: Pyrenees, European

the spring and summer rosettes and the fall and winter rosettes (such as *P. gypsicola*; Figs. 50, 98). While the leaves of the summer rosette serve carnivory and have clearly developed adhesive traps, the fall and winter rosettes are characterized by a complete loss of mucilaginous glands and are thus unable to catch prey. In addition, the summer and winter rosettes are often distinguished by their different sized leaves: species in which the summer and winter rosettes have leaves of the same size and shape are said to have "homophyllous foliage," whereas those with different

Alps, Scotland, Ireland, and Scandinavia, from sea level to about 1600 m; in swamps and spring bogs, but also on drier sites. Features: The few roots remain intact during winter and anchor the winter bud. Leaf rosette up to 6 cm in diameter, with five to eight leaves; due to a marked acuteness at the tips, these are more oblong-triangular than elliptical. White flowers up to 1.5 cm in diameter on scapes up to 10 cm high, with an orange patch; spur about 1 cm long. According to the most recent molecular genetic studies (Cieslack et al. 2005), the alpine butterwort is a close relative of the Mexican butterworts and is quite distinct from the other Northern Hemisphere species. Fig. 89

Pinguicula gypsicola Brandeg.

Distribution and habitat: Mexico (highlands); on alkaline, gypseous soils. Features: Winter rosette about 2 cm in diameter, comprised of small, finely pubescent, succulent leaves lying one over the other like roof tiles. These glandless, noncarnivorous leaves are reminiscent of houseleeks (*Sempervivum*). Summer rosette leaves pale green, up to 6.5 cm long and characteristically narrow, seldom wider than 2.5 mm. The juvenile leaves extend upward, while the older leaves lie flatter. Flowers on scapes up to 9 cm long, up to 2 cm in diameter, purplish red; petals narrow, throat white, spur 2.5 cm long and relatively well developed. Figs. 50, 98

Pinguicula moranensis H.B.K.
Syn. Pinguicula caudata Schltdl.

Distribution and habitat: Mexico (highlands), Guatemala, El Salvador; on alkaline, gypseous soils. Features: Winter rosette about 0.5 cm in diameter, half-embedded in the soil; summer rosette 20 cm in diameter, with oval to spatulate leaves, light green, reddish tinged on sunny sites, the leaves 10 cm long and about 6.5 cm wide. Scape up to 25 cm long; flower

Fig. 98, above: The new, sticky summer rosette leaves and flowers of *Pinguicula gypsicola* develop in the center of the leaves of the winter rosette, which are arranged one on top of the other, like roof tiles. I. Theisen

Fig. 99, below: Numerous sciarid flies trapped on the sticky trap leaves of the summer rosette of *Pinguicula moranensis*. W. Barthlott

about 5 cm in diameter, carmine red with several flecks and three darker veins, throat whitish, and whitish green spur 4.5 cm long. Fig. 99

Pinguicula vulgaris L.
common butterwort
Distribution and habitat: Widely distributed throughout northern Eurasia and North America. The species prefers wet, acidic soils (bogs), but will also thrive on an alkaline substrate. Features: Summer rosettes up to 16 cm in diameter, with five to eleven leaves; leaves narrow and light green. Up to six flowers on scapes about 10 cm long, flowers up to 2 cm in diameter, bluish violet with a white throat; spur about 1 cm long.

Pinguicula 'Aphrodite'
Among the butterwort hybrids, Pinguicula 'Aphrodite' deserves special mention. Winter rosette about 8 cm, summer rosette 20 cm in diameter. Flowers violet, 4 cm in diameter, spur 1.5 cm long, appearing almost year-round. A spectacular new hybrid whose parents are Pinguicula agnata and P. moctezumae, notable for its numerous violet flowers.

Cultivation

Depending on where the species is from, butterworts can be grown outdoors, in a greenhouse, or in a temperature-controlled hothouse. Butterworts are among the few carnivores that will also tolerate light additional nitrogen or phosphorous fertilization.

The Mexican highland species, which are especially easy to grow, require hot summers and cool winters (5–10°C, 40–50°F). In summer, plenty of sun and an indirect watering method (capillary action from a water-filled tray below the main container) are always nec-essary. During the winter dormancy period, from October on, the plants should be gradually watered less. A few Caribbean species require a hothouse, with temperatures of about 25°C (77°F) and high air humidity year-round. For species of temperate Eurasian and North American climates, direct sunlight must be avoided so that temperatures will not become too high. Light frost protection is necessary in winter (a leaf litter covering).

Mixtures of peat and sand have proven suitable as growing media. For species of the temperate climates of Europe, Asia, and North America that require an acidic medium, a 1:5 ratio of peat to sand should be used. Additional lime and perlite should be added for Mexican highland species.

Propagation is usually by seeds, which are planted in a peat-sand mixture as soon as they are harvested. Winter-hardy species may also be propagated by bulbils. Species such as Pinguicula heterophylla and P. primuliflora develop adventive buds at the leaf tips that already have small roots while they are still on the mother plant. Another typical method of propagation is to use leaf cuttings, which can be raised in a moist peat-sand mixture.

Genlisea A. de Saint-Hilaire
corkscrew plant

Corkscrew plants, which are cultivated only rarely, are small annual or perennial rosette plants that are mainly restricted to the tropical regions of Africa, Madagascar, and South America. Even within their native habitats, the twenty-one currently known Genlisea species are very rare.

The French botanist Auguste François César Prouvençal de Saint-Hilaire (1779–1853) named the corkscrew plant in honor of his

Fig. 100, left:
Genlisea lobata
I. Theisen

Fig. 101.
Genlisea filiformis
(with a pinhead for
scale). I. Theisen

contemporary, the writer Comtesse Stéphanie-Félicité du Crest de Saint-Aubin de Genlis (1746–1839), or "Madame de Genlis" for short, whose Paris salon was very popular among philosophers, literati, and musicians. In the first description of the species in 1833, only five South American species were known: *Genlisea aurea, G. filiformis, G. minor, G. pygmaea,* and *G. violacea. Genlisea minor,* however, is now recognized as synonymous with *G. aurea.*

Within the Lentibulariaceae, *Genlisea* is most closely related to *Utricularia* (Müller et al. 2000). Following the most recent revision of the African species (Fischer et al. 2000), the genus includes a total of twenty-one species and can be subdivided into the two subgenera *Genlisea* and *Tayloria*. Capsules that open along their long axis are characteristic of the exclusively South American subgenus *Tayloria*, which in-

cludes only three species: *G. lobata* (Fig. 100), *G. uncinata,* and *G. violacea.* By contrast, the capsules of the subgenus *Genlisea* open with a horizontally sprung capsule roof or by pores. Fromm-Trinta (1977, 1981, 1984) examined the South American *Genlisea* species in detail.

Distribution and Habitat

Mainly restricted to the tropics, the corkscrew plant is found in Africa, Madagascar, and South America (in Bolivia, Brazil, Colombia, Paraguay, and Venezuela). Olvera Garcia and Martinez (2002) reported a remarkable new find from Mexico, *Genlisea filiformis* (Fig. 101), the only species that is also found as far afield as Central America and Cuba (Fromm-Trinta 1984). On special sites, such as on white-sand savannas (quartz-sand areas) or the seepage

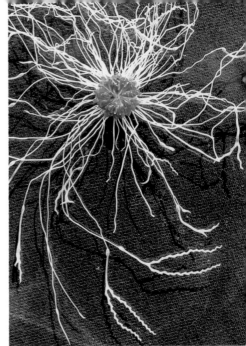

zones of inselbergs, the species grows terrestrially on low-nutrient soils that are at least seasonally moist. Less common are semi-aquatic
species (*G. repens*), which are found on the
margins of shallow waters and watercourses.

Features

The genus *Genlisea* consists of herbaceous,
mostly long-lived, perennial rosette plants
only a few centimeters high (Figs. 102, 103).
The perennial species have a narrow rhizome.
As Goebel (1891, 1893) noted, the plants have
no roots. The basal leaf rosette consists of
spatulate leaves. There are two leaf types:
aboveground, green, narrow-linear, or spatulate rosette leaves 0.5–2.0 cm long, and color-
less, underground snare leaves (rhizophylls)
modified into trapping organs whose end sections are twisted like a corkscrew (Figs. 104–
107). Individual flowers form panicles up to 50
cm high with few flowers (such as *G. uncinata*).
The yellow or violet flowers are zygomorphic
and have a spur. The opening mechanism of
the mostly spherical capsules is a means of dis-
tinguishing between the two subgenera. The
capsules of the exclusively South American
subgenus *Tayloria* open along longitudinal sutures, whereas those of the subgenus *Genlisea*
open along transverse sutures or by pores. The
numerous seeds are very small, with an average diameter of only 0.3 mm.

Trapping Mechanism, Digestion, and Prey

Darwin (1875) postulated that *Genlisea* was
carnivorous, but there was no concrete evidence for this assumption until recently, due
to a rarity of live specimens for experimental
studies. The basal, extended part of the underground leaves, which mostly emanate from a
rhizome, has a bladderlike swelling. This is
several millimeters long and presumably functions as a digestive chamber (Fig. 105). Toward
the tip, the rhizophyll becomes narrower and
divides into two arms that are angled at 90–
130° to one another. These are twisted like a
corkscrew and feature a series of narrow slit
openings (width 400 µm, height 180 µm; Fig.
107). Inside, these sections are lined with in-
ward-pointing hairs and glands (Fig. 106).

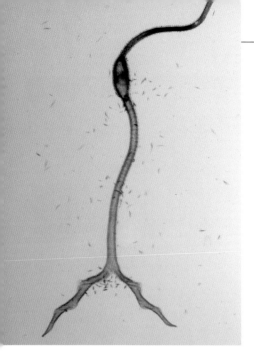

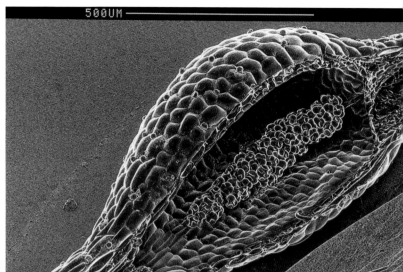

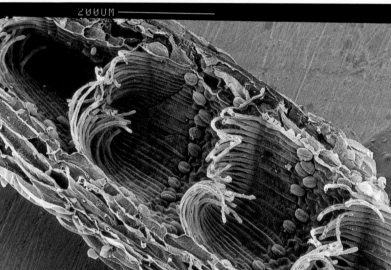

Despite exhaustive attempts, insects have never been identified as prey; only a blackish, indefinable mass has been found in the bladder-like, swollen sections of the rhizophylls leaves. Only recently have experiments shown that the rhizophylls of *Genlisea* are underground traps for protozoans, which are attracted to the snare-trap rhizophyll by an as-yet-unidentified attractant (Barthlott et al. 1998). *Genlisea* is therefore the only carnivore identified to date that has a highly specialized trap for catching protozoans, luring its prey underground by means of an attractant. The formerly widespread opinion that traps of *Genlisea* are suction traps has not been confirmed.

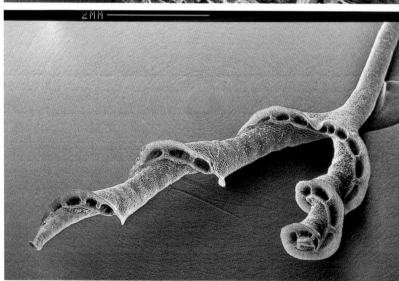

Fig. 104, above:
The corkscrew plant *Genlisea aurea*, with numerous attracted prey animals (slipper animalcules). W. Barthlott

Figs. 105–107.
Scanning electron micrographs of a corkscrew plant. Internal view of the bladderlike digestive chamber (Fig. 105). Unidirectional snare hairs alternate with glands in the trap interiors (Fig. 106). View of the Y-shaped lower section of the corkscrew plant with numerous openings that lead into the trap interiors (Fig. 107). W. Barthlott

Fig. 108, left:
Genlisea stapfii
growing in its natural
habitat in Ivory Coast.
W. Barthlott

Fig. 109, right:
Genlisea aurea
W. Barthlott

Selected Species

Genlisea aurea A. St.-Hil.

Distribution and habitat: Endemic to Brazil (from Goias to Santa Catarina); on moist, low-nutrient sites; in the Serra do Espinhaço (such as in the areas surrounding Diamantina), preferentially on quartz-sand areas. Features: Leaf rosette 3–5 cm in diameter. Inflorescences up to 40 cm high, the upper section densely covered with glandular hairs. Flowers vivid yellow, up to 2 cm long; spur twice as long as the corolla. *Genlisea aurea* is the largest and most attractive species of the yellow-flowering corkscrew plants, and it is unlikely to be mistaken for another species. Fig. 109

Genlisea guianensis N.E. Br.

Distribution and habitat: South America, from Venezuela and Guiana to Brazil (Bahia, Mato Grosso, and Goias); on seasonally moist sites. Features: A relatively impressive species. Rosette leaves narrow and ribbonlike. Flowers violet, arranged on a slightly pubescent inflorescence.

Genlisea hispidula Stapf

Distribution and habitat: Tropical Africa, from Nigeria to southern Africa; grows on constantly moist and alternately dry sites on both inselbergs and iron laterite crusts ("bowal" areas). Features: Perennial plant with spatulate rosette leaves up to 5 cm long. Inflorescence 10–25 cm high, the lower section slightly pubescent. Flower color varies between violet, blue, and pink; spur greenish or with a yellowish tinge.

Genlisea margaretae Hutch.

Distribution and habitat: Eastern Africa (Tanzania, Zambia) and Madagascar; found on moss cushions in constantly moist bogs and on watered seepage areas on inselbergs. Bosser (1958) described the Madagascar population as *Genlisea recurva*, although the species status does not appear to be justified. Features: Perennial species with rosette leaves 2–3 cm long. Numerous rhizophylls, up to 20 cm long. Inflorescence 10–30 cm high, the upper section densely covered in glandular hairs. Flowers mostly violet, with a yellowish lower lip. Figs. 102, 103

Genlisea repens Benj.

Distribution and habitat: Tropical South America (Venezuela, Guiana, Brazil, Paraguay); grows preferentially in shallow waters and watercourses. Features: Relatively small species even when fully grown, with a rosette diameter of 1.5–2.0 cm. Rhizome grows like a runner or stolon, with leaves along its entire length. Flowers small, yellow, and borne on a hairless scape.

Cultivation

To thrive, corkscrew plants need a well-lit site in a warm or temperature-controlled hothouse. The temperatures in summer should be within the range of 25–35°C (77–95°F) and in winter should not fall below 18°C (64°F). A water-permeable sand-peat mixture is suitable as a growing medium. The pots should always be set in a tray filled with water that rises into the pots by capillary action (indirect watering). The plants are best propagated by seed or by leaf cuttings.

Utricularia Linnaeus
bladderwort

The genus *Utricularia* was first described in 1753 by Carl Linnaeus. In addition to two

Fig. 110.
Utricularia vulgaris, an aquatic bladderwort. W. Barthlott

European species, three American and three Asian representatives of the genus were already known at this time. Taylor (1989) recognized 214 species, although additional species are still being discovered and described, such as *U. paulineae* (Lowrie 1998b) and *U. peter-taylorii* (Lowrie 2002). Thus, *Utricularia*, currently with 227 described species, is by far the most species-rich genus of all carnivorous plants.

The scientific name *Utricularia* is derived

Fig. 111.
Utricularia multifida growing in its natural habitat in Western Australia.
K. Reifenrath

from the Latin *utriculus* (meaning "small skin"). It refers to the tiny trapping bladders that bear a certain resemblance to waterskins or wine-skins that were formerly in widespread use.

Distribution and Habitat

As well as being the most species-rich, *Utricularia* is also the most widely distributed genus of the carnivorous plants. Bladderworts are found worldwide, with their center of distribution in the intermittently or constantly moist regions of the tropics and subtropics.

The genus reaches its northernmost limit of distribution with *Utricularia minor* in western Greenland, north of the Arctic Circle. In the south, it reaches the Cape of Good Hope in South Africa, the lower reaches of the Rio Negro (Argentina) in South America, and New Zealand's Stewart Island in Australasia. The highest elevations at which bladderworts are known is 4200 m above sea level, in the Himalayas (*U. brachiata* and *U. kumaonensis*). Because bladderworts need at least seasonally moist sites to thrive, they are absent from most of the world's arid regions. For instance, one of the few countries in which no finds have been made to date is Saudi Arabia. Bladderworts are generally also absent from oceanic islands, but exceptions include the Galapagos, New Caledonia, Guam, Palau, and some islands in the Indian Ocean.

The greatest numbers of *Utricularia* species are found in South America, with the Guiana highlands in the border area of Brazil, Venezuela, and Guiana featuring the greatest diversity. Brazil alone has fifty-nine bladderwort species, about a quarter of all species of the genus. Australia, with fifty-five species, is the second center of diversity. The tropics of Africa and Asia have markedly fewer bladderwort species, while the northern temperate lati-

tudes, northern Africa, and the Middle East have the fewest species.

The phylogenetic diversity, which describes the diversity at a taxonomic level above that of the species, shows a similar pattern to that of the distribution of species numbers. Tropical America includes twenty-one of the thirty-five sections described by Taylor (1989). Of these, fifteen sections are also restricted to this region. In Australia, New Zealand, and New Caledonia, there are eleven sections, five of which are endemic to the region. It is notable that three of the endemic Australian sections include the most primitive representatives of the genus. In Africa, too, eleven sections of *Utricularia* are represented, four of which are endemic. Asia has no endemic sections. Only the section *Utricularia*, which includes the aquatic species, is found worldwide.

Utricularia subulata (Figs. 112, 113) and *U. gibba* have the widest distributions. *Utricularia gibba* is found throughout the tropics and sub-

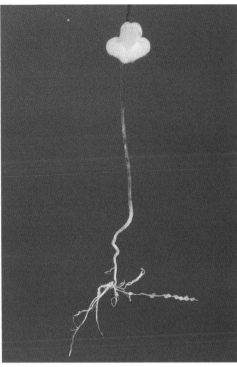

Fig. 112, left:
This *Utricularia subulata* plant, which is about 7 cm high, extends its underground trapping bladders into the moss cushion and sand. W. Barthlott

Fig. 113.
The chasmogamic form of *Utricularia subulata* has large, open flowers about 1 cm across. (The cleistogamic form is shown in Figs. 119 and 120.) W. Barthlott

tropics; in the Americas the species ranges from Canada to Argentina, it reaches the Cape of Good Hope in South Africa, and it is found in New Zealand in Australasia. Hence, *U. gibba* grows over nearly the entire area of distribution of the genus.

Other species occur over only a very small area. To date, *Utricularia steyermarkii* has been found on only two isolated table mountains (Auyan Tepui and Amaruay Tepui) in the Venezuelan state of Bolivar. *Utricularia rhododactylos* was only collected once, in the Deaf Adder Gorge in Arnhemland, Australia. In the case of *U. determannii*, only the type specimen site on a granite inselberg in Surinam is known.

There are all possible gradations between these two distributional extremes. In addition to continuous distribution patterns, there are also disjunct distribution patterns, such as that of *Utricularia stellaris*, which is widespread throughout tropical Africa and Asia, absent from the Malayan archipelago, but again present in northern Australia. *Utricularia juncea* (Figs. 19, 20), which has long been known from tropical and temperate regions of the Americas, was also discovered recently on two isolated sites in western Africa (Dörrstock et al. 1996).

Although *Utricularia* occupies a wide diversity of habitats, all of them are open and receive plenty of light. The plants are generally found on low-nutrient areas with a sparse vegetation cover. In accordance with their preferred habitats, *Utricularia* species are grouped as follows: terrestrial species, lithophytes, epiphytes, aquatic species, and rheophytes. The boundaries between these groups are somewhat unclear, but a relatively unambiguous classification is still possible for most species.

Most bladderwort species occur in terrestrial habitats, where they colonize a variety of soil types, ranging from pure quartz sands to soils with varying degrees of humus content and peat soils. Terrestrial species are found

Fig. 114, left:
Utricularia striatula,
a lithophytic bladder-
wort. I. Theisen

Fig. 115, right:
Utricularia quelchii,
an epiphytic bladder-
wort. W. Barthlott

mainly in the tropics and subtropics. They grow on sites that are constantly moist at least during their growing season. Many species prefer waterlogged substrates or seepage areas. On watercourse margins, these species also often grow underwater for a time, but they are always firmly anchored in the substrate.

Bladderworts often colonize pure quartz-sand soils, such as the quartz-sand areas of South America. The plants grow during the rainy season in moist sand that is sometimes several meters deep. These quartz sands are characterized by an extreme paucity of nutrients and therefore have only a very sparse vegetation cover. The white surface reflects the incoming solar radiation. During the dry season,

the sites dry out completely, and the plants can survive only as seeds. Many bladderworts are found in seepage zones on inselbergs, which are rocky outcrops, mostly of granite or gneiss, that rise up from the surrounding plain. These outcrops have only a minimal soil cover and are largely devoid of vegetation. Seepage zones arise on inselbergs where water continuously flows through a humus-filled accumulation of soil during the rainy season. Several *Utricularia* species may occur simultaneously in such seepage zones, in which case a particular zonation is apparent.

Lithophytic species colonize rocky outcrops or stony sites that are kept moist by water runoff. Mosses or algae are also present on these sites and allow for a degree of water storage. The lithophytic species include *Utricularia sandersonii* from southern Africa and the African-Asian *U. striatula* (Fig. 114), both of which produce many flowers and are easy to grow.

Epiphytic species grow on other plants, using them as a kind of support. They do not damage the host plant and are therefore not parasitic. Most epiphytic bladderworts colonize moss cushions that collect on the branches of tropical trees. The moss cushions ensure a constantly moist environment for the bladderworts to grow in. The epiphytic bladderworts include many spectacularly flowering species such as *Utricularia quelchii* (Fig. 115). Some South American species (such as *U. humboldtii*, Fig. 21) have developed a particular form of epiphytism: they grow in the water-filled cisterns of bromeliads, and, with the aid of long aerial stolons, they spread from one bromeliad cistern to the next. It is especially interesting that *U. humboldtii* also colonizes the cisterns of the carnivorous bromeliad *Brocchinia reducta*—a case of a carnivorous epiphyte living on another carnivore.

Aquatic bladderwort species colonize still waters and slow-moving watercourses, most of which are poor in nutrients. These plants are generally free-floating in the water. In northern latitudes, aquatic bladderworts colonize bog ponds (*Utricularia australis*, Fig. 10) and low-nutrient lakes (Fig. 110). In the tropics and subtropics, bladderworts can be found in almost every kind of water body and watercourse, including ponds in savannas, lakes, loxbow lakes, and rice paddies. The widely distributed *U. gibba* is also found in very slow-flowing, shallow water on inselbergs.

Rheophytic species also colonize water, but they occur exclusively in fast-flowing watercourses with a rocky substrate. Such a habitat forces the plants to anchor themselves firmly

to the substrate in order not to be swept away. The few highly specialized species that colonize such habitats include *Utricularia rigida*.

Features

The image that people generally have of free-floating aquatic plants with finely divided leaves is applicable to only a relatively few bladderworts. Aside from the relatively uniform leaves, the plant body itself varies enormously. The assignment of individual vegetative zones to the classical organs of shoot and leaf has been the subject of controversy among scientists for more than a century (Goebel 1889; Lloyd 1942; Troll and Dietz 1954; Rutishauser and Sattler 1989).

For the purposes of this book, the description of the features relates to the apparent nature of the plant organs. Thus, the "leaves" are plant organs that are green and flat, whereas the "shoots" are all the organs that are more or less cylindrical and bear leaves or that bear leaves where they are branched.

Bladderworts are small, herbaceous, rootless, annual or perennial plants. Most species do not attain a height or breadth of more than 30 cm. Some aquatic species may become much larger, however, such as *Utricularia macrorhiza* or *U. vulgaris*, which can attain a breadth of more than 1 m. By far the largest bladderwort is *U. humboldtii*, which grows in bromeliad cisterns (Fig. 25). It develops an inflorescence up to 1.3 m high, with large, attractive flowers.

The shoot corresponds to the form that is normally associated with flowering plants in only a few rosette-forming species, such as *Utricularia menziesii*. In most bladderwort species, the shoot is extended and is often known as a stolon. Such elongated shoots are absent only in a few, mostly primitive bladderworts (such as *U. multifida*, Fig. 111). In terrestrial species, stolons can form a dense underground network, while in aquatic species they may be branched in a regular pattern. In general, the stolons of the terrestrial species are extremely narrow and attain a length of only a few centimeters. Aquatic species, however, have stolons up to 2 mm thick and more than 1 m long. The transition from stolon to inflorescence is often covered with papillae; otherwise, the stolons are typically hairless, but often bear glands (Taylor 1989). There is a remarkable difference in biomass allocation between terrestrial and aquatic bladderworts. A high quota of green assimilating, floating shoots and leaves, with comparatively few flowers are found in aquatic species, in contrast to the achlorophyllaceous subterrestrial stolons with tiny leaves, large flowers, and many traps found in terrestrial species (Porembski et al. 2006).

Tubers represent a specialized form of the shoot and are found in several bladderwort species. Generally, these tubers develop hidden in the substrate, where they contain no chlorophyll and are either pale white or translucent. Tubers that are exposed to the light develop chlorophyll and take on a green color. The best-known tubers are those of the epiphytic species (such as *Utricularia alpina*). In 1875, Darwin demonstrated that these tubers serve water storage and not nutrient storage. From an ecological point of view, the benefits of this for epiphytic bladderworts are obvious, enabling them to withstand dry periods. The same applies to the tubers of the terrestrial species *U. menziesii*, which must survive a long dry season in its native habitats of Western Australia. Even some aquatic species, such as *U. benjaminiana*, develop tubers to survive if the waters in which they live dry out for brief periods.

Toward the end of the growing season, the aquatic bladderworts of winter-cold regions develop perennating organs, or turions, at the end of their shoots. Turions consist of a short shoot zone, ranging from a few millimeters to 2 cm in length, which is densely covered in leaves. These leaves are smaller than the normal foliage leaves and generally have wider segments. In winter, the turions sink to the substrate, rising again in the spring and growing into new plants. In addition to withstanding winter cold, turions can also survive long periods of desiccation (Wager 1928). Because the turions are relatively small and robust, they also serve as dispersal units. For example, they can be carried in the feathers of waterfowl and transported over short or long distances. Taylor (1989) noted small-scale dispersal mechanisms in *Utricularia bremii* and *U. ochroleuca* and postulated transport over greater distances in *U. australis*.

True roots are absent in *Utricularia*; instead, there are rootlike structures called rhizoids. These are not present in all bladderworts, however. Rhizoids can be simple in form, in which case they are almost impossible to distinguish from underground shoot segments, or they can be highly specialized organs in fast-flowing water that anchor the plant to the rocky substrate (such as *U. neottioides*). Many different intermediate forms exist.

The leaves of bladderworts are arranged in rosettes, whorls, or are scattered on the shoots. Some species, such as *Utricularia biovularioides*, do not develop any leaves in the vegetative zone. The leaves do not have a uniform structure, and there are many different leaf forms within the genus. One reason for this diversity is that many of the leaflike organs are, in fact, shoots that have developed a leaflike form. The form of the leaves varies from small furcate scales (*U. cymbantha*) to stalked, more or less elongated leaves (*U. subulata*), to the multipinnate leaves of aquatic species (*U. vulgaris*), to peltate leaves (*U. nelumbifolia*). The leaves are generally quite small, ranging from a few mil-

limeters to several centimeters in length. Most species have stalked, narrow, linear to obovate leaves with one or more parallel leaf nerves. The leaf surface is often very thin and flexible. The larger leaves of terrestrial and epiphytic species are generally flat, with a well-developed venation and a leathery consistency. The leaves of *U. humboldtii* are very brittle. The longest and largest leaves in the genus are found in *U. longifolia*, which can be up to 1.15 m long and 6 cm wide.

The leaves of the aquatic species, which are multipinnate, can also attain an impressive size. *Utricularia rigida*, which is native to western Africa, has leaves up to 1 m long that float in fast-flowing water. Among the species of still waters, the leaves of *U. foliosa* attain a length of 45 cm. Many aquatic species have thickened leaves filled with air at the base of the inflorescence, which lends the scape buoyancy as a free-floating body and gives it stability. In species such as *U. limosa*, the leaves are circinate

in bud, that is, the young leaf tips are rolled up like fern fronds during their development.

The traps of *Utricularia* are either on shoot sections, as in *U. multifida* and *U. reniformis*, or on leaves, as in *U. minor* and *U. sandersonii*. The trap structure is basically uniform across species and consists of a hollow space measuring 0.2–1.2 cm in length. The lengths are very constant within each species, although some species, such as *U. reniformis*, have two trap types of differing size. The traps are on a relatively long stalk and have an opening that is closed by a flap or door and a membrane or velum. The door is surrounded by different kinds of appendages. There are several hairs or bristles on the trap that trigger the opening mechanism. (A detailed description of the trap structure of *Utricularia* is given in the chapter on trapping mechanisms.) The features of the trap structure were the basis for Taylor's (1989) systematic classification of the genus.

The inflorescences of *Utricularia* are gener-

Figs. 116 and 117.
The first photographs of pollinators of *Utricularia* flowers.

Fig. 116, left:
The giant honeybee (*Apis dorsata*) on *Utricularia reticulata*.
I. Theisen

Fig. 117, right:
The convolvulus hawk moth (*Agrius convolvuli*) on *Utricularia purpurascens*.
V. D. Hoshing

Fig. 118, left: Longitudinal section of the flower of *Utricularia longifolia*. W. Barthlott

Figs. 119 and 120. The cleistogamic form of *Utricularia subulata*, a tiny bladderwort only 1 cm high (Fig. 119). In contrast to the chasmogamic form (Figs. 112, 113), the cleistogamic form has flowers only 1 mm across that are self-pollinating and do not open. W. Barthlott

ally racemose, although they may occasionally be reduced to a single flower (such as *U. menziesii*) or branched (such as *U. firmula*). The flowers have two (rarely four) fused sepals and five fused petals. The corolla is similar to that of the snapdragon, with a covered throat and a spur (see *U. longifolia* flower in Fig. 118). Aside from this common flower structure, the flower form is highly variable. The flowers color covers virtually the entire palette, with white, yellow, red, and blue flowers, and almost every imaginable shade in between. The flowers have two stamens, and the two fused carpels contain a basal placenta with numerous ovules. The flowers can be very long-lived; in the hothouse of the Botanical Gardens of the University of Bonn, for instance, a single flower of *U. menziesii* was in bloom for more than 2 months. Species such as *U. purpurascens* and *U. reticulata* offer nectar to visiting insects, including bees, hawk moths, and butterflies (Figs. 116, 117), and the flowers are sometimes scented. The fertilized flower develops into a

capsule to which the sepals remain attached and often enlarge even further. The capsule generally opens along a suture, releasing the small, variably shaped seeds.

In addition to cross-pollinated normal flowers, some bladderworts also produce cleistogamic flowers, which do not open and develop seeds through self-pollination. Such cleistogamic flowers can grow together in inflorescences, as in *Utricularia subulata* (Figs. 119, 120), or occur singly in otherwise cross-pollinated inflorescences (*U. dimorphantha*). To date, it has not been possible to clarify the factors that lead to the formation of cleistogamic flowers.

Classification

Our current knowledge of the relationships within the genus *Utricularia* is comparatively good. Supported by unambiguous molecular genetic results, Müller and Borsch (2005) proposed a new classification into three subgenera.

The subgenus *Polypompholyx* mainly contains Australian species and is the smallest group. The other species are divided between the subgenera *Bivalvia*, including *U. blanchettii*, *U. juncea*, *U. livida*, *U. nana*, *U. pubescens*, *U. rigida*, and *U. uliginosa*, and *Utricularia*, which contains the aquatic species of the Northern Hemisphere such as *U. vulgaris* and *U. purpurea*, and also epiphytic members such as *U. alpina*, and *U. reniformis*, and terrestrial species including *U. praelonga*, *U. tridentata*, and *U. subulata*. Most of the thirty-five sections elucidated by Taylor (1989) on the basis of morphological characteristics are natural groups and will therefore remain valid. At this level, the inclusion of all the species likely will lead to a complete classification in the coming years.

Special mention should be made of some of the sections. *Polypompholyx* and *Pleiochasia* are restricted to Australia and contain species that have primitive features. Many species of these sections are exclusively rosette plants that do not develop any stolons. The traps, which correspond to leaf organs, are arranged individually on the shoot, as is the case with *Genlisea*, the nearest relative of the genus *Utricularia*.

The section *Calpidisca*, which is largely restricted to Africa, contains two often-cultivated representatives, *Utricularia livida* and *U. sandersonii*. *Utricularia pubescens* is the only species of the section *Lloydia* and has peltate leaves that are otherwise found only in epiphytic species.

The epiphytic bladderworts are assigned to the sections *Chelidon*, *Orchidoides*, and *Iperua*. The name Iperua means "wonderful flower" in the language of the Arawak Indians. *Utricularia humboldtii*, which has the largest flowers of all bladderworts (Fig. 25), belongs to the section *Iperua*. The species of the sections *Orchidoides* (such as *U. quelchii*, Fig. 115) and *Iperua* may be considered the most splendid of the genus, as the names suggest.

The sections *Avesicaria*, *Avesicarioides*, *Choristothecae*, and *Mirabiles* contain only two species each. However, while adapting to their sites in fast-flowing water, these bladderworts have developed into unusual plants (rheophytes) that are firmly anchored to the rocky substrate (*U. rigida*, Fig. 121). In these sections, the number of traps is also extremely limited, and in some individuals there are none at all.

Nearly all the aquatic bladderworts are contained in the sections *Utricularia* and *Vesiculina*. These species may be considered the most

Fig. 121.
Utricularia rigida, a rheophytic species, firmly attached to the rocky substrate in a river in Ivory Coast. N. Biedinger

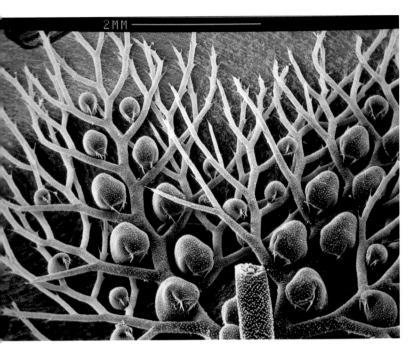

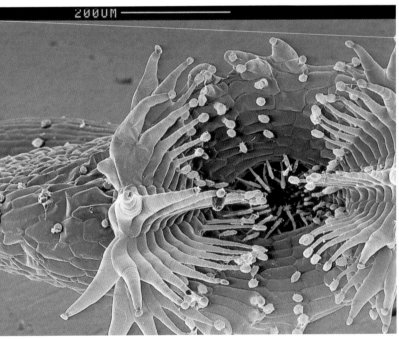

Figs. 122–124.
Scanning electron micrographs of the trapping bladders of different *Utricularia* species.

Fig. 122, above:
Utricularia australis W. Barthlott

Fig. 123, below:
Utricularia sandersonii W. Barthlott

advanced bladderworts. The section *Utricularia* contains almost all the bladderwort species of northern temperate latitudes.

Trapping Mechanism, Digestion, and Prey

Utricularia produce suction traps. This trap type is exclusive to this genus and can justifiably be considered the most sophisticated trapping mechanism found in carnivorous plants. The traps are water-filled and generate a negative pressure in their interiors. In *U. vulgaris*, Sasago and Sibaoka (1985a) measured a negative pressure of 0.14 bar in comparison with the surrounding liquid environment. If a prey animal comes into contact with the trap by brushing against the bristles of the trigger mechanism, the trap sucks water into its interior, flushing the animal in with it.

Due to the small size of the traps, it was a long time before their function was properly understood. The easily obtainable but relatively atypical aquatic species were used as study subjects. At first, it was thought that the traps were air-filled flotation devices, but Darwin (1875), Cohn (1875), and Treat (1876) independently concluded that the traps were used to catch and digest prey. Darwin and Cohn proposed that the animals had to force their way into the traps, while Treat postulated that negative pressure must play a role, given the sudden disappearance of the prey into the traps. However, it was nearly half a century before the functional principle of the traps was properly understood. Lloyd (1942) described the exciting history of the elucidation of the trap mechanism.

The main components of the traps are the stalk, trap wall, appendages (antennae), door with bristles, threshold with pavement epithelium, velum, and glandular hairs (Figs. 122–

124). All the traps are borne on relatively long stalks. The position of the stalk in relation to the trap opening differs among species and can be used for species identification.

The trap wall is typically two cell layers thick. The cells of the inner layer are usually smaller than those of the outer layer. The traps of the very primitive *Utricularia multifida* have walls that consist of several layers. On the outside, the trap wall bears spherical glands that secrete mucilage. This type of gland is found on the entire surface of bladderworts. Because the trap walls are flexible, traps that are tensioned and ready to catch prey have slightly concave walls, due to the negative pressure. If the trap is triggered, the wall suddenly returns to a resting position, in which it bulges outward. This movement increases the trap volume, flushing water together with the prey animal into the trap interior. After the prey has been caught, the trap generates negative pressure again and returns to its tensioned, concave form. The generation of negative pressure is described below.

In most bladderworts, the trap opening is surrounded by appendages (Fig. 123). The form of the appendages is characteristic of each species and is therefore an important feature for identification. Narrow appendages are also called "antennae." Together with the hairs and glands, the appendages attract the prey toward the valve opening, as Darwin (1875) postulated and Meyers and Strickler (1979) later demonstrated experimentally. In some traps, such as those of *Utricularia livida* and *U. multifida*, the appendages form a snarelike structure that serves as an anteroom for the door.

The door is generally two cell layers thick and is very flexible. It is fused to the trap wall in a semicircular fashion, while the lower, straight margin is free. In a tensioned trap, the door rests against the threshold. In the lower

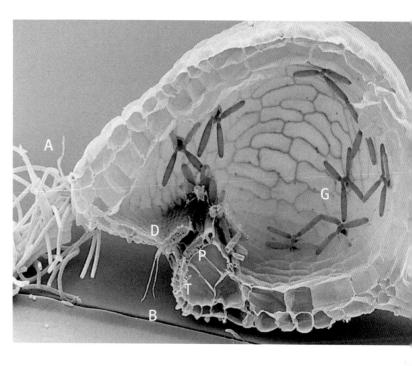

Fig. 124.
Utricularia subulata
W. Barthlott
A: appendages
G: glands
D: door
B: bristles
T: threshold
P: pavement
epithelium

part of the valve, there are several bristles that trigger the opening mechanism. Lloyd (1942) reported that a movement of the bristles bends the door until it suddenly gives way to the water pressure, resulting in the flow of water that flushes the prey animal into the trap.

The threshold forms the lower area of the trap opening. It consists of a thick, stable tissue that is several cell layers thick, forming a flat base on which the valve of the tensioned trap lies. This area features a specialized surface, the pavement epithelium, which consists of short, densely clustered glands that secrete mucilage. The pavement epithelium is also responsible for forming the velum (see below). The threshold lends the trap entrance enough stability to retain its form, even when there is negative pressure in the trap interior. The mucilage that the pavement epithelium secretes is used to seal off the trap entrance (Lloyd 1942).

The velum is a thin membrane formed by the cells of the pavement epithelium. This is the outermost envelope of cells, the cuticle, which covers the outer cell layer as a continuous film. The cuticle of the pavement epithelium is partly shed as the trap matures. It is connected with the threshold only outside the trap, and it lies over the free margin of the valve when the trap is closed (Lloyd 1942).

Bladderwort traps have different kinds of glands. In the trap interior, four-armed glands cover the entire surface and have digestion and nutrient-uptake functions. Near the opening, two-armed glands on the trap interior contribute to the buildup of negative pressure inside the trap. These absorb water from the trap interior. After transport through the trap wall near the opening, the water is then discharged to the outside (Sasago and Sibaoka 1985a, 1985b). In some *Utricularia* species, the four-armed and two-armed glands are replaced by differently shaped glands (Taylor 1989). Around the trap opening and on the appendages, there are often single rows of glands that produce sugar and mucilage.

The digestion of the trapped prey is accelerated by enzymes that the plant secretes into the trap interior. Vintejoux (1974) demonstrated that the four-armed glands in the trap interior produce proteases and acidic phosphatases that are then released into the trap; other enzymes have not yet been identified in bladderwort traps. To date, there has been no evidence of a subsequent acidification of the trap contents, although the presence of an acidic phosphatase would seem to indicate a lowering of the pH value.

The prey animals are digested relatively quickly. Slipper animalcules (ciliates) inside the traps of *Utricularia vulgaris* die within several hours (Hegner 1926). Insect larvae with relatively soft exoskeletons are largely digested after 2 days. The indigestible components of the prey remain in the traps, which cease to be functional after a certain time; the traps of *U. vulgaris*, for instance, remain active for about

50 days (Friday 1989). It is most likely that the nutrients released by digestion are resorbed into the plant via the four-armed glands. Friday and Quarmby (1994) demonstrated the uptake and further transport of nitrogen and phosphorous ions within the plant.

The prey of aquatic bladderworts consists of small animals and algae. Detailed examinations have been made for the prey of *Utricularia vulgaris*, using plants from Lake Balaton, Hungary, in which Andrikovics et al. (1988) found threadworms, snails, and a wide variety of articulates. Small crustaceans were particularly well represented, making up 90 percent of the prey animals. Mette et al. (2000), studying *U. vulgaris* and *U. macrorhiza*, obtained similar results, while also finding numerous rotifers and some planktic algae in the traps. Many of the prey animals of aquatic bladderworts are probably caught while grazing on the algal growth on the plants (Meyers and Strickler 1978, 1979).

Only a few *Utricularia* species are aquatic. Unfortunately, there is hardly any information available on the prey of terrestrial bladderworts, which make up the greater number of bladderwort species. In the traps of herbarium material, Darwin (1875) found a few remains of rhizopods and articulates. In prepared site material of *U. subulata*, Mette et al. (2000) identified rotifers, threadworms, rhizopods, and bear animalcules. Feeding attempts by Seine et al. (2002) indicated that terrestrial bladderworts attract protozoans that can then be caught. The markedly smaller trap size of terrestrial species in comparison with aquatic species supports the hypothesis that the prey spectra of these two groups are very different. The varying trap sizes and resulting prey spectra captured by different *Utricularia* species would explain the coexistence of several species in the same habitat.

Selected Species

Utricularia gibba L.
Syn. *Utricularia exoleta* R. Br.

Distribution and habitat: This species is found throughout the tropics and subtropics, extending as far north as Canada, Spain, Portugal, Israel, China, and Japan, and as far south as Argentina, South Africa, Australia, and New Zealand. Features: Perennial, aquatic plant with only a few awl-shaped (subulate) rhizoids. Relatively few, barely subdivided leaves, 0.5–1.5 cm long, on narrow, subulate stolons forming a plant about 20 cm long, either free-floating or lying as a mat on flooded ground. The traps, which are stalked, and, in comparison with *U. vulgaris*, relatively few in number, are characterized by two dorsal, much-branched appendages. The yellow flowers, which often have a reddish brown venation, are borne in numbers of two to twelve on erect inflorescences that are 10–30 cm high. This species is easy to grow and is ideal for beginners. It can be grown year-round in a small aquarium on a windowsill, at temperatures of about 18°C (64°F) and with sufficient light.

Utricularia purpurea Walt.
purple bladderwort

Distribution and habitat: Eastern North America and Central America and on the Bahamas and Cuba; in acidic and gently flowing waters. Features: Up to 60 cm long; brown stolons form free-floating, submerged mats. In contrast to most aquatic bladderworts, the shoot segments do not develop in a leaflike fashion, but instead form whorls with four to six stalks, with traps at the ends. The purplish red flowers, which are 0.8–1.8 cm long, appear on erect inflorescences 3–20 cm high.

Utricularia reniformis A. St.-Hil.

Distribution and habitat: Coastal mountain ranges in southern Brazil at elevations between 750 and 1900 m (Organ Mountains, Mount Itatiaia); terrestrial, or growing as an epiphyte between tussock grasses in moist grassland communities. Features: Leaves especially large, up to 14 cm in diameter and kidney-shaped, with stalks up to 30 cm long. The inflorescence, which is borne on a scape up to 1 m high, contains three to fourteen violet-blue flowers about 3.5 cm in diameter. The flowers are characterized by two golden yellow stripes with reddish violet margins. The traps, which are 0.7–1.5 mm across, are densely covered with glands and have two unbranched dorsal appendages. Fig. 16

Utricularia sandersonii Oliv.

Distribution and habitat: South Africa, in the northern Natal to Transkei, and in the eastern region of the Cape province; on watered rocky sites 200–1200 m above sea level. Features: Perennial species, in flower almost year-round, with spatulate leaves 3–6 cm long. Up to six light blue to white flowers, 1.0–1.5 cm long, develop on the inflorescence, which is 2–6 cm high. The upper lip is divided into two spoon-shaped petals, while the lower lip forms a spur about 2 cm long. The stalked traps have much-branched dorsal and lateral appendages. Fig. 125

Utricularia vulgaris L.
common bladderwort

Distribution and habitat: Temperate regions of Eurasia and North Africa, in still waters. Features: Forms large, submerged, free-floating mats. The stolons can attain a length of up to 2.5 m. Much branched, divided up in a fanlike fashion. Light green leaves 1–6 cm long. Traps dimorphous: (1) tiny, naked, approxi-

145

Fig. 125.
Utricularia
sandersonii
I. Theisen

mately 0.1-mm-long traps at the bases of the leaves; and (2) larger traps, 1.5–5.0 mm long, with two lateral little-branched appendages. On the erect inflorescence, which is about 20 cm high, there are six to twelve yellow flowers approximately 2 cm across. In the fall, the winter buds (turions) develop, which are typical of the temperate aquatic species, allowing the plant to overwinter on the riverbed or streambed. Fig. 110

Cultivation

Even today, bladderworts are underrepresented in carnivorous plant collections compared with, for instance, *Nepenthes* or *Sarracenia*. This may be partly due to the small size of the traps, which makes observation of the trapping process with the unaided eye impossible. Especially given their impressive flowers, however, bladderworts have enough other attractive features to make them worthwhile plants to grow.

Bladderworts need plenty of light to thrive, although excessive sun will easily damage them. A site in the morning sun and bright, indirect light for the rest of the day is recommended. Shade can be provided in sites where the sun is too strong. Aquatic species that are grown in bog beds or in containers outdoors can tolerate full sun.

The growing medium to be used depends on the plant's habit—aquatic, terrestrial, or epiphytic. Aquatic plants are best grown in weakly acidic, low-nutrient water. The water can be acidified by using peat at the base of the aquarium or by using a peat filter. Excessive nutrient levels lead to algal formation in the water and damage the plants. Terrestrial species thrive well in a potting mixture of peat and sand. Admixtures of perlite, vermiculite, or *Sphagnum* can be beneficial. Live *Sphagnum* is unsuitable, however, because it can quickly crowd out and damage smaller bladderworts. Epiphytic species can sometimes be grown in the same growing medium as terrestrial species. However, a loose mixture of peat moss, bark, and peat is more suitable. Admixtures of coconut fibers, polystyrene chips, or charcoal to loosen up the substrate further can be especially useful in a continually moist hothouse. Epiphytes can be grown in normal pots (al-

hough orchid baskets are much more attractive) or by means of true epiphytic cultivation
on a moss-covered branch.

The growing medium should be kept constantly wet. In terrestrial species, this can be
most easily achieved by placing the main container in a water-filled tray for the water to rise
by capillary action (indirect watering). An exception is the tuber-forming *Utricularia menziesii*, which requires a dry period in the summer, and tuber-forming epiphytes, which also
benefit from a dormancy period. During the
growing season, fertilizer can be applied at
one-quarter the stated strength. This is generally not necessary, however, because there are
sufficient prey animals in the soil to provide
nutrients to the plants.

High air humidity is especially important
for species with large leaves, to prevent the
leaves from drying out. Epiphytic species are
particularly demanding in this respect and
should be mist-sprayed if possible. Smaller
species whose leaves are near the soil surface
benefit from the evaporation of water from the
constantly moist substrate.

The temperatures for growth depend on the
plants' origin. Most terrestrial species thrive at
summer temperatures of 20–30°C (68–86°F)
and winter temperatures of 15–20°C (60–
68°F). In central Europe, only the aquatic species of northern temperate latitudes are frost-
resistant. These survive the cold period of the
year as turions on the bottom of a water body
that does not freeze and rise to the surface
again the following spring.

Bladderworts are very easy to propagate:
large specimens can simply be divided up.
Very vigorous species can even be allowed to
spread from one pot into another and the connection then severed. Species such as *Utricularia longifolia* can also be propagated by leaf
cuttings. Many species also produce seed,
sometimes even without pollination. The
seeds can be sown on a suitable medium at
any time of year. Seed production may ensure
that species rapidly spread within the hothouse (such as *U. subulata*). To avoid a mixing
together of cultures, species with similar vegetative forms should not be grown in close
proximity to each other.

Nepenthaceae: Asian Pitcher Plant Family

The family Nepenthaceae is native to the Old World tropics and features just one genus, *Nepenthes*, which includes about 110 species. The Asian pitcher plants have conspicuous leaves whose laminas form a pitcher-shaped container filled with liquid. The pitchers serve as passive pitfall traps with which the plants catch their prey. Nepenthaceae belongs to the extended group of the carnation-like Caryophyllidae (Meimberg et al. 2000), and the family's immediate relatives include the carnivorous hookleaf (Dioncophyllaceae) and sundew (Droseraceae) families.

Nepenthes Linnaeus
Asian pitcher plant

The name *Nepenthes* can be traced back to Carl Linnaeus (1753), who knew and described only one species, *N. distillatoria*. The name is from the Greek *nepenthes* (meaning "removal of grief and sorrow," "without pain") and is a reference to the pitcher fluid, a beverage with an intoxicating effect, as mentioned by Homer.

The most recent revision of the Asian pitcher plants by Cheek and Jebb (2001), as part of the *Flora Malesiana*, recognized eighty-seven species in the genus. In their CITES listing, Arx et al. (2002) accepted ninety-eight species and eleven natural hybrids. New species of *Nepenthes* are still being discovered and described, however, such as *N. zakriana* in Sabah, Borneo (Adam and Hafiza 2006) and *N. jamban* in Sumatra (Lee et al. 2006). Our current list counts 110 different *Nepenthes* species (see "The Carnivorous Plants of the World: A Comprehensive Listing from A to Z"). In addition,

there are more than 260 specific epithets that represent synonyms (Arx et al. 2002). The enormous interest in the genus is also reflected in the large number of horticultural crosses, comprising more than 230 hybrids.

All *Nepenthes* species are listed at least in Appendix II of CITES (Arx et al. 2002); *N. rajah* and *N. khasiana*, as Appendix I species, have been accorded the highest protection status. Without permits and trade certificates, the export or trade of live plants collected from their natural growth sites are therefore prohibited (see the chapter on nature conservation).

The systematic classification within the genus *Nepenthes* is currently being revised. Danser (1928) provided a comprehensive revision of the genus, including a classification into six sections (*Vulgatae*, *Montanae*, *Nobilis*, *Regiae*, *Insignes*, and *Urceolatae*), which has persisted to this day. Hooker (1873) and Macfarlane (1908) examined the Asian pitcher plants systematically. Jebb and Cheek (1997; Cheek and Jebb 2001) published preliminary studies relating to a forthcoming reexamination and classification of these plants. However, the preliminary results have not yet been sufficient for the authors to make a valid and unambiguous division of the genus into subgenera and sections. The most recent molecular genetic studies (Meimberg et al. 2001) are at odds with Danser's sectional classification. In addition, the species from Sri Lanka (*N. distillatoria*), the Seychelles (*N. pervillei*), Madagascar (*N. madagascariensis*, *N. masoalensis*), and India (*N. khasiana*) occupy a basal position within the genus; on the basis of their morphological features, too, these species are clearly differentiated from the others (Jebb and Cheek

1997). This led Meimberg et al. (2001) to postulate two alternative evolutionary scenarios for the Asian pitcher plants: (1) origin in the northern region of the primeval ocean Tethys, a hypothesis supported by fossil *Nepenthes* pollen finds in Europe; or (2) a Gondwanan origin, occurring at the time when India separated from Madagascar. The latter theory has since been proven by phylogenetic reconstructions (Meimberg and Heubl 2006). It is now assumed that recent Nepenthaceae originated in the Indian subcontinent. The Malaysian region with its remarkable wealth of species is considered a secondary center of diversity.

One notable feature within the Asian pitcher plants is the constant number of chromosomes. All the species that have been studied to date have a chromosome set of $n = 40$. This homogeneity is the basis for the nearly unlimited potential for hybrid crosses between different *Nepenthes* species. This lack of a genetic barrier to hybrid crossing has allowed the large number of natural and horticultural hybrids to arise.

Asian pitcher plants are used in many different ways in their regions of origin. Perhaps the best-known use is that of the pitcher liquid as a beverage. Descriptions of the taste range from "palatable" to "musty," with the plants' success in catching prey and the age of the pitchers probably being a significant factor in the taste. Macfarlane (1908) reported that *Nepenthes ampullaria* and *N. rafflesiana* are used as construction materials: the native inhabitants of Borneo use the flexible shoots of both species as cording, binding together bamboo stems to make suspension bridges. In Borneo, too, the pitchers of *Nepenthes* are used as pots for cooking rice and other foodstuffs. In the local medicine, pitcher plants are used for treating a wide range of ailments. For example, the pitcher liquid is used to treat coughs and bladder problems. Cooked root preparations are used as medication for stomach pain and dysentery,

and the cooked stems are used as a remedy for malaria. The liquid of unopened pitchers is used to treat eye diseases and skin irritations.

Fig. 126.
Nepenthes villosa
A. Weber

Distribution and Habitat

The genus *Nepenthes* is distributed from Madagascar to the Seychelles, India, and Southeast Asia and east to northeastern Australia and New Caledonia. The greatest diversity of Asian pitcher plants is found on the Malay archipelago. Most of the species have a very limited area of distribution. Nine species were not found again after their initial discovery, and are therefore known only from their type spec-

imen collections (*N. argentii, N. bellii, N. borneensis, N. boschiana, N. campanulata, N. clipeata, N. macrophylla, N. mollis,* and *N. paniculata*). Another ten species are found only on individual mountains or mountain ranges (*N. aristolochioides, N. burbidgeae, N. edwardsiana, N. mapuluensis, N. muluensis, N. murudensis, N. ovata, N. rajah, N. rhombicaulis,* and *N. villosa,* Fig. 126). Only ten species of the genus colonize an area larger than an island or a small group of islands. *Nepenthes mirabilis* has the widest distribution, extending from Indochina to Australia (Jebb and Cheek 1997).

Within their natural range, the greatest diversity of *Nepenthes* species is found in regions that never lost their permanently moist-climate vegetation during the climatic fluctuations that occurred over geological history (Steenis 1969). These areas include Sumatra and Borneo. The soil types, too, appear to have influenced the species diversity. Borneo, with its geologically highly diverse parent materials and soil types, has the richest *Nepenthes* flora worldwide, with thirty-two species (Jebb and Cheek 1997; Clarke 1997).

Nepenthes colonizes a wide variety of tropical habitats, ranging from sea level to cool, alpine mountain regions. A distinction is made between lowland species, which occur from sea level to about 1200 m, and highland species, which grow at higher elevations. Lowland species thrive in a continuously warm climate. Highland species live in climates with marked differences between daytime and nighttime temperatures and lower daily maximum temperatures. Precipitation levels and air humidity are high at nearly all *Nepenthes* growth sites.

Most *Nepenthes* species inhabit tree and shrub communities: rainforests, cloud forests, or constantly moist shrub communities only. *Nepenthes ampullaria, N. macfarlanei* (Fig. 127), and *N. mirabilis* (Fig. 128) thrive in the shade of relatively dense woody plant vegetation. The remaining Asian pitcher plants that grow in

Fig. 128.
Nepenthes mirabilis
A. Weber

tree and shrub communities prefer forest margins, clearings, or mountain ridges, where the tree cover is lower and there is more available light. The soils of these sites are generally acidic and low in nutrients (white-sand soils, sandstone, strongly weathered and leached volcanic soils, and peat soils).

Species of more brightly lit sites often colonize road cuttings, clear-cut forest areas, and fallow fields. Due to this ability to adapt, many species are able to withstand the considerable human influence in their habitats. *Nepenthes gracilis* and *N. mirabilis* actually appear to prefer anthropogenically disturbed habitats.

While most forest-dwelling *Nepenthes* species are rooted in the soil and grow from there into the surrounding woody vegetation, epiphytes, such as *N. inermis,* live without any contact with the soil. They are often rooted in moss cushions that, in turn, grow on the supporting trees.

Several Asian pitcher plants colonize savanna-like grass communities that generally occur on continuously moist, sandy soils. Be-

Fig. 127, facing page:
Nepenthes macfarlanei
T. Borsch

cause these are very open habitats, the pitcher plants receive plenty of light. *Nepenthes thorelii* colonizes grassland with a marked dry period in the lower Mekong River region in Vietnam. The plant has a thickened shoot base that Kurata (1976) interpreted as a water-storage organ. Phillipps and Lamb (1996) reported that cultivated specimens of *N. anamensis* (syn. *N. kampotiana*), which is native to the monsoon regions of Thailand, lose their leaves in the winter and undergo a dormancy period.

Swamps on sandy soils or peat are also home to several *Nepenthes* species. The soil is acidic, and the plants have plenty of available light. Such habitats are colonized by *N. ampullaria*, *N. madagascariensis*, and *N. mirabilis*, for example. *Nepenthes mirabilis* is also found on the margins of slow-flowing rivers and streams (Kurata 1976). The highest known site for the genus is a swamp: *N. lamii* grows at an elevation of 3520 m on Dorman Top in New Guinea. At this elevation, the temperature may fall below freezing during the early morning hours.

Other unusual habitats also are colonized. *Nepenthes albomarginata*, *N. mirabilis*, *N. reinwardtiana*, and *N. treubiana* grow on beaches, within the spray zone. These species, therefore, can withstand the high ionic concentrations on salt-containing soils. By contrast, *N. argentii*, *N. burbidgeae*, *N. danseri*, *N. macrovulgaris*, and *N. rajah* are found exclusively on soils that contain heavy metals. Although the plants tolerate the heavy-metal content of the soils, they do not require the heavy metals for their survival. Their restriction to these sites is probably due to the reduced competition to which the species are exposed on these soils.

Inselbergs are home to *Nepenthes clipeata* (Mount Kelam, eastern Borneo) and *N. pervillei* (the islands of Mahé and Silhouette, Seychelles). Due to the shallow soil cover and the bare rock of the inselbergs, sunny conditions quickly lead to desiccation and low air humidity (Porembski and Barthlott 2000). *Nepenthes*

campanulata and *N. northiana* grow as climbers on steep limestone rock faces. These plants prefer areas in which there is continuous water seepage and use their root systems to anchor themselves into cracks in the rock.

Features

Nepenthes species are perennial, lignifying (wood-forming) plants and are mostly lianas. The nonclimbing species grow as small, erect shrubs or creep along the ground. The climbing species can reach a considerable height: for example, *N. bicalcarata* and *N. edwardsiana* can be up to 15 m long. Most species are much smaller, however, less than 10 m long. Young plants have a short shoot and leaves arranged in a rosette. The shoots of older plants grow much longer, yielding a shrub or vine. Especially in the highland species, the rosette form may persist for many years. The young shoots of Asian pitcher plants are generally green and often bear nectar glands. After several months, the shoots turn brown. The older shoots are no longer very flexible and sometimes become brittle over time. Most Asian pitcher plants have cylindrical shoots, but three-cornered shoots are also known (such as in *N. tentaculata*). The shoots of species such as *N. gracilis* have decurrent leaf bases and therefore appear winged.

Despite their considerable length, the species that grow as lianas have a shoot thickness ranging from only a few millimeters (such as *Nepenthes fusca*) to about 3 cm (such as *N. rafflesiana*). The shoot of the mostly epiphytic, climbing *N. veitchii* often dies off at ground level, while the growth of the tip continues (Macfarlane 1908). Creeping, prostrate shoots are found among species such as *N. rajah* and *N. villosa*. *Nepenthes ampullaria* develops not only prostrate rhizomes, which bear leaf rosettes at intervals, but also climbing shoots.

The shrub species *Nepenthes pervillei* (Fig. 129) and *N. madagascariensis* (Figs. 130, 131)

Fig. 129.
Nepenthes pervillei
growing on the
island of Mahé
(Seychelles).
N. Biedinger

develop leaning to erect shoots that are more than 1 m long.

The roots of the seedlings branch freely at an early stage. Compared with the roots of most other carnivorous plants, the root systems of *Nepenthes* are well developed. The roots are not very flexible, however, and break easily. The root networks of older plants do not have a taproot, instead being spread out flat.

Three leaf zones can be distinguished: (1) the flat basal part of the leaf, attached to the shoot; (2) the rounded stalk leading to the pitcher; and (3) the pitcher at the end of the leaf (Fig. 131). These three zones fulfill different functions. The foliage leaflike part primarily serves photosynthetic requirements, and hence the plant's energy supply. In most species, the pitcher stalk is developed as a tendril and is

Fig. 130, left:
*Nepenthes
madagascariensis*
and the Madagascar
traveler's tree
(*Ravenala madagas-
cariensis*) in their
natural environment
near Fort Dauphin
in southeastern
Madagascar.
W. Barthlott

Fig. 131, right:
*Nepenthes
madagascariensis*
W. Barthlott

153

Figs. 132 and 133. Pitcher dimorphism in *Nepenthes ramispina*: hanging pitcher (Fig. 132) and ground pitcher (Fig. 133). A. Weber

used to anchor the plant to the surrounding vegetation. The pitcher itself is used for catching prey (details of its structure and function are dealt with in the chapter on trapping mechanisms).

Although the leaves of pitcher plants appear totally unlike normal foliage leaves, it is still possible to describe them in terms of the basic leaf form. The green, foliage-like basal section is developed from the normally inconspicuous leaf base; it is very large and flat. The pitcher stalk corresponds to a normal petiole; it is a tendril that can wind itself around neighboring plants, but is coiled only once. The pitcher stalk ensures that the pitcher is in an optimal position. The pitcher is a completely transformed leaf lamina, the normally flat part of the leaf that makes up the greater part of the foliage leaf. The pitchers of the different species exhibit a wide variation in form and color. The largest pitchers are found in *Nepenthes rajah*, which may contain up to 2 L of liq-

uid. All pitchers have a tubular section with a prominent rim (peristome), a lid, two wing ribs, and a spur behind the lid, which is the actual leaf tip. The lid is often interpreted as a protection against incoming rainwater, but there are also species with a backward-pointing lid (such as *N. ampullaria*) or comparatively small lid (such as *N. fusca*). In both cases, the lid of the pitcher is unable to provide any protection against incoming rainwater.

The cotyledons of Asian pitcher plants do not bear any pitchers and have a simple, elliptical form. All subsequent leaves develop a pitcher. The initial leaves of a young plant do not develop a long pitcher stalk; instead, their pitchers sit atop a short stalk tapering off of the flat, basal part of the leaf. Young plants bear their leaves in a scattered, rosette-shaped arrangement. The leaves of the elongated shoots that later develop are also arranged in a scattered fashion, but are separated from one another by longer shoot internodes. An excep-

Figs. 134 and 135. Pitcher dimorphism in *Nepenthes rafflesiana*: hanging pitcher (Fig. 134) and ground pitcher (Fig. 135). A. Weber

tion is *Nepenthes veitchii*, whose leaves are arranged in two rows.

Most *Nepenthes* species develop different pitcher forms on the leaves near the ground (lower pitcher form) and on the elongated stalks (upper pitcher form), a phenomenon known as "leaf dimorphism." The differences between the lower and upper pitcher forms within a single plant are often so great that the two forms could be mistaken for pitchers of two different species (such as *N. lowii*, *N. rafflesiana*; see Figs. 134, 135). This dimorphism is repeated at lateral shoots, which begin by forming the rosette-shaped standing leaves of the lower pitcher form; as the lateral shoots elongate, leaves of the upper pitcher form develop.

As a rule, the lower pitcher form has a shorter, straight pitcher stalk and wide, stout pitchers with conspicuous wings. By contrast, the upper pitcher form has a long, mostly coiled pitcher stalk, a narrow, cylindrical or amphora-shaped pitcher, and relatively small, inconspicuous wings. The dimorphism in *Nepenthes ampullaria* and *N. pectinata* is particularly marked: the leaves with the lower pitcher form have only a short, flat leaf section and almost spherical pitchers, whereas the leaves with the upper pitcher form have a large, assimilating leaf section and usually no pitcher at all.

Pitcher plants are dioecious, which means that the male and female flowers develop on separate plants. The racemose or paniculate inflorescences of the individual species are very different in length (Fig. 136), ranging from 10–15 cm in *Nepenthes bongso* to about 1 m in *N. rajah*. In the male inflorescences, the individual flowers survive only a few days. If unpollinated, female flowers can remain fresh for several weeks. An individual flower generally has four petals that bear many nectar glands on the inner side. The ovaries of the female flowers consist of four carpels, and the male flowers have eight stamens (Fig. 137).

Fig. 136, left: Male inflorescence of *Nepenthes ampullaria*. A. Weber

Fig. 137, right: Male flower (top) and female flower of *Nepenthes alata*. W. Barthlott

Macfarlane (1908) reported on a heavy, unpleasant scent emanating from *Nepenthes* flowers, describing small flies and beetles as the pollinators. Pollinated female flowers develop into capsules that release hundreds of awl-shaped seeds. A single inflorescence of *N. gracilis* can produce more than 10,000 seeds. The seeds are wind-dispersed and generally germinate quickly on a moist growing medium.

Trapping Mechanism, Digestion, and Prey

The traps of the Asian pitcher plant are passive pitfall traps that do not move. In general, as the common name suggests, they are shaped like a pitcher or jug.

Despite its thin walls, the pitcher is remarkably stable. This stability is achieved by the thickened cell walls of the epidermal cells and greatly hardened leaf nerves. In addition, there are scattered, specialized, elongated cells in the tissue of the pitcher walls whose cell walls are spirally thickened. The stability of the pitcher wall ensures that even powerful prey animals cannot break free by damaging the pitcher. The lid of the pitcher is closed only in the early stages of the pitcher's development; once open, the lid does not close again.

Nectar, color, and occasionally scent are used to attract the prey. The aboveground parts of Asian pitcher plants are sparsely covered with nectar glands. Their sugar-containing secretions attract many animals that then approach the traps. In addition, Moran (1996) noted olfactory signals: the pitfall traps often emit a sweet scent; the traps usually have a conspicuous coloration or variegation as well.

Nepenthes pitfall traps can be divided into three zones with different functions, the attraction zone, pitfall zone, and digestion zone.

Attraction zone This comprises the lid and the peristome (rim of the trap opening) of the pitfall trap. The lid underside and the inner margin of the peristome are covered with many nectar glands that range in diameter from about 0.1 to 3.0 mm. The external wings of the pitcher also help to attract prey and generally have a larger number of nectar glands than the remaining exterior pitcher surfaces. The sugar-containing secretions of the glands attract the prey to the trap opening (Moran 1996). The number and arrangement of the nectar glands on the lid underside varies from one species to another and can be used as a characteristic for identifying plants. For instance, *Nepenthes ampullaria* has only a very few glands or none at all.

The peristome or pitcher rim, which is more or less T-shaped in cross-section, has a ribbed surface. The horizontal bars of the peristome are often bent inward. On the inner side of the pitcher, the ribs of the peristome usually end in spines with nectar glands between them. Animals that stand on the peristome and reach down toward the glands lose their footing and fall into the trap interior. The form of the peristome is characteristic for each species, but within a species it can often vary between the upper and lower pitchers. The peristome of *Nepenthes tentaculata* is very weakly developed; it is 2 mm wide and a plain green. By contrast, the peristomes of *N. edwardsiana* and *N. macrophylla* are very wide and have extreme ribs. The most extreme expression of individual peristome ribs is found in *N. bicalcarata*; two ribs at the base of the lid are elongated into free-standing "fangs."

The often-conspicuous coloration or variegation of the lid and the peristome also likely contributes to the attraction of prey animals. A marked pubescence that may force animals toward the trap opening is found on the lid underside of *Nepenthes lowii* (Fig. 138). In Asian pitcher plants, scent only seldom plays a role in attracting prey. The underside of the lid of *N. rafflesiana* emits a heavy, sweet scent, whereas *N. lowii* occasionally secretes an unpleasant-smelling substance from the same location.

Pitfall zone This zone begins directly beneath the nectar glands at the rim of the peristome. In the pitfall zone, the epidermis features several half-moon-shaped, somewhat protruding cells. These cells are reduced stomata that give the surface a shingled, downward-pointing structure. Even with the unaided eye, the pitfall zone is visible as a whitish or bluish, sometimes iridescent surface, which is caused by a waxy secretion that is composed of two layers. The inner layer consists of waxy strands arranged in a net, while the layer above it consists of scale-shaped crystals. When touched, the crystals slough off, making a firm foothold on the surface impossible (Martin and Juniper 1970; Gaume et al. 2004; Gorb et al. 2004, 2005; Gorb and Gorb 2006; Riedel et al. 2003).

In almost all *Nepenthes* species, the pitfall zone in the upper pitchers is much less well developed than in the lower pitchers. *Nepenthes reinwardtiana* has two wax-free spots in the upper part of the pitfall zone; nothing is known about their function. In older traps, the waxy layer is sometimes so badly eroded that prey animals are able to climb back up the pitcher walls. In some species,

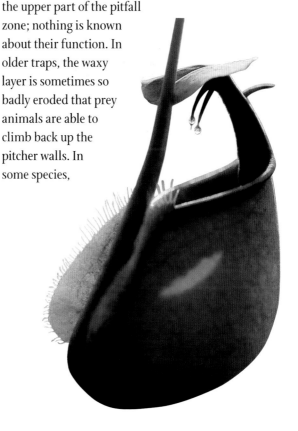

completely wetted, even if their surface normally causes water to run off. Hence, the victims drown in the liquid very quickly. To date, there have not been any reliable investigations of the nature and composition of the wetting agents in the trap fluid.

The digestion of the prey animals begins as soon as they have drowned in the pitcher fluid. The digestion of the soft parts of the victim proceeds quickly and takes only about 2 days. The chitin exoskeletons of insects can be at least partially digested, although this process takes longer.

The trap fluid of unopened *Nepenthes* pitchers already contains various enzymes and has a moderately acidic pH of about 5.5. It may sometimes have a viscous consistency like that of glycerin. When the trap opens, the fluid is generally diluted by rainwater and is therefore thinned. Through chemical stimulation, such as by proteins, the pH value falls to about 3 and increased digestive enzyme production is triggered. A mechanical stimulation of the pitcher interior does not cause any increase in enzyme production, however.

The digestive glands of *Nepenthes* produce a variety of enzymes, including esterases, phosphatases, proteases, aminopeptidases, peroxidases, and ribonucleases, which serve to digest the soft tissue of the prey animals. In addition to their own enzymes, to assist with digestion of the prey Asian pitcher plants also make use of the digestive secretions of bacteria that live in the pitchers. In addition, chitinase has been identified in the pitcher fluid, without any direct evidence of the enzyme in the glands. This enzyme is able to dissolve the extremely resistant exoskeletons of insects and other arthropods that generally pass undigested through the digestive tract of birds, for example.

The digestive glands are also involved in nutrient uptake into the plant body. Schulze et al. (1997) demonstrated that the nitrogen

including *N. ampullaria*, the pitfall zone is absent altogether.

Digestive zone The zone at the bottom of the pitcher serves digestion and lies beneath the surface of the digestive fluid. The trap wall bears numerous sunken digestive glands that are round or oval and generally covered by a slightly projecting margin. In this zone, too, prey animals cannot gain a foothold to climb back up. The size of the glands within the digestive zone generally increases from top to bottom.

The trap fluid contains surface-active substances that ensure that the prey animals are

taken up from the pitcher fluid is transported within the plant to the developing leaves.

Prey

The prey of Asian pitcher plants mainly consists of arthropods. Ants and other insects are the main victims, while spiders, scorpions, and centipedes are also regularly found. Snails and frogs are among the more unusual prey animals.

The composition of the prey is highly variable. In ten pitchers, Erber (1979) found nearly 2000 prey animals belonging to 150 species. Among most Asian pitcher plants, pitchers do not appear to be specialized for particular prey animals. *Nepenthes albomarginata* (Fig. 139), however, is specialized to catch termites (Merbach et al. 2002). Attracted by a white ring of edible hairs beneath the peristome, thousands of termites fall to their deaths in the pitfall traps. If no termites are available at the site, there are relatively few prey animals that will be caught because *N. albomarginata* does not secrete nectar at the pitcher rim as an attractant.

Perhaps the most spectacular prey animals recovered from Asian pitcher plants are rats that were found in the pitchers of *Nepenthes rajah* on Mount Kinabalu. It is thought that the animals fell into the pitchers during a dry spell while looking for drinking water and could not escape once having fallen in. Vertebrates are certainly not the Asian pitcher plants' usual prey but must be regarded as occasional accidental captures.

Selected Species

Nepenthes alata Blanco

Distribution and habitat: Philippines (highlands). Features: Pitchers up to 20 cm long and up to 3 cm wide; almost cylindrical in the up-

per half, stout below, on the underside with two weakly developed, serrated wings. The rim of the pitcher opening is narrow. Pitcher and lid light green to yellow, partly reddish tinged, with a glandular crest beneath the lid. The species is very heat-tolerant and is suitable for growing on a windowsill.

Nepenthes ampullaria Jack

Distribution and habitat: Malay archipelago (lowlands). Features: Small, white to red leaves in a basal leaf rosette. Pitcher traps up to 11 cm long, barrel-shaped, green, with a prominent wing on the front side; the small oval lid is directed completely backward. The species

Fig. 139.
*Nepenthes
albomarginata*
A. Weber

thrives in a hothouse or warm terrarium; the long shoots can easily be cut back, which then encourages the further development of traps on basal rosettes. The traps take on a good coloration even in shady sites. Suitable for growing by beginners. Fig. 140

Nepenthes bicalcarata Hook. f.

Distribution and habitat: Borneo (lowlands). Features: Two different pitcher types (pitcher dimorphism): lower pitchers up to 10 cm long, stout, with two fringed wings. Upper pitchers up to 15 cm long with a marked funnel shape, with two ribs instead of the fringed wings. The peristomes of both pitcher types have two spines about 2 cm long that secrete nectar. The species needs hot, moist conditions. Because it grows to be very large, however, *Nepenthes bicalcarata* is suitable for large greenhouses only. Fig. 141

Nepenthes gracilis Korth.

Distribution and habitat: Borneo, Sumatra, Sulawesi (lowlands). Features: Lower pitchers light green, up to 7.5 cm long, upper pitchers dark red to brown and up to 15 cm long. Unlike the pitchers of *Nepenthes alata*, which are very similar, the pitchers of *N. gracilis* do not have a glandular crest beneath the lid. The species is suitable for warm terrariums on a windowsill. They can be cut back and root easily in water. Suitable for growing by beginners.

Nepenthes rajah Hook. f.

Distribution and habitat: Borneo (highlands). Features: This species has the largest pitchers of the entire genus. Pitchers scarlet red, up to 40 cm long and 18 cm wide; peristome deep red and markedly ringed; lid oval, extraordinarily large, covering the entire oblique pitcher mouth. Both this species and *Nepenthes khasiana* have been accorded CITES Appendix I protection.

Cultivation

Asian pitcher plants were first brought to Europe by Sir Joseph Banks in 1789. Interest in

Fig. 140.
Nepenthes ampullaria
A. Weber

Nepenthes grew steadily throughout the nineteenth century, and in the second half of the century the plants became fashionable among the gentry. They were not as expensive as orchids, but were nevertheless unaffordable for the majority of people. Asian pitcher plants had a permanent place in the famous greenhouses of the Victorian Age, although this golden age of *Nepenthes* cultivation came to an abrupt end with the outbreak of World War I.

When growing *Nepenthes*, it is important to be aware of the geographic origin of the species (see the appendix). About 30 percent of *Nepenthes* species are from the lowlands and need hot days and warm nights. The remaining 70 percent colonize highland sites and prefer warm days and cooler nights.

All *Nepenthes* species require high air humidity with sufficient ventilation. Most species prefer light to sunny sites; in summer, shading should be provided in greenhouses to avoid scorching of the leaves. A soil that retains water well is the most suitable, although stagnant water should be avoided. The soil, too, should be well aerated, which means that there should be sufficient coarse material. Most species thrive on acidic soils, so that a mixture of peat moss (which retains water), bark, charcoal, and vermiculite, among other media, is suitable. Clay pots, which allow evaporation, ensure that the growing medium is cooled, which can be particularly useful for highland species. Cultivation in orchid baskets is also recommendable if an adequate air humidity can be ensured and if the plants are watered frequently and sufficiently. Fertilization is not necessary for *Nepenthes*. However, an occasional application of orchid food as leaf fertilizer during the summer, diluted to half strength, will benefit growth.

Older plants with several long shoots and rosettes can be cut back, and they can similarly be cut well back for repotting. It is impor-

tant that one or more rosettes remain on the plant. Pitcher formation on long shoot leaves can be promoted by using climbing aids to which the tendrils can attach.

Propagation is mainly achieved by cuttings. Long shoots should be cut into several pieces, each with three nodes. Remove the leaf from the lowest node, and cut the remaining leaves in half. Dip the cuttings in fungicide and rooting hormone before planting out. The following media are recommended for raising the

Fig. 141.
Nepenthes bicalcarata
W. Barthlott

161

Fig. 142.
Nepenthes sanguinea
A. Weber

cuttings: *Sphagnum*, a mixture of *Sphagnum* and vermiculite, or pure rock wool. The medium must not be allowed to dry out. The cuttings should be kept in light, humid conditions, but not in direct sunlight.

Reproduction by seeding requires the presence of flowers. Because *Nepenthes* plants are dioecious, male and female flowers are not always available together. Carnivorous plant societies often organize pollen exchanges (see the list of societies at the end of the book). The seeds are tiny and are capable of germination for only a very brief time, although they can be stored for several weeks. They should be sown on a fine-grained medium and kept in moist and light, but not sunny, conditions. The temperatures should be adjusted to meet the requirements of the adult plants.

Roridulaceae: Bug Plant Family

This family contains just one genus, *Roridula*, the bug plant. With two perennial species, this genus is restricted to the mountainous areas of the South African Cape region.

According to molecular genetic studies, the Roridulaceae are related to the heather family (Ericaceae), as well as the families of the tea plants, primroses, and ebonies. It was previously believed that the closest relatives of the bug plants were the Australian rainbow plants (*Byblis*), with which they were included in a common family, the Byblidaceae (Cronquist 1988). Instead, it is now clear that the American pitcher plants (Sarraceniaceae) and the Asian-American kiwifruits (Actinidiaceae) are the closest relatives of Roridulaceae (Anderberg et al. 2002). When Linnaeus (1764) first described this genus, the bug plant (*Roridula dentata*) was still included among the sundews (Droseraceae). It was only 160 years later that Engler and Gilg (1924) raised the status of both the species (*R. dentata* and *R. gorgonias*, the latter described by Planchon in 1848) to that of an independent family.

Bug plants catch their prey with passive adhesive traps. Because they lack any digestive enzymes of their own, however, they are able to obtain the nutrients only with the aid of assassin bugs and spiders, with which they live in a symbiotic relationship. Hence, the Roridulaceae—in a manner akin to *Brocchinia* and *Catopsis* of the Bromeliaceae—are among the precarnivorous plants. Lloyd (1942) determined that the glands' secretions are resinous and not aqueous. Because water is required for enzymatic activity, he felt that *Roridula* should not be included among the carnivorous plants.

Roridula Linnaeus
bug plant

The genus includes two species, *Roridula dentata* L. (Fig. 143) and *R. gorgonias* Planch. (Fig. 144). The generic name derives from the Latin word *roridus* ("wet with dew") and refers to the mucilaginous secretions of the trapping leaves. On his travels though southern Africa in 1773, the botanist Carl Peter Thunberg (1743–1828) reported that *Roridula* was collected in the Cape region and used to catch flies in the houses there, due to its sticky leaves. In this region, the plants still bear the name *vlieëbos* ("fly-bush") to this day.

Distribution and Habitat

Endemic to the South African Cape region, the two *Roridula* species are found only in the mountainous regions of the Cedar Mountains and the Hermanus district. Here, the local, open, heathlike vegetation, known as *fynbos*, is subject to frequent outbreaks of fire. *Roridula* is well adapted to this habitat and can easily regenerate from seed after fire. These regular fires, which occur every few years, serve to rejuvenate *Roridula* stands and suppress competing species that would otherwise crowd out the habitat. The predominantly seasonally moist and sandy sites, which are located between quartzite rocks, are extremely low in nutrients.

Features

Both species are subshrubs up to 2 m high. The lignified shoots have few branches. The plants have a well-developed root system with numerous, fine, fibrous roots. The alternate foliage leaves, which are yellowish green and astipulate, are concentrated at the ends of the shoots, as the older, dried-up leaves are shed. In the prefoliation phase, the leaves are rolled up in a circinate fashion. The leaves, which are insensitive to stimuli, are densely covered with sticky, stalked glandular tentacles of varying lengths that project from the leaf margins at different angles. The quinate flowers, which are borne in the leaf axils, are pink or whitish and consist of five sepals, five petals, five stamens, and three fused carpels. The pollinators include a bug that stabs the sugar-containing tissue at the base of the stamens, which then open up and release the pollen. The trilocular capsules open along longitudinal sutures and release numerous seeds, which are about 5 mm and have a very fleshy endosperm. The morphology of the seeds is different for the two species: *Roridula dentata* has ovate seeds, whereas *R. gorgonias* has irregular polygonous seeds (Lobova 1999).

Trapping Mechanism, Digestion, and Prey

The extremely sticky glands, which glisten in the sunlight like drops of nectar, are attractive to insects, which both in the wild and in cultivation land on the leaves in large numbers and are trapped there. As mentioned earlier, *Roridula* is not a carnivorous plant in the strictest sense. As early as 1903, Rudolf Marloth (1855–1931) showed that animals were caught but that the plant produced no enzymes to digest the prey. The bug plant is often designated as precarnivorous or as a primitive carnivore, be-

cause it is seen as still on the evolutionary path to true carnivory. It must be asked, however, whether the principle that *Roridula* employs, to have helpers (in this case bugs and spiders) working for it, is perhaps more favorable in terms of energy, which means that further evolutionary steps toward true carnivory can be dispensed with.

Although *Roridula* does not have digestive enzymes of its own, the plants benefit from their catches through a remarkable symbiosis with bugs (*Pameridea marlothii* and *P. roridulae*) and spiders (*Synaema marlothii*). These highly specialized animals, which are found exclusively on *Roridula* plants, use the sticky plants in two ways: they feed on the prey that the plants have caught, and the plants serve as a refuge and habitat. In return, the bug plants benefit from the bugs' excretions, which act as manure and are taken up directly by the leaf surface (cuticle). In this way, it is ultimately possible for the plants to resorb the nutrients contained in the insects that they have caught (Dolling and Palmer 1991; Ellis and Midgley 1996; Midgley and Stock 1998). It was only recently that Anderson and Midgley (2002), using radioactively labeled prey animals, were able to demonstrate the role of the spiders in this mutualistic triangle. Although it was previously understood that both the spiders and bugs contributed to the plants' nutrition through their excretions, Anderson and Midgley showed that the proportion of nitrogen in the plant from prey animals varied from about 70 percent (with many bugs and no spiders) to only 30 percent (with few bugs and many spiders).

The prey animals are mainly flying insects, such as flies and wasps and other hymenopterans. Because the mucilaginous secretions of *Roridula* are extraordinarily effective and extremely sticky, larger flying insects, such as butterflies or dragonflies, can also be caught.

Overview of Species

Roridula dentata L.

Distribution and habitat: South African Cape region; in mountainous areas 900–1200 m above sea level in the Tulbagh, Ceres, and Clanwilliam districts. Features: Lignified shrub up to 2 m high. Leaves up to 5 cm long and 3 mm wide; unlike *Roridula gorgonias*, the leaves of *R. dentata* are toothed (dentate). Inflorescence up to 10 cm long, petals up to 12 mm long. Fig. 143

Roridula gorgonias Planch.

Distribution and habitat: South African Cape region, on cloud-covered mountain slopes from 100 to 900 m above sea level in the region around Sommerset West, Stellenbosch, Caledon, and Swellendam. Features: Lignified shrub up to 1.8 m high. Leaves up to 12 cm long and 5 mm wide, with entire margins. Inflorescences shorter than in *Roridula dentate*, about 4–6 cm long; petals about 15 mm long. Fig. 144

Cultivation

The plants are best grown in a 3:1 mixture of peat and quartz sand. The acidic substrate should be kept only moderately moist to avoid the risk of root rot, but it should never be allowed to dry out completely. Only lime-free water should be used for watering. *Roridula* needs a sunny place with moderate temperatures. In winter, the plants may be kept in an unheated room. The plants can be propagated by sowing seed.

Fig. 143.
Roridula dentata
W. Barthlott

Fig. 144.
Roridula gorgonias
W. Barthlott

Sarraceniaceae: American Pitcher Plant Family

The family Sarraceniaceae includes three genera with twenty-one species and numerous subspecies, varieties, forms, and hybrids whose distribution is restricted to North America and northern South America. Sarraceniaceae is comprised of the genera *Darlingtonia* (the cobra lily), *Heliamphora* (South American pitcher plants), and *Sarracenia* (North American pitcher plants). In all American pitcher plants, the leaves are modified into tubular pitfall traps with fluid at the base into which the trapped prey falls and dies.

The American pitcher plant family is not closely related to most of the other carnivorous plants. There is only a close kinship only with the Roridulaceae: both families belong to the order Ericales, which includes the heathers (Ericaceae) and primroses (Primulaceae). Within the Sarraceniaceae, molecular genetic studies have revealed *Darlingtonia* to be the most primitive genus compared to the more advanced species of the genera *Heliamphora* and *Sarracenia* (Bayer et al. 1996).

Darlingtonia Torrey
cobra lily

The genus *Darlingtonia* features just one species, *D. californica* Torr. (syn. *Chrysamphora californica* [Torr.] Greene), which was first discovered in 1841 by J. D. Brackenridge in the upper reaches of the Sacramento River, during a research expedition from Oregon to San Francisco led by Captain Wilkes.

John Torrey named the species in 1853 in honor of his friend William Darlington, a distinguished physician based in West Chester, Pennsylvania. In 1891, however, Edward Greene discovered that the name *Darlingtonia* had already been assigned to a legume genus, thus breaching the valid nomenclatural rules. From then on, the valid name for the cobra lily, as chosen by Greene, was *Chrysamphora californica*. In 1954, after the individual species of the legume genus in question had been reassigned to other genera, a commission of the International Code of Botanical Nomenclature declared that the old, hitherto invalid but extremely popular name *Darlingtonia californica* should regain its validity and that *Chrysamphora californica* be declared a synonym.

The common name, cobra lily, is a reference to the characteristic tubular leaf, which resembles a raised cobra head and even has a forked tongue. The cobra lily does not have glands that secrete digestive enzymes into the pitfall trap fluid. To digest the prey, the plant must rely on the assistance of bacteria living in the trap. Hence, similar to *Roridula* and *Brocchinia*, *Darlingtonia* is among the precarnivorous plants.

Distribution and Habitat

The cobra lily is found mainly in the Sierra Nevada and adjacent mountain ranges (including the Klamath, Siskiyou, Salmon, and Trinity Mountains) near the Pacific coast in northwestern California and southwestern Oregon. There is evidently also a planted population near Seattle, Washington. The plants mainly grow on open sites in montane regions at elevations up to 2500 m, but in Oregon they are also found at sea level (Fig. 145). Preferred sites include *Sphagnum* bogs, moist meadows, and river valleys. In northwestern California, *Darlingtonia californica* often grows in pine-dominant forests (pine savannas, especially those with *Pinus monticola* and *P. contorta*) in which other carnivorous species are also present (such as *Drosera rotundifolia* and *Pinguicula vulgaris*). *Darlingtonia* characteristically forms large stands that grow in soils that are moist from seepage for the greater part of the year. Nevertheless, cobra lily sites are also subject to regular fires, which, if not too intense, can be easily withstood by the plants. Most *Darlingtonia* sites have serpentine soils.

Features

Darlingtonia is a more or less evergreen, long-lived perennial herb (Fig. 145). It contains an underground, horizontal, runner-forming, lignified rhizome about 1.5–2.0 cm in diameter, which develops a pitcher and roots at every node. There is no primary root, but instead numerous fibrous roots. The funnel-shaped, tubular leaves exhibit a spiral torsion, on average 180° (90–270°). They generally grow stiffly upright and attain a maximum height of 1 m. On average, however, they are 20–60 cm high. The upper parts of the traps are yellowish green, and the lower parts are dark green. In strong sunlight, red and yellow flecks develop on the upper parts of the traps. Most unusual for a member of the dicotyledonous flowering plants (Dicotyledoneae; see Fig. 43), newly germinated seedlings of *Darlingtonia* have three cotyledons, instead of the usual two. In contrast to the subsequently developing juvenile leaves, the cotyledons are not tubular in form. The five to ten juvenile leaves arranged in a rosette already bear a hood-shaped zone that arches over the tips of the tubular leaves as well as the trap opening (peristome). The most char-

acteristic feature of the pitchers is the forked appendage ("fishtail" or "snake's tongue") that hangs down from the downwardly directed trap opening (Fig. 146).

In its natural habitat, the cobra lily is in flower from April to August, depending on the site's elevation. The inflorescence, which at 1 m is only a little higher than the surrounding trap leaves, features about a dozen pink to light green subtending leaves, 1.0–1.5 cm long, that end in a single flower. The yellowish sepals of the radially symmetrical flowers are longer than the reddish petals, which are curled over at their tips, allowing the pollinat-

Fig. 145.
Darlingtonia californica, the cobra lily, growing in its natural habitat in northern California. K. Müller

167

ing insects access to the flower interior. During the fruit-ripening stage, the ovary, in the initially pendulous flower, develops into a capsule containing hundreds of tiny, pubescent seeds 2–3 mm long. The seeds ripen within 10 weeks after pollination. In its natural habitat, *Darlingtonia* reproduces vegetatively more frequently than it does by seed. In each leaf axil, there is a bud that can develop into a lateral rhizome branch and later separate.

Trapping Mechanism, Digestion, and Prey

The tubular, passive pitfall traps can be subdivided into six functional zones (Fig. 147).

Zone 1 This area comprises the paired appendages that, in particular, bear numerous nectaries on their undersides. In addition, hairs direct potential prey animals toward the trap opening.

Zone 2 This area comprises the peristome rim, which also bears nectaries. In this area, the leaf margin is rolled inward, forming a nectar roll that encircles the entire peristome.

Zone 3 This is an arched zone that is characterized by conspicuous light windows (fenestrations) in an irregular pattern. This part of the pitcher, as well as the back of the pitcher wall, is dotted with numerous translucent flecks. In these fenestrations, chlorophyll is broken down during leaf development, which means that sunlight can penetrate almost undiminished in intensity into the trap interior. Hairs and stomata are absent.

Zone 4 There is a smooth transition between zones 3 and 4. Zone 4 is characterized by areas in which epicuticular waxes form a slick layer adjacent to dense, downwardly directed hairs.

Zone 5 The downwardly directed hairs are densest in this zone; only few areas are covered in wax.

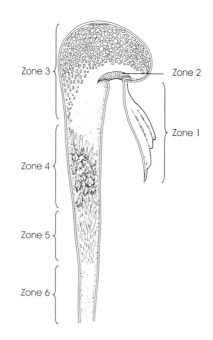

Fig. 147.
Pitcher zonation of *Darlingtonia californica*. I. Theisen

Zone 6 This is the basal section of the pitcher. Hairs are largely absent in this section, and there are no digestive glands at all.

The traps are filled with water secreted by the pitcher. The volume of fluid increases when insects or nitrogen-containing substances are added (Lloyd 1942). The first traps that are produced after flowering are generally the largest. One to two large traps can be produced each year, in addition to a medium-sized trap and three to five very small ones. The small traps mostly lie prostrate, with the fishtail in contact with the ground and acting as an entranceway for insects.

The prey insects are attracted by the traps' coloration and nectar secretions, produced by nectaries on the fishtail and peristome. Nectar production is particularly high on the inner side of the nectar roll, and light shines through the fenestrations. Both these factors encourage insects to penetrate deeper into the trap interior. Once the waxy and very pubescent conduction zone (zone 4 in Fig. 147) has been reached, it is almost impossible for the insects to make their way back out again. Ultimately they drop into the trap liquid, from which they

Fig. 146, facing page:
Pitcher leaves of *Darlingtonia californica*, with a hood-shaped entrance zone and tongued appendage.
W. Barthlott

only very seldom escape. Because the cobra lily produces no digestive enzymes of its own, the prey is broken down by microbial action, and the pitchers then resorb the nutrients.

More than twenty insect species have made the traps of *Darlingtonia* their home (see the chapter "Guests at the Carnivores' Table"). For example, the larvae of some dipteran species feed on the trapped insects. Several species of spider enter the traps to catch victims. Often, however, the pitchers fall victim themselves to insects that lay their eggs in them. These insect larvae then feed exclusively on the pitcher leaf tissue.

Cultivation

It is relatively easy to grow *Darlingtonia californica* in a temperature-controlled greenhouse. The plants grow best in a well-lit spot in a mixture of peat moss (*Sphagnum*) and lime-free sand. When temperatures increase during the summer, the plants should be given light shade. The air humidity must always be kept high and the plants given plenty of water, although it is important to avoid a waterlogged substrate that could lead to root rot. Temperatures in summer should not exceed 30°C (86°F); in late fall and winter, the plants should be kept at 12–15°C (54–60°F). Temperatures as low as 0°C (32°F) are tolerated. When cultivated, the plants flower between May and July.

The plants can be propagated both vegetatively and by seed. For example, young plants developing on the rhizomes can be separated. The rhizomes also can be divided up, and young plants soon develop from them. As soon as possible after harvesting, the seeds should be sown and kept at a temperature of 12–15°C (54–60°F) for 3 to 6 weeks to break their dormancy. The seeds are best sown in the fall, in a growing medium of 2:1 peat moss and lime-free sand. Because *Darlingtonia* needs light to germinate, the seed containers should not be covered. The young plants are sensitive to desiccation.

Heliamphora Bentham
South American pitcher plant

The genus *Heliamphora* comprises twelve species whose distribution is exclusively restricted to the flat-topped sandstone formations of the South American Guiana plateau in the border region between Venezuela, Brazil, and Guiana.

The South American pitcher plant was first discovered in 1838 by the German naturalist Robert Hermann Schomburgk (1804–1865), who, with his brother, Moritz Richard Schomburgk (1811–1891), was commissioned to survey the border zone between British Guiana and Venezuela. George Bentham (1800–1884)

first described the species *Heliamphora nutans* in 1840, the only species known at that time, working with plant material that Schomburgk had collected. The generic name refers to the growth site and tubular leaves of the South American pitcher plant. As Bentham's original description states: "I now proceed to give the technical character of the *Heliamphora nutans*, of which I have derived the generic name from ελοζ [eloz], a marsh, and αμφορευζ [amforeuz, or amphora], a pitcher" (Bentham 1840, p. 432). (The English designation "sun pitcher plants" is wrongly derived from the similar-sounding Greek word *helios*, meaning "sun.") Because the plants are difficult to grow and their natural growth sites are remote, *Heliamphora* is found in plant collections only occasionally.

Distribution and Habitat

The plants' area of distribution is restricted to the Guiana plateau in northern South America. In particular, they colonize the summit plateaus of the Precambrian sandstone massifs known as *tepuis*, which occur in the border zone between Venezuela, Brazil, and Guiana. These are table-shaped inselbergs about 1800–2700 m (highest elevation: Sierra de la Neblina, 3014 m above sea level) that tower above the surrounding area, which is about 500–1500 m above sea level. The species colonize infertile soils on sites that are kept constantly moist by fog, with high levels of sunlight.

Features

The various species of *Heliamphora* are long-lived, evergreen perennial herbs that develop simple or branched shoots from a rhizome. The plant has a well-developed root system. Sword-shaped (gladiate) or tubular leaves, sometimes in a rosette arrangement, develop from the shoots. The tubular leaves are the trapping organs, which show considerable variety of sizes within the genus. The pitchers of *Heliamphora* typically have the following form. At the tip of the leaves, which are rounded or oval in cross-section, there is a curved rudimentary lid (often called a "spoon") with nectar glands on its underside. These glands emit an intense scent that may play a role in attracting prey. Immediately below this is a narrow, peripheral region that is densely covered with downwardly directed hairs. This merges into a lower, smooth zone that is densely covered with nectar glands whose scent, possibly together with light-reflecting characteristics, attracts prey animals. The lower half of the pitcher consists of an upper zone with stiff hairs that leads down to a zone that is densely covered with downwardly directed hairs.

The flowers are arranged on racemose inflorescences on long stalks. The corolla generally has four (more rarely, five or six) white, greenish, or pinkish tepals. The highly pubescent ovary is surrounded by ten or more stamens. The capsules contain numerous endosperm-containing seeds.

Trapping Mechanism, Digestion, and Prey

The funnel-shaped pitchers, which are filled with water, are formed as pitfall traps into which the insects fall and drown. *Heliamphora* does not secrete digestive enzymes into the pitchers. Instead, the insects are digested with the aid of bacteria that live in the pitcher liquid. Hence, South American pitcher plants are precarnivorous, comparable with *Brocchinia* and *Roridula*.

Fig. 148, above:
Heliamphora hispida C. Scherber

Fig. 149, below:
Heliamphora nutans W. Barthlott

Selected Species

Heliamphora heterodoxa Steyerm.

Distribution and habitat: Southern Venezuela (state of Bolivar), on the Auyan Tepui at elevations above 2000 m and in areas of the Gran Sabana. The species grows in bright sunlight and prefers to colonize continuously moist plant cushions. Features: Pitchers up to 30 cm high, with a constriction about halfway up.

Heliamphora ionasi Maguire

Distribution and habitat: Southern Venezuela, on the Ilu Tepui. Features: Pitchers more than 50 cm high in the wild, constricted in the upper half with a relatively large rudimentary lid on top. Flowers initially white, later turning reddish.

Heliamphora minor Gleason

Distribution and habitat: Southern Venezuela, on the Auyan Tepui. Features: Pitchers 6–8 cm high, constricted in the upper section. Small rudimentary lid, reddish on the inside.

Heliamphora nutans Benth.

Distribution and habitat: In the border zone between Venezuela, Guiana, and Brazil, on the Roraima, Kukenan, Ilu, and Tramen Tepuis. Features: Pitchers up to 15 cm high, with a constriction near the top. The inside of the rudimentary lid is vivid red. Flowers initially white, later turning to red. Fig. 149

Heliamphora tatei Gleason

Distribution and habitat: This species forms large stands in the white-sand savannas in the south of Venezuela and in Guiana; occasionally found together with the carnivorous bromeliad *Brocchinia reducta*. Features: Stems up to 4 m tall, especially on exposed sites. Shoots branched, with pubescent pitchers on the in-

Fig. 150.
Heliamphora sarracenioides
T. Carow

ner sides that are up to 40 cm long. Flowers initially white, later turning to red.

Heliamphora tatei var. *nebulinae* (Maguire) Steyerm. is found only on the Pico de la Neblina, whose summit marks the border between Venezuela and Brazil. It is distinguished from the type species by its stouter growth, shorter pitchers, and white, greenish, or delicate pink flowers.

Cultivation

All *Heliamphora* species are difficult to grow and are best left to experienced carnivore specialists. The plants are best grown in a greenhouse. They need a very brightly lit site, but overheating must be avoided in summer (such as by using a fog machine). Temperatures in summer should not exceed 25°C (77°F). In winter, temperatures should not exceed 15°C (60°F) or fall below 3°C (37°F); these lower temperatures in winter benefit flowering. At this time of year, additional artificial light is helpful, with a diurnal illumination of 13 hours. *Sphagnum* or a mixture of *Sphagnum* and lime-free sand are suitable as growing me-

dia. The plants react very sensitively to fertilizer, so fertilizing should be avoided at all costs. *Heliamphora* species require a constantly high air humidity. The plants should be given enough water so that the peat moss remains a fresh green and the lower parts of the pitchers are filled with water. Especially in summer, they should be watered several times a day, while taking care to avoid root rot.

It is relatively easy to propagate *Heliamphora* species vegetatively, and this is best carried out in early summer by dividing up the plants. Propagation by seed is more difficult and takes much longer. Seeds should be sown in *Sphagnum* moss at a temperature of about 20°C (68°F) in the shade. The first seedlings, which grow very slowly, appear after 1 to 2 months, but it may also take more than 6 months for them to appear.

Sarracenia Linnaeus
North American pitcher plant

The genus *Sarracenia*, which is found exclusively in eastern North America, probably awakened the interest of the early European settlers due to its remarkable leaves. The first illustration of a *Sarracenia* plant was made in 1576 by Mathias de L'Obel (Lobelius 1538–1616), in his *Nova Stirpium Adversaria*. The genus was named in honor of Dr. Michel S. Sarrazin (1659–1735), who sent live specimens of *Sarracenia purpurea* from Quebec to the French botanist Joseph Pitton de Tournefort (1656–1708). The generic name, as it appeared in Tournefort's original 1700 description, was included by Carl Linnaeus in his work *Species Plantarum* (1753), which listed two species (*S. purpurea* and *S. flava*). The strange growth habit and the large numbers of dead insects found in a watery fluid inside the pitchers led some early naturalists to suspect that *Sarracenia* might be carnivorous. It was Hepburn et al. (1920, 1927) who first provided direct evidence that insects were not only caught but also digested.

Today, the genus *Sarracenia* comprises eight species (including fifteen subspecies, varieties, and forms and eighteen natural hybrids), for which there are more than 130 synonymous specific epithets (see the CITES checklist in Arx et al. 2002). North American pitcher plants are extraordinarily popular among carnivore enthusiasts, as the very large number of hybrids and cultivars (about 100) makes abundantly clear. All the *Sarracenia* species are listed at least in Appendix II of CITES (Arx et al. 2002). *Sarracenia rubra* ssp. *alabamensis*, *S. rubra* ssp. *jonesii*, and *S. oreophila* are listed in Appendix I and are thus accorded the highest protection status. Without permits and trade certificates, the collection of live plants from their natural habitats or the trade or export of such plants are prohibited (see the chapter on nature conservation).

Distribution and Habitat

North American pitcher plants are mainly restricted to eastern North America, in particular the southeastern United States (Alabama, Georgia, South Carolina, North Carolina, and Virginia). *Sarracenia purpurea* occurs as far north as Labrador and northwestern Canada (Schnell 2002). This species has also become artificially established at a few sites in Europe: Ireland, England (Lakes District), and Switzerland (such as Jura; Lauber and Wagner 2001). In Germany, a growth site has been identified in the Bavarian Forest region (Fürsch 2001). *Sarracenia* preferentially colonizes open sites on mostly acidic soils.

Features

Sarracenia plants are long-lived perennial herbs with underground rhizomes and leaves arranged in a rosette. Generally, a large number of fibrous roots are produced, and the main root is reduced early in the development. The foliage leaves are formed as pitchers ranging from 10 cm to 1.2 m high. Flattened, elongated leaves that consist of widened petioles (phyllodia) are found regularly in only two species, *S. oreophila* and *S. flava*. Leaves of this type (known as "winter leaves") develop in the late summer and persist during the cold period of year. The most conspicuous feature of North American pitcher plants, however, is their typically attractively colored and variegated tubular leaves, which have a winglike seam, or ala, along their adaxial long axis. The openings of the pitchers are located beneath an immobile, arched, hoodlike section that serves to attract prey animals and acts as a lid, preventing excessive rainwater from collecting in the traps.

The single flowers, borne at the end of very

long scapes (in some cases up to 70 cm), hang downward. The umbrella-shaped style is elongated into five V-shaped, split lobes that bear the small stigmata (Fig. 151). The style, which bulges downward, has five cleft points with the pendulous petals hanging between them. The rounded ovary and the numerous stamens therefore lie within a cavity, which is sealed off by the petal bases and the sepals. The pollinators of *Sarracenia* are mostly bees, which land on the base of the petals and ultimately penetrate through a small opening into the interior of the flower cavity, brushing the pollen they carry onto the stigma lobes. The bees, moving around on the inside of the umbrella-shaped style, ultimately take up the pollen that dusts down from the stamens. The capsules contain numerous tiny seeds.

Fig. 151.
A *Sarracenia flava* flower, with long, pendulous petals and an umbraculate stigma. W. Barthlott

Trapping Mechanism, Digestion, and Prey

The traps of North American pitcher plants have several features that allow them to attract prey. The generally horizontal hood is densely covered with nectar glands and inwardly directed hairs and has a prominent color pattern. Just how much the odorous substances that emanate from the traps help to attract prey is still a matter of debate. The next section inward includes the narrow, rolled pitcher tube margin, as well as a directly adjacent zone that is also covered with nectar glands and hairs. The following conduction zone, which is clearly demarcated from the previous one and forms the largest part of the trap interior, is densely covered with epicuticular waxes and glands in which insects cannot gain a footing. In the traps, the level of the watery liquid tends to reach as far as the digestive zone. It is free of waxes, and instead there are numerous digestive glands that produce enzymes and

hairs that prevent the prey from escaping. In addition to the digestive enzymes that the plants produce, however, bacteria living in the trap liquid are probably involved with breaking down and digesting the prey. There are considerable variations between individual *Sarracenia* species in terms of the traps' effectiveness in catching prey. The erect traps, in particular, are often filled to the brim with trapped insects (Fig. 31).

Aside from the prey animals, various organisms that are unaffected by the digestive fluid are also found in the pitchers. These include protozoa and various insect larvae that live as commensals with the plants. The most notable examples include the larvae of some mosquito species, such as *Wyeomyia smithii*, which develop in the traps of several *Sarracenia* species. The larvae of the fly genus *Sarcophaga* are resistant to the digestive enzymes in the traps and feed on the decaying insect corpses. The larvae of the moth *Exyra* develop in the traps of several *Sarracenia* species. The

Fig. 152.
Sarracenia flava growing in its natural habitat in South Carolina. K. Müller

adult moths are able to move on the slick, wax-covered conduction zone of the trap interiors without danger, and they lay one egg per trap. The larva produces a dense web directly beneath the trap entrance that keeps out rainwater and other insects. The larva feeds on the interior wall of the trap, among other things, causing the trap section above to dry out and collapse. It is possible to tell the level of *Exyra* infestation of a plant population from a distance on the basis of the collapsed traps. Before pupating, the larva bites two holes in the lower part of the trap. The fully developed adult moth uses the upper hole as an exit, while the lower hole allows any water that may have penetrated into the trap interior to drain away. Because many *Exyra* larvae overwinter in the traps, fires during this time reduce the level of moth infestation in *Sarracenia* populations.

Selected Species

Sarracenia alata Wood
Distribution and habitat: Gulf Coast of the United States (Texas, Louisiana, Mississippi, Alabama); on sandy and loamy soils. Features:

Pitchers erect, up to 75 cm long. In some regions, such as around Mobile Bay, the species can be mistaken for *Sarracenia flava*. Unlike that species, however, the traps of *S. alata* do not have a bell-shaped bulge below the opening, and the lid is smaller, with the margins not bent back. The traps of *S. alata* are yellowish green, with a fine red venation. Petals yellowish white to pale yellow, oval (in *S. flava* linear).

Sarracenia flava L.
Distribution and habitat: In Alabama, Florida, Georgia, South Carolina, North Carolina, and Virginia on sandy soils and in bogs. Features: Pitchers striking in appearance, erect, up to 90 cm high; wing (ala) not wider than 3 mm; lid round, larger than the trap opening, with the margins bent back. There are great variations between individual plants in terms of the trap form and coloration. In particular, the upper part of the pitcher varies from light green to pale yellow and golden yellow, and the colors of the lid range from deep red to chestnut brown. All the different colors and shapes can occur in close proximity at a single site. Sword-shaped (gladiate) winter leaves develop in late summer and persist during the cold period of the year. The large, yellow flowers (diameter up to 10 cm) emit a strong scent. Figs. 151, 152

Sarracenia leucophylla Raf.
Distribution and habitat: In Mississippi, Alabama, Florida, and Georgia, in *Sphagnum* bogs and on sandy soils. Features: Pitchers erect, up to 1 m high, with an only weakly developed wing; variable size of trap opening. The upper half of the trap is often a conspicuously luminous white, but the trap color varies from one plant to another; traps often with conspicuous green or red venation. Flowers large, vivid red, with a sweet scent. This species is widely con-

sidered the most attractive of the entire genus. Fig. 153

Sarracenia minor Walt.

Distribution and habitat: From North Carolina south to Florida, found both on infertile sandy soils in pine forests and in *Sphagnum* bogs. *Sarracenia minor* is the only North American pitcher plant radiating further south into peninsular Florida (Lake Okeechobee). Features: Pitchers erect, with an average height of 25–30 cm, sometimes up to 80 cm; typical for the species are the pronounced wing and the hoodlike form of the lid, which covers the trap opening; traps greenish to reddish, with translucent flecks (fenestrations) on the rear side that have a light-window function similar to that of *Sarracenia psittacina* and *Darlingtonia californica*. Flowers odorless, pale yellowish green, usually opening together with the new pitchers. The prey of *S. minor* are generally ants, which seek out the nectar glands at the rim of the trap opening and then fall into the trap interior.

Sarracenia oreophila (Kearney) Wherry

Distribution and habitat: In the mountainous regions of Alabama and Georgia (where they are presumed extinct) and into North Carolina, on moist sites along streams and rivers on different soil types. Features: Pitchers up to 75 cm high, light green (slightly reddish when older), erect, with a relatively wide opening; lid more or less erect (more so than in *S. flava*), occasionally with venation. In late summer, sickle-shaped phyllodia ("winter leaves") form in the upper half. Flowers yellowish green, weakly scented.

Sarracenia psittacina Mich.

Distribution and habitat: From Georgia to Florida and extending as far as southern Mis-

sissippi, on seasonally flooded sandy soils and in continuously moist *Sphagnum* bogs. Features: Pitchers up to 20 cm (rarely 30 cm) long, lying prostrate on the ground when mature, forming a rosette; winged seam easily visible; under normal sunlight conditions, pitchers bent forward, with a helmet-shaped or globose hood (often referred to as a "parrot beak") that closes off part of the trap opening; upper part of the pitchers mostly tinged dark red, at the back with numerous translucent flecks (fenestrations). The long hairs in the trap interior, which point toward the base of the traps, have the most complex form of all

Fig. 153.
A *Sarracenia leucophylla* cultivar featuring conspicuous red-veined lids of the pitfall traps.
W. Barthlott

Fig. 154.
A *Sarracenia psittacina* cultivar in flower. W. Barthlott

Sarracenia species, being intertwined. These pitcher hairs prevent captured insects from exiting the traps, thus hindering their escape. There is also a collar just inside the pitcher opening that works like a lobster trap, preventing prey egress. When submerged by flooding, the decumbent pitchers are able to trap water animals, which are unable to swim out of the opening. Flowers relatively small, with dark to vivid red petals; weakly scented. Fig. 154

Sarracenia purpurea L.

Distribution and habitat: Throughout most of Canada and into the southeastern United States, in *Sphagnum* bogs but also on infertile sandy soils. *Sarracenia purpurea* has the largest distribution of all North American pitcher plants. It is also found as a locally introduced exotic species in Switzerland (in the St. Gallen, Waadt, Jura, Neuenberg, and Bern cantons) and in Germany (Bavarian Forest region). Features: Tubular traps lying almost prostrate, curved, with a wing, up to 45 cm long; with a hood (as in *Sarracenia psittacina*), whose margins are strongly wavy (sinuate) and whose inner surfaces are densely covered with stiff hairs; base of the hood pulled down over the trap opening on two sides but hood erect; form and coloration of the traps extraordinarily variable, with typical features depending on the subspecies; the trap color ranges from greenish yellow to deep purple. Flower color pink to dark red. Fig. 155

Sarracenia rubra Walt.

Distribution and habitat: Southeastern United States (discontinuously from North and South Carolina to Alabama); found mainly on coastal plains. Features: Pitchers relatively slender, 15–30 cm high and erect; fully grown traps copper-colored with brown to light red venation; rich production of nectar, which may trickle down the traps. Often two leaf types: weakly phyllodiform leaves in spring and typical pitchers in summer. Flowers light red, often several flowers on each plant, strongly and pleasantly scented. This extraordinarily variable species evidently consists of a complex of geographically isolated taxa that are sometimes described as individual species (such as the synonym *Sarracenia jonesii*) or subspecies (*S. rubra* subsp. *jonesii*).

Cultivation

Assuming certain basic principles are followed, most *Sarracenia* species can be recommended for beginners, although *S. oreophila* presents more of a challenge. A temperature-controlled greenhouse or outdoor flowerbeds are suitable for growing North American pitcher plants.

The plants require a well-lit site, but should be protected from excessive direct sun, especially in summer. Because North American pitcher plants are not very sensitive to frost, in some places they can be overwintered in a frame outdoors, although it is best to overwinter them within the temperature range of 5–8°C (40–46°F). North American pitcher plants can tolerate high temperatures during the summer months. Young plants can be cultivated throughout the winter, without the need for a dormancy period. The air humidity should be high, although the plants do not react very sensitively to occasional dry spells. Peat or a mixture of peat, sand, and perlite (in a 4:1:1 ratio) are recommended as growing media. The plants can be moderately fertilized during the growth period; the weak fertilizer should be added to the water that is used for watering.

It is easy to propagate *Sarracenia* species by dividing up the rhizomes. Each rhizome section should include several growth points. To avoid fungal infestation, the cut surfaces should be disinfected, for instance, with charcoal powder. Growing North American pitcher plants from seed is a longer and more difficult process. Before sowing, the seed must be stored under damp conditions for 6 to 8 weeks in a refrigerator to break the dormancy.

Fig. 155.
Sarracenia purpurea
in flower. W. Barthlott

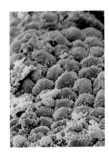

Animal-Trapping Liverworts

All of the approximately 630 species of carnivorous plants that have been identified to date are flowering plants (angiosperms). Does this mean that carnivory developed only very late in evolutionary history, in a modern plant group, or could the catching of animal prey be an older phenomenon?

As early as the nineteenth century, there was speculation as to whether certain liverworts (Hepaticae) caught animals. From leaves or leaf tips, some liverworts form pitcher or beaker-shaped organs on their undersides. These are generally interpreted as water-storage organs in which tiny animals (bryozoans, nematodes, and especially rotifers) may also live. Like mosses, liverworts lead a periodically moist existence and can withstand dry periods in a dormant state. In general, however, most liverworts do not have traplike

Fig. 156.
Colura zoophaga,
an animal-trapping,
epiphytic liverwort.
W. Barthlott

organs. Such organs are found in only two predominantly tropical liverwort genera: *Colura* and *Pleurozia* (Barthlott et al. 2000; Frahm 2001; Hess et al. 2005).

Colura Dumort. (Lejeuneaceae)
These are exclusively epiphytic liverworts that have a tropical distribution, with approximately sixty species worldwide. Fig. 156

Pleurozia Dumort. (Pleuroziaceae)
This genus of liverworts, which live epiphytically on trees or grow on bare ground, includes twelve species. They are found primarily in the Old World tropics, while two species extend as far south as South America and one species (*Pleurozia purpurea*) as far north as Great Britain and Norway.

Trapping Mechanism

The traplike structures in the liverwort leaves were described in exact detail by Goebel (1893). These structures somewhat resemble *Utricularia* traps, but are microscopic. In *Colura*, the upper leaf margin is rolled inward and is fused to the rest of the leaf, forming a spacious, elongated water sac (Figs. 157, 158). Between this and the lower leaf margin, there is a funnel-shaped channel. At the end of the channel, there is a small opening in the water sac, sealed by a movable lid that opens only inward. A threshold at the edge of the opening prevents the lid from being pushed open outward. As in the pitcher-shaped organs of other liverworts, small animals were found inside

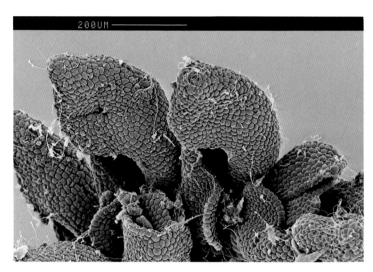

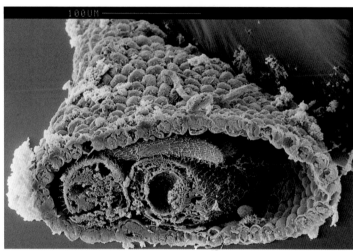

the water sacs of *Colura*, and this stimulated the imaginations of some botanists. Kerner von Marilaun, for example, in his *Pflanzen-leben* (1922), gave detailed descriptions of how *Colura* caught prey, although no one had ever observed this process.

What at first looked like a perfect trapping mechanism, however, had some inexplicable characteristics. The leaves of the liverwort *Colura* are no more than 1 mm long, the whole plant is only a few millimeters in size, and it lives exclusively as an epiphyte on tree trunks and narrow twigs. It was only the discovery that carnivory also includes the capture of protozoans (Barthlott et al. 1998) that allowed a new interpretation of this trapping mechanism. It is difficult to imagine that such a complicated mechanism, specific to liverworts, could have simply arisen for no apparent reason. But what if the mechanism were used for trapping protozoans?

To test this hypothesis, plants of a newly described species from the African highlands, *Colura zoophaga* Eb. Fischer, were grown and fed with the ciliate *Blepharisma americana*. Barthlott et al. (2000) showed that the ciliates graze the surface of the liverwort plant for bacteria, as well as the groove formed by the lower leaf margin, which leads to the lid in the water sac. Due to the ciliate's movement, the lid is pushed inward, so that the animal can penetrate into the interior, but then cannot get out again. Barthlott et al. observed the trapping of up to fourteen ciliates in a water sac in this way. The ciliates have only a limited life expectancy; after a while they die, and their cell bodies burst, releasing the contents into the water sac. Here the observations that point to the capture of animals (zoophagy) come to an end; the actual consumption of animal tissue (carnivory) has not yet been demonstrated. It is probably reasonable to assume that *Colura* does not have any enzymes that break down

proteins (proteases), with which it could then digest the ciliates. These may not be required, however, as we have seen in species of *Heliamphora*, which also do not have such enzymes. The remains of the ciliates are presumably broken down by bacteria and resorbed by the plant. In view of the epiphytic mode of life of *Colura*, which is otherwise solely dependent on nutrients dissolved in rainwater, this would be a welcome additional source of nutrition.

Figs. 157 and 158. *Colura zoophaga*: scanning electron micrographs of the tube-shaped leaves (above); the trapped and partly sectioned slipper animalcules (paramecia) can be seen in longitudinal section (below).
W. Barthlott

Animal-Trapping Fungi

Many people associate fungi only with edible mushrooms. However, many pathogens, such as the fungus that causes athlete's foot, as well as molds and yeasts, belong to this huge group of more than 100,000 species.

Although they were traditionally assigned to the plant kingdom, fungi are not actually plants at all, because, unlike green plants, they have no chlorophyll or plastids. Hence, fungi are unable to meet their nutritional requirements through photosynthesis and derive their nutrition through heterotrophic means. As decomposers, they occupy a variety of ecological niches: saprophytes feed on dead plant material (such as white rot and red ring-root on wood), while many other species derive their nutrition as parasites, feeding on the living tissue of their host, often causing plant diseases (such as potato blight, mildews, and smut fungus). Many species live as micorrhizal fungi in a symbiotic relationship with higher plants, while others have been able to form a symbiotic relationship with algae, yielding lichens.

The fungi, or Mycetes, are classified into three divisions: Myxomycota, slime molds; Oomycota, algal fungi; and Eumycota, true fungi (including Chytridiomycetes, Zygomycetes, Ascomycetes, and Basidiomycetes). These divisions differ from one another in various ways. Apart from the plasma masses of the primitive slime molds (Myxomycota), which have no cell walls and move in an amoeboid fashion, fungi consist of a network of microscopically fine cellular threads (hyphae) that together make up the vegetative body (mycelium) and the macroscopically visible fruiting bodies, such as those of the Ascomycetes and Basidiomycetes, from which spores are released.

At present, there are some 160 known species of carnivorous or "zoophagous" fungi, with threadworms (nematodes) representing the most important prey group in terms of numbers. However, nematodes are not the only victims of these nematophagous fungi. In addition to large numbers of unicellular animals (protozoans) in the soil, rotifers and springtails (*Collembola*) in particular are also caught.

Most animal-trapping fungi inhabit the uppermost soil layer, with fewer representatives colonizing the surfaces of small standing waters. They are also found living in moss, compost, and manure, but not in peat. With the aid of resting spores, these fungi are able to withstand extreme environmental conditions, such as drought and frost, undamaged.

> Another ecological group of fungi attack and kill insects. These entomophagous fungi include *Empusa muscae*, which feeds on flies, and *Cordyceps myrmecophila*, an ant-killing fungus. Infection of a prey animal is the result of fungal spores either being swallowed or becoming attached to the animal body. This fungal group, however, is not included among the animal-trapping fungi.

They are mainly found in neutral to weakly alkaline, moist soils, in which a thin film of water allows the victims to move and trapping organs to develop.

Zoophagous fungi mostly live saprophytically in the soil and develop special organs on their hyphae for trapping prey animals. Digestive hyphae penetrate from the points of contact into the trapped animals, devouring their contents. Dowe (1987) provided a comprehensive overview of the mode of life and diversity of predatory fungi.

Trapping Mechanism

The special trapping organs of the animal-trapping fungi are quite varied, but they can be classified into several types (Drechsler 1933; Lysek and Nordbring-Hertz 1983; Dowe 1987). Apart from some species that can form adhesive substances at any point on their mycelium, the range of trapping organs includes three-dimensional adhesive nets, hyphal branches, hyphal knobs, and noncontracting and contracting rings.

Three-Dimensional Adhesive Nets

This form of trapping mechanism is widespread in nature. Due to their spatial structure, three-dimensional adhesive nets are able to catch a particularly large number of prey and are more effective than a two-dimensional net. The adhesive substance, which consists of lectins, is found both on the hoops and on the conidium-bearing hyphae. The trapping hyphae are about four to five times as thick as normal hyphae, with a mean diameter of 20–59 μm. Many species of the genus *Arthrobotrys* (Ascomycetes, Moniliales) feature this trap-

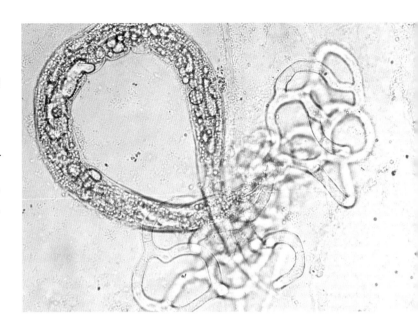

ping mechanism, including *A. oligospora* (Fig. 159).

Adhesive Hyphal Branches

The bearing hyphae form one- to three-celled hyphal branches that are coated with adhesive substances; individual adhesive hyphal branches can come into contact with neighboring trapping hyphae and form a mesh (such as in *Monacrosporium gephyropagum*, Ascomycetes, Moniliales) with which nematodes can be trapped more effectively. Struggling vigorously after having been caught, the nematodes become stuck in several places and can no longer break free. Other species of this type include *Monacrosporium cionopagum* and *Dactylella lobata* (Ascomycetes, Moniliales).

Hourglass-Shaped, Adhesive Knobs

This special trapping type is found only in the genus *Nematoctonus* (Basidiomycetes). The traps grow on short, noncellular stalks and have especially strong adhesive properties.

Fig. 159.
A nematode caught in the adhesive net of *Arthrobotrys oligospora*. R. Sikora

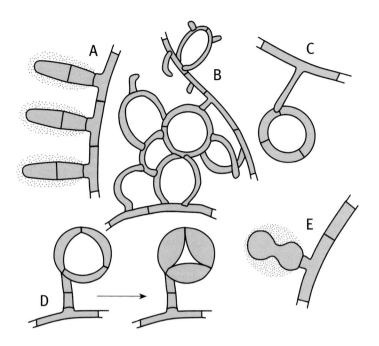

phae grow from these broken-off rings into the prey animal, killing it. *Dactylaria candida* and *D. leptospora* (Ascomycetes, Moniliales) use this type of prey capture.

Contracting Rings

Like noncontracting rings, contracting rings are always three-celled and stalked; they develop in the same way and are of a similar size. The trapping action occurs when the ring swells, jamming the prey, which is triggered by contact with the inside of the ring. An example of this type is *Arthrobotrys dactyloides* (Ascomycetes, Moniliales).

Cultivation

Growing predatory fungi is very much the domain of specialists. First, it is not easy to gain access to the fungi, because they are nearly impossible to obtain commercially. Only larger institutes in universities and the German Institute of Microorganisms in Braunschweig (DSMZ) maintain permanent cultures of these species, which are unavailable to private enthusiasts. Moreover, nematophagous fungi can be kept only in sterile cultures under strictly controlled conditions of pH, temperature, and nutrients. Nevertheless, Cooke and Godfrey (1964) described a method for raising predatory fungi with the aid of agar plates covered in soil and then isolating them.

Fig. 160.
Trapping mecha-
nisms in animal-
trapping fungi:
(A) adhesive hyphal
branches; (B) three-
dimensional adhe-
sive nets; (C) non-
contracting rings;
(D) contracting rings;
and (E) hourglass-
shaped adhesive
knobs (after Dowe
1987). I. Theisen

Unlike spherical adhesive knobs, they remain attached to the stalk.

Noncontracting Rings

While forming a stalked, three-celled ring, a hyphal branch elongates and bends itself backward to join up with the point of elongation. Trapping rings usually consist of three to four cells, and the ring opening has a mean diameter of 20–50 µm. The rings are able to catch prey without the need for adhesive substances, as the prey animal becomes trapped while trying to squeeze through the ring. Because the connection between the stalk and the ring is weak, the nematode may also help to disperse the fungus if the ring breaks off. Digestive hy-

The Carnivorous Plants of the World: A Comprehensive Listing from A to Z

More and more carnivorous plant species from around the world are now finding their way into the trade. Although they are often referred to by their correct scientific names, unfortunately, invalid names (so-called synonyms) are also used. This section gives a complete overview of the carnivorous plants' currently valid generic names and specific epithets, together with their synonyms and the most common hybrids. Valid specific epithets are given in italics. In addition to the alphabetically listed names of species, the table contains information such as the names of the taxonomic authorities, the years that the species were first

described, and their geographic distributions. For hybrids, parental specific epithets are given in brackets. Species marked with an asterisk (*) are listed under CITES Appendix I, which includes species threatened with extinction that can be or are endangered by trade. This information will help interested readers to learn more about the plants' growing requirements and details of the individual species, with reference to further literature sources. The many species of animal-trapping fungi, which are not in fact plants at all, have been omitted here.

Aldrovanda L. 1753: waterwheel plant (Droseraceae)
verticillata Roxb. 1832 = *vesiculosa*
vesiculosa L. 1753; Euras., Afr., N–SE Austral.
 – var. australis Darwin 1876 = *vesiculosa*

Biovularia Kamienski 1890 = Utricularia (Lentibulariaceae)

Brocchinia Schult. f. 1830 (total of 18 species) (Bromeliaceae)
reducta Baker 1882, Venez. Guia.

Byblis Salisb. 1808: rainbow plant (Byblidaceae)
aquatica Lowrie & Conran 1998; NW Austral.
 – 'Darwin Red' D'Amato 1998
caerulea R. Br. ex Planch. 1848 = *liniflora*
'Cataby' (see *gigantea*)
'Darwin Red' (see *aquatica*)
'Eneabba' (see *gigantea*)

filifolia Planch. 1848; NW Austral.
gigantea Lindl. 1839; SW Austral.
 – 'Cataby' D'Amato 1998
 – 'Eneabba' D'Amato 1998
lamellata Conran & Lowrie 2002; SW Austral.
lindleyana Planch. 1848 = *gigantea*
liniflora Salisb. 1808; N Austral., New Guin.
 – subsp. occidentalis Conran & Lowrie 1993 = *filifolia*
rorida Lowrie & Conran 1998; NW Austral.

Catopsis Griseb. 1864 (total of 17 species) (Bromeliaceae)
berteroniana (Schult. f.) Mez 1896; S Fla., Caribb., Central Am.–E Braz.

Cephalotus Labill. 1806: Australian pitcher plant (Cephalotaceae)
follicularis Labill. 1806; SW Austral.

Chrysamphora Greene 1891 = Darlingtonia (Sarraceniaceae)

californica (Torr.) Greene 1891 = *Darlingtonia californica*

Colura Dumort. 1835 (total of 20 species) (Lejeuneaceae)

zoophaga Eb. Fisch. 1999; Kenya

Darlingtonia Torr. 1853: cobra lily (Sarraceniaceae)

californica Torr. 1853; U.S.A. (Ore., Calif.)

Dionaea Sol. ex J. Ellis 1768: Venus flytrap (Droseraceae)

'Akai Ryu' (see *muscipula*)

corymbosa Raf. 1840 = *muscipula*

'Fused Tooth' (see *muscipula*)

muscipula J. Ellis 1768; U.S.A. (N.C., S.C.)
  – 'Akai Ryu' R. Gagliardo 1996
  – 'Fused Tooth' D'Amato 1998

sensitiva Salisb. 1796 = *muscipula*

sessiliflora Raf. 1840 = *muscipula*

uniflora Raf. 1833 = *muscipula*

Drosera L. 1753: sundew (Droseraceae)

The following is an overview of the sundew species, their distribution, and their systematic classification. The classification is not the result of a revision of the genus, but instead has been compiled on the basis of literature comparisons, whereby the classification concept of the "Carnivorous Plant Database" (available at http://www.omnisterra.com/bot/cp_home.cgi) has been aligned with the classification of Seine and Barthlott (1994). In its present form, the section *Drosera* does not represent a natural group; thus, it is likely that species that have been assigned to the section *Drosera* eventually will be reclassified.

acaulis L. f. 1781; sect. *Ptycnostigma*; Cape

adelae F. Muell. 1864; sect. *Drosera*; NE Austral. (N Queensl.)

admirabilis Debbert 1987 = *cuneifolia*

affinis Welw. ex Oliv. 1871; sect. *Drosera*; trop. central, S Afr.

afra Debbert 2002; sect. *Drosera*; Cape

alba E. Phillips 1913; sect. *Drosera*; Cape

aliciae Raym.-Hamet 1905; sect. *Drosera*; Cape

americana Willd. 1809 = *intermedia*

andersoniana W. Fitzg. ex Ewart & Jean White 1909; sect. *Ergaleium*; SW Austral.

androsacea Diels 1904; sect. *Bryastrum*; SW Austral.

anglica Huds. 1778; sect. *Drosera*; Eur., N Asia, N Jap., Kor., N Am., Hawaii

angustifolia F. Muell. 1855 = *indica*

annua E. L. Reed 1915 = *brevifolia*

arcturi Hook. 1834; sect. *Drosera*; SE Austral., Tasm., New Zeal.

arenicola Steyerm. 1952; sect. *Drosera*; Venez.
  – var. *occidentalis* Maguire & Wurdack 1957; Venez.

ascendens A. St.-Hil. 1824 = *villosa*

atra Colenso 1899 = *arcturi*

atrostyla Debbert 1991 = *pauciflora*

auriculata Backh. ex Planch. 1848 = *peltata* subsp. *auriculata*

×*badgerupii* Cheek 1993; [*nitidula* × *occidentalis*]

banksii R. Br. ex DC. 1824; sect. *Lasiocephala*; N & NE Austral. (Queensl.), Moluc., New Guin.

barbigera Planch. 1848; sect. *Bryastrum*; SW Austral.
  – subsp. *silvicola* (Lowrie & Carlquist) J. Schlauer 1996; SW Austral.

bequaertii Taton 1945; sect. *Drosera*; trop. Afr. (Angola, Congo)

bicolor Lowrie & Carlquist 1992 = *peltata*

biflora Willd. ex Roem. & Schult. 1820; sect. *Drosera*; Venez.

binata Labill. 1804; sect. *Phycopsis*; SE Austral., Tasm., New Zeal.

brasiliensis Mart. ex J. A. Schmidt 1872 = *graminifolia*

brevicornis Lowrie 1996; sect. *Lasiocephala*; N Austral.

brevifolia Pursh 1814; sect. *Drosera*; U.S.A. (Va.–Tex., Fla.), Cuba, Mex., Belize, Braz., Urug.

broomensis Lowrie 1996; sect. *Lasiocephala*; NW Austral.

browniana Lowrie & N. G. Marchant 1992; sect. *Erythrorhizae*; SW Austral.

bulbigena Morrison 1903; sect. *Ergaleium*; SW Austral.

bulbosa Hook. 1841; sect. *Erythrorhizae*; SW Austral.

  – subsp. *major* (Diels) N. G. Marchant & Lowrie 1992; SW Austral.

burkeana Planch. 1848; sect. *Drosera*; trop. central & S Afr., Madag.

burmannii Vahl 1794; sect. *Thelocalyx*; Ind.–Jap. south to N Austral., Malays., Micrones.

caduca Lowrie 1996; sect. *Lasiocephala*; NW Austral.

×*californica* Cheek 1993; [*filiformis* × *filiformis* var. *tracyi*]

callistos N. G. Marchant & Lowrie 1992; sect. *Bryastrum*; SW Austral.

calycina Planch. 1848 = *microphylla*

camporupestris Rivadavia 2003; sect. *Drosera*; Braz.

capensis L. 1753; sect. *Drosera*; Cape

capillaris Poir. 1804; sect. *Drosera*; U.S.A. (Va.–Tex., Fla.), West Ind., Mex.–Braz.

cayennensis Sagot ex Diels 1906; sect. *Drosera*; Venez., Guai., Braz.

cendeensis Tamayo & Croizat 1949; sect. *Drosera*; Venez.

chiapasensis Matuda 1956 = *brevifolia*

chrysolepis Taub. 1893; sect. *Drosera*; SE Braz. (Minas Gerais)

circinervia Colenso 1984 = *peltata* subsp. *auriculata*

cistiflora L. 1760; sect. *Ptycnostigma*; Cape

citrina Lowrie & Carlquist 1992; sect. *Bryastrum*; SW Austral.

  – var. *nivea* (Lowrie & Carlquist) J. Schlauer 1996; SW Austral.

closterostigma N. G. Marchant & Lowrie 1992; sect. *Bryastrum*; SW Austral.

coccipetala Debbert 2002 = *cistiflora*

collinsiae N. E. Br. ex Burtt Davy 1924; sect. *Drosera*; S Afr. (Lesotho, Nat., Transv.)

colombiana A. Fernández 1965; sect. *Drosera*; Col.

communis A. St.-Hil. 1824; sect. *Drosera*; Venez., Col., Braz., Parag.

  – var. *pauciflora* Eichler 1872; Arg., Braz.

compacta Exell & J. R. Laundon 1955 = *bequaertii*

congolana Taton 1945 = *madagascariensis*

×*corinthiaca* R. Gibson & E. Green 1999; [*aliciae* × *glabripes*]

corsica Maire 1904 = *rotundifolia*

cuneifolia L. f. 1781; sect. *Drosera*; SW Cape

cunninghamii Walp. 1842 = *binata*

curvipes Planch. 1848 = *madagascariensis*

curviscapa Salter 1939 = *aliciae*

darwinensis Lowrie 1996; sect. *Lasiocephala*; N Austral.

derbyensis Lowrie 1996; sect. *Lasiocephala*; NW Austral.

dichrosepala Turcz. 1854; sect. *Bryastrum*; SW Austral.

  – subsp. *enodes* (N. G. Marchant & Lowrie) J. Schlauer 1996; SW Austral.

dielsiana Exell & J. R. Laundon 1956; sect. *Drosera*; S Afr. (Transv., Nat.), Moz., Malawi, Zimb.

dietrichiana Rchb. f. 1871 = *burmannii*

dilatatopetiolaris K. Kondo 1984; sect. *Lasiocephala*; NW Austral.

drummondii Planch. 1848 = *menziesii* subsp. *penicillaris*

echinoblastus N. G. Marchant & Lowrie 1992; sect. *Bryastrum*; SW Austral.

elongata Exell & J. R. Laundon 1955; sect. *Drosera*; Angola

eneabba N. G. Marchant & Lowrie 1992; sect. *Bryastrum*; SW Austral.

enodes N. G. Marchant & Lowrie 1992 = *dichrosepala* subsp. *enodes*

ericksoniae N. G. Marchant & Lowrie 1992; sect. *Bryastrum*; SW Austral.

erythrogyne N. G. Marchant & Lowrie 1992; sect. *Ergaleium*; SW Austral.

erythrorhiza Lindl. 1839; sect. *Erythrorhizae*; SW Austral.

  – subsp. *collina* N. G. Marchant & Lowrie 1992; SW Austral.

  – subsp. *magna* N. G. Marchant & Lowrie 1992; SW Austral.

Drosera continued

erythrorhiza continued
  – subsp. *squamosa* (Benth.) N. G. Marchant
    & Lowrie 1992; SW Austral.
esmeraldae (Steyerm.) Maguire & Wurdack
    1957; sect. *Drosera*; Col., Venez.
esterhuyseniae (Salter) Debbert 1991 = *aliciae*
falconeri K. Kondo 1984; sect. *Lasiocephala*;
    NW Austral.
felix Steyerm. & L. B. Smith 1974; sect. *Dro-
    sera*; Venez.
filicaulis Endl. 1837 = *menziesii*
filiformis Raf. 1808; sect. *Drosera*; U.S.A.
    (Mass.–Del., S.C.–La., Fla.)
  – var. *tracyi* Diels 1906; SE U.S.A. (Miss.–
    Fla.)
filipes Turcz. 1854 = *huegelii*
fimbriata De Buhr 1975; sect. *Stoloniferae*; SW
    Austral.
flabellata Benth. 1864 = *platypoda*
flagellifera Colenso 1891 = *binata*
flexicaulis Welw. ex Oliv. 1871 = *affinis*
fulva Planch. 1848; sect. *Lasiocephala*; N
    Austral.
gigantea Lindl. 1839; sect. *Ergaleium*; SW
    Austral.
  – var. *geniculata* (N. G. Marchant & Lowrie)
    J. Schlauer 1996; SW Austral.
glabripes (Harv.) Stein 1886; sect. *Drosera*;
    Cape
glanduligera Lehm. 1844; sect. *Coelophylla*;
    S Austral., Tasm.
graminifolia A. St.-Hil. 1824; sect. *Drosera*;
    Braz. (Minas Gerais)
graniticola N. G. Marchant 1982; sect. *Erga-
    leium*; SW Austral.
grantsaui Rivadavia 2003; sect. *Drosera*; Braz.
graomogolensis T. R. S. Silva 1997; sect. *Drosera*;
    Braz. (Minas Gerais)
grievei Lowrie & N. G. Marchant 1992; sect.
    Bryastrum; SW Austral.
hamiltonii C. R. P. Andrews 1903; sect. *Dro-
    sera*; SW Austral.
hartmeyerorum J. Schlauer 2001; sect. *Drosera*;
    N Austral.
helianthemum Planch. 1848 = *cistiflora*

helodes N. G. Marchant & Lowrie 1992; sect.
    Bryastrum; SW Austral.
heterophylla Lindl. 1839; sect. *Ergaleium*; SW
    Austral.
hilaris Cham. & Schltdl. 1826; sect. *Drosera*;
    Cape
hirtella A. St.-Hil. 1824; sect. *Drosera*; Braz.
    (Minas Gerais)
hirticalyx R. Duno & Culham 1995; sect. *Dro-
    sera*; Venez.
huegelii Endl. 1837; sect. *Ergaleium*; SW
    Austral.
humbertii Exell & J. R. Laundon 1956; sect.
    Drosera; E Madag.
humilis Planch. 1848 = *stolonifera* subsp.
    humilis
×*hybrida* Macfarl. 1899; [*filiformis* × *inter-
    media*]
hyperostigma N. G. Marchant & Lowrie 1992;
    sect. *Bryastrum*; Austral.
indica L. 1753; sect. *Drosera*; trop. Afr., E
    Madag., Asia (Ind.–Jap., Korea, Indomal.),
    Austral.
insolita Taton 1945; sect. *Drosera*; Congo
intermedia Hayne 1800; sect. *Drosera*; Eur.,
    E N Am., S Am. (Venez., Guai., Braz.),
    West Indies
intricata Planch. 1848; sect. *Ergaleium*; SW
    Austral.
kaieteurensis Brumm.-Ding. 1955; sect. *Dro-
    sera*; Guai., Venez.
×*kansaiensis* Debbert 1996 = ×*tokaiensis*
katangensis Taton 1945; sect. *Drosera*; Congo
kenneallyi Lowrie 1996; sect. *Lasiocephala*; NW
    Austral.
×*kihlmanii* Ikonn. 2001; [*linearis* × *rotundifolia*]
lanata K. Kondo 1984; sect. *Lasiocephala*; N &
    NE Austral.
lasiantha Lowrie & Carlquist 1992; sect. *Bryas-
    trum*; SW Austral.
leioblastus N. G. Marchant & Lowrie 1992 =
    paleacea subsp. *leioblastus*
leionema Raf. 1836 = *filiformis*
leucantha Shinners 1962 = *brevifolia*
leucoblasta Benth. 1864; sect. *Bryastrum*; SW
    Austral.

ligulata Colenso 1899 = *arcturi*

linearis Goldie 1822; sect. *Drosera*; E Can.
(Queb., Ont.), U.S.A. (Great Lakes)

liniflora Debbert 2002 = *cistiflora*

longifolia L. 1753 = *intermedia*

longiscapa Debbert 2002 = *madagascariensis*

loureirii Hook. & Arn. 1841 = *spatulata*

lovellae F. M. Bailey 1893 = *spatulata*

lowriei N. G. Marchant 1992; sect. *Erythrorhizae*; SW Austral.

lusitanica L. 1753 = *Drosophyllum lusitanicum*

macedonica Kosanin 1922 = *anglica*

macloviana Gand. 1913 = *uniflora*

macrantha Endl. 1837; sect. *Ergaleium*; SW
Austral., Tasm.

macrophylla Lindl. 1839; sect. *Erythrorhizae*;
SW Austral.

madagascariensis DC. 1824; sect. *Drosera*; trop.
Afr., E Madag.

makinoi Masam. 1932 = *indica*

mannii Cheek 1990; sect. *Bryastrum*; SW
Austral.

marchantii De Buhr 1975; sect. *Ergaleium*; SW
Austral.

– subsp. *prophylla* N. G. Marchant & Lowrie
1992; SW Austral.

maritima A. St.-Hil. 1824 = *brevifolia*

menziesii R. Br. ex DC. 1824; sect. *Ergaleium*;
SW Austral.

– subsp. *basifolia* N. G. Marchant & Lowrie
1992; SW Austral.

– subsp. *penicillaris* (Benth.) N. G. Marchant
& Lowrie 1992; SW Austral.

– subsp. *thysanosepala* (Diels) N. G. Marchant 1982; SW Austral.

meristocaulis Maguire & Wurdack 1957; sect.
Meristocaules; Venez.–Braz. (Cerro de la
Neblina)

metziana Gand. 1913 = *indica*

microphylla Endl. 1837; sect. *Ergaleium*; SW
Austral.

microscapa Debbert 1991 = *occidentalis* var.
microscapa

miniata Diels 1904; sect. *Bryastrum*; SW
Austral.

minutula Colenso 1889 = *spatulata*

moaensis C. Panfet Valdés 1991 = *brevifolia*

modesta Diels 1904; sect. *Ergaleium*; SW
Austral.

montana A. St.-Hil. 1824; sect. *Drosera*; Venez.,
Braz., Bol.

– var. *schwackei* Diels 1906; Braz.

– var. *tomentosa* (A. St.-Hil.) Diels 1906;
Braz.

moorei (Diels) Lowrie 1999; sect. *Ergaleium*;
SW Austral.

myriantha Planch. 1848; sect. *Ergaleium*; SW
Austral.

×*nagamotoi* Cheek 1993; [*anglica* × *spatulata*]

natalensis Diels 1906; sect. *Drosera*; S Afr.,
Moz., E Madag.

neesii Lehm. 1978; sect. *Ergaleium*; SW Austral.

– subsp. *borealis* N. G. Marchant 1982; SW
Austral.

neocaledonica Raym.-Hamet 1906; sect. *Drosera*; New Caled.

nidiformis Debbert 1991; sect. *Drosera*; S Afr.
(Nat.)

nipponica Masam. 1933 = *peltata*

nitidula Planch. 1848; sect. *Bryastrum*; SW
Austral.

– var. *allantostigma* (N. G. Marchant & Lowrie) J. Schlauer 1996 = *allantostigma*

– var. *leucostigma* (N. G. Marchant &
Lowrie) J. Schlauer 1996 = *leucostigma*

– subsp. *omissa* (Diels) N. G. Marchant &
Lowrie 1992; SW Austral.

nivea Lowrie & Carlquist 1992 = *citrina* var.
nivea

oblanceolata Y. Z. Ruan 1981; sect. *Drosera*;
SE China

occidentalis Morrison 1912; sect. *Bryastrum*;
SW Austral.

– subsp. *australis* N. G. Marchant & Lowrie
1992; SW Austral.

– var. *microscapa* (Debbert) J. Schlauer 1996;
SW Austral.

omissa Diels 1906 = *nitidula* subsp. *omissa*

orbiculata N. G. Marchant & Lowrie 1992; sect.
Erythrorhizae; SW Austral.

ordensis Lowrie 1994; sect. *Lasiocephala*; NW
Austral.

Drosera continued

oreopodion N. G. Marchant & Lowrie 1992;
sect. *Bryastrum*; SW Austral.

paleacea DC. 1824; sect. *Bryastrum*; SW
Austral.
– subsp. *leioblastus* (N. G. Marchant &
Lowrie) J. Schlauer 1996; SW Austral.
– subsp. *roseana* (N. G. Marchant & Lowrie)
J. Schlauer 1996; SW Austral.
– subsp. *stelliflora* (Lowrie & Carlquist) J.
Schlauer 1996; SW Austral.
– subsp. *trichocaulis* (Diels) N. G. Marchant
& Lowrie 1992; SW Austral.

pallida Lindl. 1839; sect. *Ergaleium*; SW
Austral.

panamensis Correa & A. S. Taylor 1976; sect.
Drosera; Pan.

paradoxa Lowrie 1997; sect. *Lasiocephala*; NW
Austral.

parvifolia A. St.-Hil. 1824 = *communis* var.
pauciflora

parvula Planch. 1848; sect. *Bryastrum*; SW
Austral.
– subsp. *sargentii* (Lowrie & N. G. Marchant)
J. Schlauer 1996; SW Austral.

pauciflora Banks ex DC. 1824; sect. *Ptycnostigma*; SW Cape

pedicellaris Lowrie 2002; sect. *Bryastrum*; SW
Austral.

peltata Thunb. 1797; sect. *Ergaleium*; Asia
(Ind.–Jap., Korea, S to Indomal., New
Guin., Austral., Tasm.)
– subsp. *auriculata* (Backh. ex Planch.) B. J.
Conn 1981; SE Austral., Tasm., New
Zeal.

penicillaris Benth. 1864 = *menziesii* subsp.
penicillaris

peruensis T. R. S. Silva & M. D. Corrêa 2002;
sect. *Drosera*; Peru

petiolaris R. Br. ex DC. 1824; sect. *Lasiocephala*; N Austral., New Guin.

pilosa Exell & J. R. Laundon 1956; sect. *Drosera*; trop. Afr. (Guin., Camer., Kenya,
Tanz.)

planchonii Hook. f. ex Planch. 1848 =
macrantha

platypoda Turcz. 1854; sect. *Stoloniferae*; SW
Austral.

platystigma Lehm. 1844; sect. *Bryastrum*; SW
Austral.

polyneura Colenso 1890 = *arcturi*

porrecta Lehm. 1844 = *stolonifera* subsp.
porrecta

praefolia Tepper 1892 = *whittakeri*

preissii (Lehm.) Planch. 1848 = *heterophylla*

prolifera C. T. White 1940; sect. *Drosera*; NE
Austral. (Queensl.)

prostratoscaposa Lowrie & Carlquist 1990; sect.
Erythrorhizae; SW Austral.

pulchella Lehm. 1844; sect. *Bryastrum*; SW
Austral.

pumilla E. Santos 1986 = *colombiana*

pusilla Kunth 1821 = *biflora*

pycnoblasta Diels 1904; sect. *Bryastrum*; SW
Austral.

pygmaea DC. 1824; sect. *Bryastrum*; SW–SE
Austral., Tasm., New Zeal.

radicans N. G. Marchant 1982; sect. *Ergaleium*;
SW Austral.

ramellosa Lehm. 1844; sect. *Stoloniferae*; SW
Austral.

ramentacea Burch. ex DC. 1824; sect. *Ergaleium*; SW Cape

rechingeri Strid 1987; sect. *Bryastrum*; SW
Austral.

regia Stephens 1926; sect. *Regiae*; Cape

roraimae (Klotzsch ex Diels) Maguire & J. R.
Laundon 1957; sect. *Drosera*; Braz.,
Venez., Guai.

roridula Thunb. 1797 = *Roridula dentata*

roseana N. G. Marchant & Lowrie 1992 = *paleacea* subsp. *roseana*

rosulata Lehm. 1844; sect. *Erythrorhizae*; SW
Austral.

rotundifolia L. 1753; sect. *Drosera*; Eur., N Asia,
Jap., N Am.

ruahinensis Colenso 1896 = *arcturi*

rubiginosa Heckel 1906 = *neocaledonica*

rubrifolia Debbert 2002 = *aliciae*

rubripetala Debbert 1991 = *cistiflora*

salina N. G. Marchant & Lowrie 1992; sect.
Ergaleium; SW Austral.

sanariapoana Steyerm. 1952 = *cayennensis*

sargentii Lowrie & N. G. Marchant 1992 = *parvula* subsp. *sargentii*

schizandra Diels 1906; sect. *Drosera*; NE Austral. (Queensl.)

scorpioides Planch. 1848; sect. *Bryastrum*; SW Austral.

septentrionalis Stokes 1812 = *rotundifolia*

sessilifolia A. St.-Hil. 1824; sect. *Thelocalyx*; Braz., Guai., Venez.

sewelliae Diels 1904; sect. *Bryastrum*; SW Austral.

silvicola Lowrie & Carlquist 1992 = *barbigera* subsp. *silvicola*

slackii Cheek 1987; sect. *Drosera*; Cape

spatulata Labill. 1804; sect. *Drosera*; Asia (Jap., Taiw., S China) S to Indomalays., New Guin., E Austral., Tasm., New Zeal.
  – var. *gympiensis* R. A. Gibson & I. Snyder 2005; NE Austral (Queensl.)

speciosa C. Presl. 1844 = *cistiflora*

spilos N. G. Marchant & Lowrie 1992; sect. *Bryastrum*; SW Austral.

spiralis A. St.-Hil. 1824 = *graminifolia*

squamosa Benth. 1864 = *erythrorhiza* subsp. *squamosa*

stenopetala Hook. f. 1853; sect. *Drosera*; New Zeal.

stolonifera Endl. 1837; sect. *Stoloniferae*; SW Austral.
  – subsp. *compacta* N. G. Marchant 1982; SW Austral.
  – subsp. *humilis* (Planch.) N. G. Marchant 1982; SW Austral.
  – subsp. *monticola* Lowrie & N. G. Marchant 1992; SW Austral.
  – subsp. *porrecta* (Lehm.) N. G. Marchant & Lowrie 1992; SW Austral.
  – subsp. *prostrata* N. G. Marchant & Lowrie 1992; SW Austral.
  – subsp. *rupicola* N. G. Marchant 1982; SW Austral.

stricticaulis (Diels) O. H. Sarg. 1913; sect. *Ergaleium*; SW Austral.
  – subsp. *eremaea* (N. G. Marchant & Lowrie) J. Schlauer 1996; SW Austral.

stylosa Colenso 1896 = *peltata* subsp. *auriculata*

subhirtella Planch. 1848; sect. *Ergaleium*; SW Austral.

subtilis N. G. Marchant 1982; sect. *Ergaleium*; N Austral.

sulphurea Lehm. 1844; sect. *Ergaleium*; SW Austral.

tentaculata Rivadavia 2003; sect. *Drosera*; Braz.

thysanosepala Diels 1906 = *menziesii* subsp. *thysanosepala*

×tokaiensis (Komiya & C. Shibata) T. Nakam. & K. Ueda 1991; [*spatulata* × *rotundifolia*]

tomentosa A. St.-Hil. 1824 = *montana* var. *tomentosa*

tracyi Macfarl. ex Diels 1906 = *filiformis* var. *tracyi*

triflora Colenso 1890 = *spatulata*

trinervia Spreng. 1820; sect. *Drosera*; Cape

tubaestylis N. G. Marchant & Lowrie 1992; sect. *Erythrorhizae*; SW Austral.

uniflora Willd. 1809; sect. *Drosera*; Patag., Tierra d. Fueg.

variegata Debbert 2002 = *cistiflora*

venusta Debbert 1987 = *natalensis*

villosa A. St.-Hil. 1824; sect. *Drosera*; E Braz.

violacea Willd. 1809 = *cistiflora*

viridis Rivadavia 2003; sect. *Drosera*; Braz.

walyunga N. G. Marchant & Lowrie 1992; sect. *Bryastrum*; SW Austral.

whittakeri Planch. 1848; sect. *Erythrorhizae*; SE Austral.

yutajensis R. Duno & Culham 1995; sect. *Drosera*; Venez.

zigzagia Lowrie 1999; sect. *Ergaleium*; SW Austral.

zonaria Planch. 1848; sect. *Erythrorhizae*; SW Austral.

Drosophyllum Link 1806: Portuguese sundew (Drosophyllaceae)

lusitanicum (L.) Link 1806; Port., Spain, Moroc.

Freatulina Chrtek & Slavikova 1996 = *Drosera* subgen. *Regiae* (Droseraceae)

Freatulina continued

regia (Stephens) Chrtek & Slavikova 1996 =
    Drosera regia

Genlisea A. St.-Hil. 1833: corkscrew plant
    (Lentibulariaceae)
africana Oliv. 1865; subgen. *Genlisea*; Angola,
    Congo, Zambia, Zimb.
    – subsp. stapfii (A. Chev.) P. Taylor 1972 =
        stapfii
anfractuosa Tutin 1934 = *filiformis*
angolensis R. D. Good 1924; subgen. *Genlisea*;
    Angola, Congo
aurea A. St.-Hil. 1833; subgen. *Genlisea*; Braz.
barthlottii Porembski, Eb. Fisch. & Gemmel
    1996; subgen. *Genlisea*; Guin.
biloba Benj. 1847 = *violacea*
esmeraldae Steyerm. 1953 = *pygmaea*
filiformis A. St.-Hil. 1833; subgen. *Genlisea*;
    Belize, Boliv., Braz., Guat., Guai., Col.,
    Cuba, Mex., Nicar., Venez.
glabra P. Taylor 1967; subgen. *Genlisea*; Venez.
glandulosissima R. E. Fr. 1916; subgen. *Genli-
    sea*; Zambia, Zimb.
guianensis N. E. Br. 1900; subgen. *Genlisea*;
    Boliv., Braz., Guai., Venez.
hispidula Stapf 1904; subgen. *Genlisea*; Angola,
    Camer., Kenya, Congo, Malawi, Moz.,
    Nig., Zambia, S. Afr., Tanz., C. Afr. Rep.,
    Zimb.
lobata Fromm 1989; subgen. *Tayloria*; Braz.
luetzelburgii Merl & Luetzelb. 1923 =
    guianensis
luteoviridis Wright 1869 = *filiformis*
margaretae Hutch. 1946; subgen. *Genlisea*;
    Madag., Zambia, Tanz.
minor A. St.-Hil. 1833 = *aurea*
nigrocaulis Steyerm. 1948 = *pygmaea*
ornata Mart ex Benj. 1847 = *aurea*
oxycentron P. Taylor 1954 = *pygmaea*
pallida Fromm & P. Taylor 1985; subgen. *Gen-
    lisea*; Angola, Zambia
pulchella Tutin 1934 = *repens*
pusilla Warm. 1923 = *repens*
pygmaea A. St.-Hil. 1833; subgen. *Genlisea*;
    Braz., Guai., Col., Venez.
recurva Bosser 1958 = *margaretae*

reflexa Benj. 1847 = *violacea*
repens Benj. 1847; subgen. *Genlisea*; Braz.,
    Guai., Parag., Surin., Venez.
roraimensis N. E. Br. 1901; subgen. *Genlisea*;
    Braz., Guai., Venez.
sanariapoana Steyerm. 1953; subgen. *Genlisea*;
    Venez.
stapfii A. Chev. 1912; subgen. *Genlisea*;
    Burkina Faso, Ivory C., Gabun, Guin.,
    Camer., Congo, Liber., Mali, Seneg., Sierra
    Leo., C. Afr. Rep.
subglabra Stapf 1906; subgen. *Genlisea*;
    Burundi, Congo, Malawi, Zambia, Tanz.
subviridis Hutch. 1946 = *africana*
taylorii Eb. Fisch., Porembski & Barthlott
    2000; subgen. *Genlisea*; Angola
uncinata P. Taylor & Fromm 1983; subgen.
    Tayloria; Braz.
violacea A. St.-Hil. 1833; subgen. *Tayloria*;
    Braz.

Heliamphora Benth. 1840: South American
    pitcher plant (Sarraceniaceae)
chimantensis Wistuba, Carow & Harbarth
    2002; Venez. (Chimanta Tepui)
elongata Nerz 2004; Venez. (Ilu Tepui)
folliculata Wistuba, Harbarth & Carow 2001;
    Venez. (Los Testigos: Murosipan Tepui,
    Aparaman Tepui, Kamarcaibarai Tepui)
heterodoxa Steyerm. 1951; Venez. (Ptari Tepui)
    – var. exappendiculata Maguire & Steyerm.
        1978 = *exappendiculata*
    – f. glabella Steyerm. 1984 = *glabra*
    – f. *glabra* (Maguire) Steyerm. 1984; Venez.
        (Mt. Serra do Sol)
hispida Wistuba & Nerz 2000; Braz.–Venez.
    (Sierra de la Neblina)
ionasi Maguire 1978; Venez. (Ilu Tepui,
    Yuruani Tepui)
macdonaldae Gleason 1931 = *tatei* f.
    macdonaldae
minor Gleason 1939; Venez. (Auyan Tepui,
    Chimanta Tepui)
    – f. *laevis* Steyerm. 1984; Venez. (Auyan
        Tepui, Chimanta Tepui)

neblinae Maguire 1978 = *tatei* var. *neblinae*

– var. parva Maguire 1978 = *tatei* var. *neblinae* f. *parva*

– var. viridis Maguire 1978 = *tatei* var. *neblinae*

nutans Benth. 1840; Braz., Guai., Venez. (Roraima Tepui, Kukenan Tepui, Ilu Tepui, Tramen Tepui)

pulchella Wistuba, Carow, Harbarth & Nerz 2005; Venez. (Chimanta Tepui, Euroda Tepui)

sarracenioides Carow, Wistuba & Harbarth 2005; Venez. (Gran Sabana)

tatei Gleason 1931; Venez. (Duida-Marahuaca Massif)

– f. *macdonaldae* (Gleason) Steyerm. 1984; Venez. (Cerro de Duida)

– var. *neblinae* (Maguire) Steyerm. 1984; Braz., Venez. (Sierra de la Neblina, Cerro Aracamuni)

– var. *neblinae* f. *parva* (Maguire) Steyerm. 1984; Braz., Venez. (Sierra de la Neblina)

tyleri Gleason 1931 = *tatei*

Nepenthes L. 1753: Asian pitcher plant (Nepenthaceae)

The elevation ranges (above sea level) of the wild populations have been included below, because they are quite relevant for cultivation. Elevation values in parentheses represent single records.

adnata Tamin & M. Hotta ex J. Schlauer 1994; Indones. (Sum.); 700–1000 m

alata Blanco 1837; Phil.; 400–2400 m

alba Ridl. 1924 = *gracillima*

albolineata F. M. Bailey 1898 = *mirabilis*

albomarginata T. Lobb ex Lindl. 1849; Brun., Indones. (Born., Sum.), Malays.; 0–1100 m

alicae F. M. Bailey 1898 = *mirabilis*

×*alisaputrana* J. H. Adam & C. C. Wilcock 1992; [*burbridgeae* × *rajah*]; Malays. (Born.); 500–2200 m

×*amabilis* hort. G. Nicholson 1888; [(*rafflesiana* × *ampullaria*) × *rafflesiana*]

ampullaria Jack 1835; Brun., Indones. (Born., Sum., Irian Jaya), Malays., Papua New G., Singap., Thail.; 0–1000 (–2100) m

anamensis Macfarl. 1908; Indoch. (Camb., Thail., Vietn.); 1500 m

angasanensis R. G. Maulder, D. Schubert, B. R. Salmon & B. Quinn 1999; Indones. (Sum.); 2500 m

angustifolia Mast. 1881 = *gracilis*

argentii Jebb & Cheek 1997; Phil.; 1400 m

aristolochioides Jebb & Cheek 1997; Indones. (Sum.); 2000–2200 m

armbrustae F. M. Bailey 1905 = *mirabilis*

×*atro-sanguinea* hort. Veitch ex Mast. 1882; [*distillatoria* × (*gracilis* × *khasiana*)]

×*balfouriana* hort. Veitch ex Mast. 1899; [(*northiana* × *maxima*) × (*sanguinea* × *khasiana*)]

beccariana Macfarl. 1908; Indones. (Nias, Sum.); 0–1000 m

bellii K. Kondo 1969; Phil.; 250–800 m

benstonei C. Clarke 1999; Malays. (Penins.); 450–600 m

bernaysii F. M. Bailey 1881 = *mirabilis*

bicalcarata Hook. f. 1873; Brun., Indones. (Born.), Malays. (Born.); 0–950 m

blancoi Blume 1852 = *alata*

bongso Korth. 1839; Indones. (Sum.); 1000–2700 m

borneensis J. H. Adam & C. C. Wilcock 1989 = *boschiana*

boschiana Korth. 1839; Indones. (Born.); 780–1880 m

brachycarpa Merr. 1915 = *philippinensis*

burbidgeae Hook. f. ex Burb. 1882; Malays. (Born.); 1200–2250 m

burkei Mast. 1889; Phil.; 1300–1600 m

campanulata Sh. Kurata 1973; Indones. (E Born.), Malays. (E Born.); 300 m

carunculata Danser 1928 = *bongso*

celebica Hook. f. 1873 = *maxima*

chaniana C. Clarke, Chi C. Lee & S. McPherson 2006; Malays. (Born.: Sabah); 1600 m

×*chelsonii* hort. Veitch ex Mast. 1872; [(*rafflesiana* × *hirsuta*) × (*rafflesiana* × *ampullaria*)]

cholmondeleyi F. M. Bailey 1900 = *mirabilis*

Nepenthes continued

×*cincta* Mast. 1884; [*northiana* × *albomarginata*]; Malays. (Born.); 0–500 m

clipeata Danser 1928; Indones. (W Born.); 600–800 m

copelandii Merr. ex Macfarl. 1908; Phil. (Mind.); 400–2000 m

×*courtii* hort. Veitch 1877; [(*gracilis* × *rafflesiana*) × *hirsuta*]

curtisii Mast. 1887 = *maxima*

curtisii subsp. *zakriana* J. H. Adam & Wilcock 1993 = *zakriana*

×*cylindrica* hort. Veitch 1887; [*distillatoria* × *veitchii*]

danseri Jebb & Cheek 1997; Indones. (Irian Jaya, Moluc.); 0–300 m

deaniana Macfarl. 1908; Phil.; 1300–1500 m

decurrens Macfarl. 1925 = *northiana*

densiflora Danser 1940; Indones. (Sum.); 1700–3000 m

dentata Kurata 1984 = *hamata*

×*deslogesii* Desloges 1905; [(*maxima* × *veitchii*) × (*northiana* × *maxima*)]

diatas Jebb & Cheek 1997; Indones. (Sum.); 2400–2600 m

×*dicksoniana* Linds. 1855; [*rafflesiana* × *veitchii*]

distillatoria L. 1753; Sri Lanka; 0–700 m

×*dominii* hort. Veitch ex Mast. 1842; [*rafflesiana* × *hirsuta*]

×*dormanniana* hort. B. S. Williams ex Mast. 1882; [(*mirabilis* × *gracilis*) × *khasiana*]

dubia Danser 1928; Indones. (Sum.); 1000–2500 m

dyak S. Moore 1880 = *bicalcarata*

echinostoma Hook. f. 1873 = *mirabilis*

edgeworthii Rchb. f. ex Beck 1895 = *edwardsiana*

×*edinensis* Linds. 1888; [*rafflesiana* × {(*rafflesiana* × *hirsuta*) × (*rafflesiana* × *ampullaria*)}]

edwardsiana Low ex Hook. f. 1859; Malays. (Born.); 1500–2700 m

ephippiata Danser 1928; Indones. (Born.); 1000–1900 m

eustachya Miq. 1858; Indones. (Sum.); 0–1600 m

×*excelsior* hort. B. S. Williams 1885; [*rafflesiana* × (*rafflesiana* × *ampullaria*)]

eymae Sh. Kurata 1984; Indones. (Celebes); 1500–2000 m

faizaliana J. H. Adam & C. C. Wilcock 1991; Malays. (Born.); 600–1600 m

fallax Beck 1895 = *stenophylla*

×*ferrugineomarginata* Sh. Kurata 1982; [*reinwardtiana* × *albomarginata*]; Malyas., Indones. (Born., Sum.); 0–1000 m

fimbriata Blume 1852 = *mirabilis*

×*formosa* hort. Veitch 1986; [{(*rafflesiana* × *hirsuta*) × (*rafflesiana* × *ampullaria*)} × *distillatoria*]

fusca Danser 1928; Indones. (Born.); 800–2500 m

garrawayae F. M. Bailey 1905 = *mirabilis*

geoffrayi Lecomte 1909 = *anamensis*

glabrata J. R. Turnbull & A. T. Middleton 1984; Indones. (Celebes); 1600–2000 m

glandulifera Chi C. Lee 2004; Malays. (Born.); 1200–1600 m

globamphora Sh. Kurata & Toyosh. 1972 = *bellii*

gracilis Korth. 1839; Brun., Indones. (Born., Celebes, Sum.), Malays., Singap., Thail.; 0–800 m

gracillima Ridl. 1908; Malays.; 1300–2100 m

gymnamphora Nees 1824; Indones. (Java, Sum.); 1000–2700 m

hamata J. R. Turnbull & A. T. Middleton 1984; Indones. (Celebes); 1400–2500 m

×*harryana* Burb. 1882; [*villosa* × *edwardsiana*]; Malays. (Born.); 2400–2700 m

×*henryana* hort. B. S. Williams 1882; [(*gracilis* × *khasiana*) × (*rafflesiana* × *ampullaria*)]

hirsuta Hook. f. 1873; Brun., Indones. (Born.), Malays. (Born.); 500–1100 m

hispida Beck 1895; Brun., Malays. (Born.); 100–800 m

×*hookeriana* Lindl. 1848; [*rafflesiana* × *ampullaria*]; Brun., Indones. (Born., Sum.), Malays., Singap.; 0–1000 m

hurrelliana Cheek & A. L. Lamb 2003; Malays. (Born.); 1300 m

×*hybrida* hort. Veitch ex Mast. 1872; [*gracilis* × *khasiana*]

inermis Danser 1928; Indones. (Sum.); 2300–2600 m

infundibuliformis J. R. Turnball & A. T. Middleton 1984 = *eymae*

insignis Danser 1928; Indones. (Irian Jaya); 0–850 m

×*intermedia* hort. ex Veitch 1875; [*rafflesiana* × *hirsuta*]

izumiae Troy Davis, C. Clarke & Tamin 2003; Indones. (Sum.) 1700–1800 m

jacquelineae C. Clarke, Troy Davis & Tamin 2001; Indones. (Sum.); 1700–2200 m

jamban Chi C. Lee, Hernawati & P. Akhriadi 2006; Indones. (Sum.); uplands

jardinei F. M. Bailey 1897 = *mirabilis*

junghuhnii Macfarl. 1917 nom. nud.; Indones. (Sum.); 2600 m

kampotiana Lecomte 1909 = *anamensis*

kennedyana F. Muell. 1865 = *mirabilis*

kennedyi Benth. 1873 = *mirabilis*

khasiana* Hook. f. 1873; Ind. (Assam); 1000 m

×*kinabaluensis* Sh. Kurata ex J. H. Adam & C. C. Wilcock 1984; [*rajah* × *villosa*]; Malays. (Born.); 2400–3000 m

klossii Ridl. 1916; Indones. (Irian Jaya); 1000–2000 m

korthalsiana Miq. 1908 = *reinwardtiana*

×*kuchingensis* Sh. Kurata 1982; [*ampullaria* × *mirabilis*]; Indones. (Born., Irian Jaya, Sum.), Malays., Papua New G.; 0–1000 m

laevis Lindl. 1848 = *gracilis*

lamii Jebb & Cheek 1997; Indones. (Irian Jaya); 1500–3500 m

lanata hort. Linden 1876 = *veitchii*

lavicola Wistuba & Rischer 1996; Indones. (Sum.); 2000–2600 m

×*lawrenciana* hort. B. S. Williams ex Mast. 1880; [*mirabilis* × (*rafflesiana* × *ampullaria*)]

×*lecouflei* Kusak. 1983; [*mirabilis* × *thorelii*]

leptochila Danser 1928 = *hirsuta*

lindleyana Low ex W. Baxt. 1850 nom. dub.; Malays. (Born.)

lingulata Chi C. Lee, Hernawati & P. Akhriadi 2006; Indones. (Sum.); uplands

longifolia Nerz & Wistuba 1994; Indones. (Sum.); 300–1100 m

longinodis Beck 1895 = *gracilis*

lowii Hook. f. 1859; Brun., Malays. (Born.); 1600–2600 m

×*lyrata* hort. Veitch ex Wilson 1877; [(*khasiana* × *gracilis*) × *rafflesiana*]

macfarlanei Hemsl. 1905; Malays. (Penins.); 1000–2100 m

macrophylla (Marabini) Jebb & Cheek 1997; Malays. (Born.); 2200–2400 m

macrostachya Blume 1852 = *mirabilis*

macrovulgaris J. R. Turnbull & A. T. Middleton 1987; Malays. (Born.); 300–1200 m

madagascariensis Poir. 1797; SE Madag.; 0–100 m

mapuluensis J. H. Adam & C. C. Wilcock 1990; Indones. (E Born.); 700–800 m

masoalensis Schmid-Hollinger 1977; E Madag.; 30–400 m

×*mastersiana* hort. Veitch ex Mast. 1881; [*sanguinea* × *khasiana*]

maxima Reinw. ex Nees 1824; Indones. (Irian Jaya, Moluc., Celebes), Papua New G.; 600–2500 m

melamphora Reinw. ex Blume 1852 = *gymnamphora*

merrilliana Macfarl. 1911; Phil.; 20–1700 m

mikei B. R. Salmon & R. G. Maulder 1995; Indones. (Sum.); 1100–2500 m

mindanaoensis Sh. Kurata 2001; Phil.; 200–300 m

mira Jebb & Cheek 1998; Phil. (Palawan); 1600 m

mirabilis (Lour.) Druce 1916; trop. SE Asia, China, Austral. (Queensl.), Indones. Malays., Micronesia, Phil., Papua New G.; 0–1000 (–1500) m

×*mixta* hort. Veitch ex Mast. 1893; [*northiana* × *maxima*]

mollis Danser 1928; Indones. (Born.); 1800 m

moluccensis Oken 1841 = *mirabilis*

×*morganiana* hort. Veitch ex Wilson 1881; [*mirabilis* × (*rafflesiana* × *ampullaria*)]

muluensis Hotta 1966; Malays. (Born.); 1700–2400 m

murudensis Culham ex Jebb & Cheek 1997; Malays. (Born.); 2200–2500 m

Nepenthes continued

naquiyuddinii J. H. Adam & Hafiza 2006; Malays. (Born.: Sabah); 1400m

neglecta Macfarl. 1908 = *hirsuta*

neoguineensis Macfarl. 1911; Indones. (Irian Jaya), Papua New G.; 0–900 (–1400) m

×*nobilis* hort. Veitch ex Mast. 1910; [*sanguinea* × *maxima*]

northiana Hook. f. 1881; Malays. (Born.); 0–800 m

×*northisii* Veitch 1892; [*northiana* × *maxima*]

oblanceolata Ridl. 1916 = *maxima*

×*outramiana* hort. B. S. Williams ex Denny 1879; [(*gracilis* × *khasiana*) × (*rafflesiana* × *ampullaria*)]

ovata Nerz & Wistuba 1994; Indones. (Sum.); 1800 m

×*pangulubauensis* hort. B. R. Salmon & R. G. Maulder ex Mann 1996; [*mikei* × *gymnamphora*]; Indones. (W Sum.); 1100–2500 m

paniculata Danser 1928; Indones. (Irian Jaya); 1500 m

papuana Danser 1928; Indones. (Irian Jaya); 200–900 m

×*paradisae* hort. B. S. Williams ex G. Nicholson 1888; [*mirabilis* × (*rafflesiana* × *ampullaria*)]

pascoensis F. M. Bailey 1905 = *mirabilis*

pectinata Danser 1928 = *gymnamphora*

pervillei Blume 1852; Seych.; 350–500 m

petiolata Danser 1928; Phil.; 1500–1700 m

philippinensis Macfarl. 1908; Phil.; 0–500 m

phyllamphora Willd. 1805 = *mirabilis*

pilosa Danser 1928; Indones. (Born.); (1000–) 1600–1800 m

platychila Chi C. Lee 2002; Malays. (Born.); 900–1400 m

pumila Griff. 1854 = *sanguinea*

pyriformis Sh. Kurata 2001; Indones. (Sum.); 1600–2000 m

rafflesiana Jack 1835; Brun., Indones. (Born., Sum.), Malays.; 0–300 (–1000) m

rajah* Hook. f. 1859; Malays. (Born.); 1500–2600 m

ramispina Ridl. 1909; Malays. (Penins.); 900–2000 m

×*ratcliffiana* hort. Veitch ex Mast. 1882; [*mirabilis* × (*rafflesiana* × *ampullaria*)]

reinwardtiana Miq. 1851; Brun., Indones. (Born., Sum.), Malays. (Born.); 0–1500 (–2100) m

rhombicaulis Sh. Kurata 1973; Indones. (Sum.); 1700–1900 m

rigidifolia Akhriadi, Hernawati & Tamin 2004; Malays., Indones. (Sum.); 1000–1500 m

×*robusta* B. S. Williams ex Mast. 1880; [*mirabilis* × (*rafflesiana* × *ampullaria*)]

rosulata Tamin & M. Hotta 1986 = *gymnamphora*

rowanae F. M. Bailey 1897 = *mirabilis*

rubromaculata Sh. Kurata 1984 = *glabrata*

×*rubro-maculata* hort. Veitch ex Wilson 1877; [*gracilis* × (*khasiana* × *veitchii*)]

×*rufescens* hort. Veitch ex Mast. 1888; [{*gracilis* × (*rafflesiana* × *hirsuta*)} × *distillatoria*]

sandakanensis J. H. Adam & C. C. Wilcock 1996 = *fallax*

sanderiana Burb. 1904 = *rafflesiana*

sanguinea Lindl. 1849; Malays. (Penins.), Thail.; 900–1800 m

saranganiensis Sh. Kurata 2003; Phil. (Mindanao); uplands

×*sarawakiensis* J. H. Adam, C. C. Wilcock & Swaine 1993; [*tentaculata* × *muluensis*]; Malays. (Born.); 1700–2100 m

×*sedeni* hort. Veitch ex Mast. 1872; [*distillatoria* × *ventricosa*]

sibuyanensis Nerz 1998; Phil.; 1300–1800 m

singalana Becc. 1886; Indones. (Sum.); 1900–2800 m

smilesii Hemsl. 1895 = *mirabilis*

smithii Beck 1895 = *distillatoria*

spathulata Danser 1935; Indones. (Sum.); 1500–2200 m

spectabilis Danser 1928; Indones. (Sum.); 1400–2000 m

spinosa Tamin & M. Hotta 1986 = *sumatrana*, *gymnamphora*

spuria Beck 1895 = *northiana*

stenophylla Mast. 1890; Brun., Indones. (Born.), Malays. (Born.); 1000–2600 m

sumatrana (Miq.) Beck 1895; Indones. (Sum.); 0–1000 m

surigaoensis Elmer 1915 = *merrilliana*

talangensis Nerz & Wistuba 1994; Indones. (Sum.); 1800–2500 m

tentaculata Hook. f. 1873; Brun., Indones. (Born., Celebes), Malays. (Born.); (800–) 1200–2100 (–2500) m

tenuis Nerz & Wistuba 1994; Indones. (Sum.); 1000 m

teysmanniana Miq. 1858 = *albomarginata*

thorelii Lecomte 1909; Indochina (Camb., Thail., Vietn.); 0–200 m

×*tiveyi* hort. Veitch ex Mast. 1897; [*maxima* × *veitchii*]

tobaica Danser 1928; Indones. (Sum.); 1000–2700 m

tomentella Miq. 1855 = *albomarginata*

tomoriana Danser 1928; Indones. (Celebes); 0–400 m

treubiana Warb. 1891; Indones. (Irian Jaya); 0–500 m

×*trichocarpa* Miq. 1858; [*gracilis* × *ampullaria*]; Indones. (Born., Sum.), Malays., Singap.; 0–800 m

truncata Macfarl. 1911; Phil.; 200–600 m

×*trusmadiensis* Marabini 1983; [*macrophylla* × *lowii*]; Malays. (Born.); 2200–2400 m

tubulosa Macfarl. 1908 = *mirabilis*

veitchii Hook. f. 1859; Brun., Indones. (Born.), Malays. (Born.); 700–1800 m

ventricosa Blanco 1837; Phil.; 1200–1500 m

vieillardii Hook. f. 1873; New Caled.; 30–800 m

villosa Hook. f. 1852; Malays. (Born.); 2400–3200 m

vogelii Schuit. & de Vogel 2002; Indones. (Born.); 1000 m

wilkiei Jebb & Cheek 1998 = *philippinensis*

×*williamsii* hort. Veitch ex Mast. 1880; [(*gracilis* × *khasiana*) × (*rafflesiana* × *ampullaria*)]

×*wrigleyana* hort. Veitch ex Mast. 1880; [*mirabilis* × (*rafflesiana* × *ampullaria*)]

xiphioides B. R. Salmon & R. G. Maulder 1995 = *gymnamphora*

zakriana (J. H. Adam & Wilcock) J. H. Adam & Hafiza 2006; Malays. (Born.: Sabah); 1200–1500 m

zeylanica (Burm. ex Brongn.) Raf. 1836 = *distillatoria*

Pinguicula L. 1753: butterwort (Lentibulariaceae)

acuminata Benth. 1839; sect. *Heterophyllum*; Mex.

agnata Casper 1963; sect. *Agnata*; Mex.

albanica Griseb. 1844 = *crystallina* subsp. *hirtiflora*

albida Wright ex Griseb. 1866; sect. *Agnata*; Cuba

algida Malyschev 1966; sect. *Micranthus*; Russ. (NE Sib.)

alpina L. 1753; sect. *Micranthus*; Euras. (Arct., Alp., Him.)

antarctica J. Vahl 1827; sect. *Ampullipalatum*; Patag. (Chile, Arg.)

'Aphrodite' J. Flisek & K. Pasek 2000; [*agnata* × *moctezumae*]

arctica Eastw. 1902 = *vulgaris*

auricolor Arv.-Touv. 1871 = *alpina*

australis Chapm. 1860 = *caerulea*

'Ayautla' (see *gigantea*)

balcanica Casper 1962; sect. *Pinguicula*; Balk.
  – subsp. *pontica* Casper 1970; Russ., Turk. (Black Sea)
  – var. *tenuilaciniata* Casper 1962; Balk.

barbata Zamudio & Rzed. 1986 = *clivorum*

benedicta Barnhart 1920; sect. *Agnata*; Cuba

bissei Casper 2004; sect. *Agnata*; Cuba

bohemica Krajina 1927 = *vulgaris*

buswellii Moldenke 1945 = *pumila*

caerulea Walter 1788; sect. *Isoloba*; SE U.S.A. (N.C., S.C., Ga., Fla.)

calderoniae Zamudio 2001; sect. *Longitubus*; Mex.

calyptrata Kunth 1817; sect. *Ampullipalatum*; Andes (Col., Ecua.)

caryophyllacea Casper 2004; sect. *Agnata*; Cuba

casabitoana J. Jimenez Alm 1960; sect. *Discoradix*; Dom. Rep.; epiphytic

Pinguicula continued

caudata Schltdl. 1832 = *moranensis*

chilensis Clos 1849; sect. *Ampullipalatum*;
  Chile, Arg.

cladophila A. Ernst 1961 = *casabitoana*

clivorum Standl. & Steyerm. 1944; sect. *Temnoceras*; Mex., Guat.

colimensis McVaugh & Mickel 1963; sect.
  Orcheosanthus; Mex.

conzattii Zamudio & van Marm 2003; sect.
  Heterophyllum; Mex.

corsica Bernard & Gren. ex Gren. & Godr.
  1850; sect. *Pinguicula*; France (Cors.)

crassifolia Zamudio 1988; sect. *Longitubus*;
  Mex.

crenatiloba A. DC. 1844; sect. *Temnoceras*;
  Mex.–Pan.

crystallina Sibth. & Sm. 1806; sect. *Cardiophyllum*; Turk., Cyp.
  – subsp. *hirtiflora* (Ten.) Strid 1991; Med.
    SE Eur.

cubensis Urquiola & Casper 2003; sect. *Agnata*;
  Cuba

cyclosecta Casper 1963; sect. *Orcheosanthus*;
  Mex.

debbertiana Speta & F. Fuchs 1992; sect. *Crassifolia*; Mex.

dertosensis (Cañig.) G. Mateo Sanz & M. B.
  Crespo Villalba 1995 = *longifolia* subsp.
  dertosensis

diversifolia Cuatrec. 1945 = *elongata*

ehlersiae Speta & F. Fuchs 1982; sect. *Crassifolia*; Mex.

elatior Michx. 1803 = *caerulea*

eliae Sennen 1936 = *grandiflora*

elizabethiae Zamudio 1999; sect. *Orcheosanthus*; Mex.

elongata Benj. 1847; sect. *Ampullipalatum*;
  Venez., Col.

emarginata Zamudio & Rzed. 1986; sect. *Temnoceras*; Mex.

esseriana B. Kirchn. 1981; sect. *Crassifolia*;
  Mex.

filifolia Wright ex Griseb. 1866; sect. *Agnata*;
  Cuba

fiorii Tammaro & Pace 1987 = *longifolia* subsp.
  reichenbachiana

flavescens Flörke ex Hoppe 1800 = *alpina*

floridensis Chapm. 1883 = *pumila*

fontiqueriana Romo, Peris & Stübing 1996 =
  vulgaris

gigantea H. Luhrs 1995; sect. *Agnata*; Mex.
  – 'Ayautla' D'Amato 1998

glandulosa Trautv. & Mey. 1856 = *variegata*

gracilis Zamudio 1992; sect. *Temnoceras*; Mex.

grandiflora Lam. 1789; sect. *Pinguicula*; W Eur.
  (Irel., France, Spain, Swed.), Moroc.
  – subsp. *rosea* (Mutel) Casper 1962; France

greenwoodii Cheek 1994; sect. *Homophyllum*;
  Mex.

gypsicola Brandegee 1911; sect. *Orcheosanthus*;
  Mex.

hellwegeri Murr 1897 = *leptoceras*

hemiepiphytica Zamudio & Rzed. 1991; sect.
  Longitubus; Mex.

heterophylla Benth. 1839; sect. *Heterophyllum*;
  Mex.

hintoniorum B. L. Turner 1994 = *ehlersiae*

hirtiflora Ten. 1836 = *crystallina* subsp.
  hirtiflora

'Huahuapan' (see *moranensis*)

huilensis Cuatrec. 1945 = *calyptrata*

×hybrida Wettst. 1919; [alpina × vulgaris]

ibarrae Zamudio 2004; sect. *Agnata*; Mex.

imitatrix Casper 1963; sect. *Heterophyllum*; Mex.

immaculata Zamudio & Lux 1992; sect. *Temnoceras*; Mex.

inaequilobata Sennen 1936 = *grandiflora*

infundibuliformis Casper 2003; sect. *Agnata*;
  Cuba

involuta Ruiz & Pav. 1798; sect. *Ampullipalatum*;
  Bol., Peru

ionantha R. K. Godfrey 1961; sect. *Isoloba*;
  U.S.A. (Fla.)

jackii Barnhart 1930; sect. *Homophyllum*; Cuba

jaraguana Casper 2003; sect. *Agnata*; Cuba

jaumavensis Debbert 1991; sect. *Crassifolia*;
  Mex.

jorgehintonii B. L. Turner 1994 = *rotundiflora*

kondoi Casper 1974; sect. *Heterophyllum*; Mex.

laeta Pant. 1873 = *crystallina* subsp. *hirtiflora*

lateciliata McVaugh & Mickel 1963 = *cyclosecta*

laueana Speta & F. Fuchs 1989; sect. *Longitubus*;
  Mex.

laxifolia H. Luhrs 1995; sect. *Orchioides*; Mex.

leptoceras Rchb. 1823; sect. *Pinguicula*; Alp.

'L'Hautil' L. Legendre & S. Lavayssiere 1993; [(*ehlersiae* × *moranensis*) × *moranensis*]

lignicola Barnhart 1920; sect. *Discoradix*; Cuba; epiphytic

lilacina Schltdl. & Cham. 1830; sect. *Isoloba*; Mex., Central Am. (Belize, Guat.)

longifolia Ram. ex DC. 1805; sect. *Pinguicula*; France, Spain

– subsp. *caussensis* Casper 1962; France

– subsp. *dertosensis* (Cañig.) J. Schlauer 1994; Spain

– subsp. *reichenbachiana* (Schindler) Casper 1962; France, Ital.

louisii Markgr. 1926 = *crystallina* subsp. *hirtiflora*

lusitanica L. 1753; sect. *Isoloba*; W Eur., NW Afr. (Alger., Moroc.)

lutea Walter 1788; sect. *Isoloba*; SE U.S.A.

macroceras Link 1820; sect. *Pinguicula*; arct. Pacific nations: Can., U.S.A., Jap., Russ. (Kuril Is., Kamtch.)

– subsp. *nortensis* J. Steiger & H. Rondeau 1997; U.S.A. (N Calif., Ore., Wash.)

macrophylla Kunth 1817; sect. *Orcheosanthus*; Mex.

macrostyla Benj. 1847 = *involuta*

martinezii Zamudio 2004; sect. *Agnata*; Mex.

medusina Zamudio & Studnicka 2000 = *heterophylla*

merinoana Sennen 1936 = *grandiflora*

mesophytica Zamudio 1997; sect. *Orcheosanthus*; Central Am. (Guat., Hond., El Salv.)

mexicana Bonpl. ex Casper 1966 = *moranensis*

mirandae Zamudio & Salinas 1996; sect. *Heterophyllum*; Mex.

'Mitla' hort. A. Slack 1986; [*gypsicola* × *moranensis*]

moctezumae Zamudio & R. Ortega 1994; sect. *Orcheosanthus*; Mex.

moranensis Kunth 1817; sect. *Orcheosanthus*; Mex.

– 'Huahuapan' hort. A. Slack 1986

mundi Blanca, M. Jamilena, Ruiz Rejon & R. Zamora 1996; sect. *Pinguicula*; Spain

nevadensis (Lindbg.) Casper 1962; sect. *Pinguicula*; Spain

norica Beck 1912 = *vulgaris*

oblongiloba A. DC. 1844; sect. *Orcheosanthus*; Mex.

orchidioides A. DC. 1844; sect. *Orcheosanthus*; Mex., Guat.

parvifolia Robinson 1894; sect. *Heterophyllum*; Mex.

pilosa Luhrs, Studnicka & Gluch 2004; sect. *Agnata*; Mex.

planifolia Chapm. 1897; sect. *Isoloba*; U.S.A. (Fla., Miss.)

poldinii J. Steiger & Casper 2001; sect. *Pinguicula*; Ital.

potosiensis Speta & F. Fuchs 1989; sect. *Orcheosanthus*; Mex.

primuliflora C. E. Wood & R. K. Godfrey 1957; sect. *Isoloba*; SE U.S.A.

pumila Michx. 1803; sect. *Isoloba*; SE U.S.A., Baham.

ramosa Miyoshi ex Yatabe 1890; sect. *Micranthus*; Jap.

rectifolia Speta & F. Fuchs 1989; sect. *Orcheosanthus*; Mex.

reichenbachiana Schindler 1908 = *longifolia* subsp. *reichenbachiana*

reticulata F. Fuchs ex J. Schlauer 1991; sect. *Heterophyllum*; Mex.

reuteri Genty 1891 = *grandiflora*

rosei W. Watson 1911 = *moranensis*

rotundiflora Studnicka 1985; sect. *Heterophyllum*; Mex.

scopulorum Brandegee 1908 = *lilacina*

×*scullyi* Druce 1922; [*grandiflora* × *vulgaris*]

sharpii Casper & Kondo 1977; sect. *Isoloba*; Mex.

sibirica Vest ex A. DC. 1841 = *alpina*

sodalium F. Muell. ex E. Fourn. 1873 = *moranensis*

stolonifera H. Luhrs 1995 = *orchidoides*

submediterranea Blanca, M. Jamilena, Ruiz Rejón & R. Zamora 1996 = *longifolia* subsp. *dertosensis*

takakii Zamudio & Rzed. 1986; sect. *Isoloba*; Mex.

Pinguicula continued

'Titan' L. Song 2001; [*agnata × macrophylla*]

utricularioides Zamudio & Rzed. 1991; sect. *Longitubus*; Mex.; known only from herbarium specimen

vallisneriifolia Webb 1853; sect. *Pinguicula*; Spain

variegata Turcz. 1840; sect. *Micranthus*; Russ. (E Sib.)

villosa L. 1753; sect. *Nana*; N Euras., Can., U.S.A. (Alaska)

vulgaris L. 1753; sect. *Pinguicula*; Euras., N Am.
 – var. floribunda S. Watanabe & A. Takeda 1997 = *macroceras*

zecheri Speta & F. Fuchs 1982; sect. *Orcheosanthus*; Mex.

Pleurozia Dumort. 1835 (about 12 species in total) (Pleuroziaceae)

purpurea Lindb. 1877; coastal regions of Norw., Scotl., Irel.

Polypompholyx Lehm. 1844 = *Utricularia* subgen. *Polypompholyx* (Lentibulariaceae)

Roridula L. 1764: bug plant (Roridulaceae)

×*brachysepala* Gand. 1913; [*dentata × gorgonias*]

crinita Gand. 1913 = *gorgonias*

dentata L. 1753; Cape

gorgonias Planch. 1848; Cape

verticilliata (L.) Pers. 1815 = *dentata*

Sarracenia L. 1753: North American pitcher plant (Sarraceniaceae)

acuta Raf. 1840 = *rubra* subsp. *rubra*

adunca Sm. 1804 = *minor*

×*ahlesii* C. R. Bell & Case 1956; [*alata × rubra*]; U.S.A. (Ala., Miss.)

alabamensis Case & R. B. Case 1974 = *rubra* subsp. *alabamensis*
 – subsp. wherryi Case & R. B. Case 1976 = *rubra* subsp. *wherryi*

alata (A. W. Wood) A. W. Wood 1863; U.S.A. (Ala., La., Miss., Tex.)

×*areolata* Macfarl. 1917; [*leucophylla × alata*]; U.S.A. (Ala., Miss.)

calceolata Nutt. 1834 = *psittacina*

×*catesbaei* Elliott 1824; [*flava × purpurea*]; U.S.A. (Ala., Fla., Ga., N.C., S.C., Va.)

×*chelsonii* auct. non hort. Veitch ex Wilson: Mast. 1880; [*purpurea × rubra*]; U.S.A. (Ala., Fla., Ga., N.C., S.C.)

×*courtii* hort. Veitch ex Wilson 1881; [*purpurea × psittacina*]; U.S.A. (Ala., Fla., Ga., Miss.)

drummondii Croom 1848 = *leucophylla*

×*excellens* hort. G. Nicholson 1885; [*leucophylla × minor*]; U.S.A. (Fla., Ga.)

×exculta hort. Savage Garden 1885 = ×*moorei*

×*exornata* hort. Savage Garden 1885; [*purpurea × alata*]; U.S.A. (Ala., Miss.)

×*farnhamii* hort. Farnham 1892; [*leucophylla × rubra*]; U.S.A. (Fla.)

flava L. 1753; U.S.A. (N.C., S.C., Va.)
 – var. *atropurpurea* (hort. Bull) C. R. Bell 1949; U.S.A. (Fla., N.C., S.C.)
 – var. catesbaei C. Mohr 1897 = *oreophila*
 – var. *cuprea* D. E. Schnell 1998; U.S.A. (Fla., N.C., S.C.)
 – var. *maxima* hort. Bull ex Mast. 1881; U.S.A. (Fla., N.C., S.C.)
 – var. media Macfarl. 1908 = *flava* var. *maxima*
 – var. oreophila Kearney 1900 = *oreophila*
 – var. ornata hort. Bull ex Mast. 1881; U.S.A. (Fla., N.C., S.C.)
 – var. *rubricorpora* D. E. Schnell 1998; U.S.A. (Fla.)
 – var. *rugelii* (Shuttlew. ex A. DC.) Mast. 1881; U.S.A. (Fla., Ga.)

×*formosa* hort. Veitch ex Mast. 1881; [*minor × psittacina*]; U.S.A. (Fla., Ga.)

gibbosa Raf. 1840 = *purpurea*

×*gilpinii* C. R. Bell & Case 1956; [*rubra × psittacina*]; U.S.A. (Ala., Fla., Ga., Miss.)

gronovii A. W. Wood 1861 = *alata, flava, leucophylla, rubra*

×*harperi* C. R. Bell 1952; [*flava × minor*]; U.S.A. (Fla., Ga., N.C., S.C.)

heterophylla Eaton 1824 = *purpurea* f. *heterophylla*

jonesii Wherry 1929 = *rubra* subsp. *jonesii*

laciniata Kerner 1888 = *leucophylla*

lacunosa Bartr. 1794 = *leucophylla, minor*

leucophylla Raf. 1817; U.S.A. (Ala., Fla., Ga.)

×*maddisoniana* hort. Savage Garden 1885 = ×*formosa*

media Bartr. ex Macfarl. 1908 = *rubra*

minor Walter 1788; U.S.A. (Fla., Ga., N.C., S.C.)
 – var. *okefenokeensis* D. E. Schnell 2002; U.S.A. (Ga.)

×*mitchelliana* hort. ex G. Nicholson 1885; [*leucophylla* × *purpurea*]; U.S.A. (Ala., Fla., Ga., Miss.)

×*moorei* hort. Veitch ex Mast. 1874; [*flava* × *leucophylla*]; U.S.A. (Ala., Fla., Ga.)

nutans (Benth.) D. Dietr. 1843 = *Heliamphora nutans*

*oreophila** (Kearney) Wherry 1933; U.S.A. (Ala., Ga., N.C.)

parviflora Raf. 1840 = *purpurea* subsp. *venosa*

×*popei* hort. Moore ex Mast. 1881; [*flava* × *rubra*]; U.S.A. (Ala., Fla., Ga., N.C., S.C.)

psittacina Michx. 1803; U.S.A. (Ala., Fla., Ga., La., Miss.)

pulchella Croom 1834 = *psittacina*

purpurea L. 1753; Can., E U.S.A.
 – var. *burkii* D. E. Schnell 1993; U.S.A. (Gulf Coast: Ala., Fla., Ga.)
 – subsp. gibbosa Wherry 1933 = *purpurea*
 – f. *heterophylla* (Eaton) Fernald 1922; Can. (Newfoundl., Nova Scotia), U.S.A. (Mich., N.J., N.Y., Va.)
 – f. *incisa* J. Rousseau & Rouleau 1957 = *purpurea*
 – f. *luteola* Hanrahan & Miller 1998; U.S.A. (Ala.)
 – var. *montana* D. E. Schnell & Determann 1997; U.S.A. (Ga., N.C., S.C.)
 – f. plena (Klawe) Erskine 1955 = *purpurea*
 – var. ripicola B. Boivin 1951 = *purpurea*
 – var. stolonifera Macfarl. 1933 = *purpurea*
 – var. terrae-novae Bach. Pyl. 1827 = *purpurea*
 – var. typica Macfarl. 1908 = *purpurea*
 – subsp. *venosa* (Raf.) Wherry 1933; U.S.A. (N.J., Va., Ga., N.C., S.C.)
 – var. venosa (Raf.) Fernald 1936 = *purpurea*

×*readii* C. R. Bell 1952; [*leucophylla* × *rubra*]; U.S.A. (Ala., Fla., Ga., Miss.)

×*rehderi* C. R. Bell 1952; [*minor* × *rubra*]; U.S.A. (Fla., Ga., N.C., S.C.)

rosea Naczi, Case & R. B. Case 1999 = *purpurea* var. *burkii*

rubra Walter 1788; U.S.A. (Ga., N.C., S.C.)
 – subsp. *alabamensis** (Case & R. B. Case) D. E. Schnell 1978; U.S.A. (Ala.)
 – subsp. *gulfensis* D. E. Schnell 1979; U.S.A. (Fla.)
 – subsp. *jonesii** (Wherry) Wherry 1972; U.S.A. (N.C., S.C.)
 – subsp. *wherryi* (Case & R. B. Case) D. E. Schnell 1978; U.S.A. (Ala., Miss.)

rugelii Shuttlew. ex A. DC. 1873 = *flava* var. *rugelii*

sledgei Macfarl. 1908 = *alata*

×*swaniana* W. J. Rob. 1833; [*minor* × *purpurea*]; U.S.A. (Fla., Ga., N.C., S.C.)

×*tolliana* G. Nicholson 1887 = ×*moorei*

undulata Decne. 1852 = *leucophylla*

variolaris Michx. 1803 = *minor*

venosa Raf. 1840 = *purpurea* subsp. *venosa*

×*williamsii* hort. Bull ex Mast. 1874 = ×*catesbaei*

×*wrigleyana* hort. Savage Garden 1887; [*leucophylla* × *psittacina*]; U.S.A. (Ala., Fla., Ga., Miss.)

Sondera Lehm. 1844 = *Drosera* subgen. *Ergaleium* (Droseraceae)

Triphyophyllum Airy Shaw 1952: hookleaf (Dioncophyllaceae)

peltatum (Hutch. & Dalz.) Airy Shaw 1952; Ivory C., Liber., Sierra Leo.

Utricularia L. 1753: bladderwort (Lentibulariaceae)

aberrans Bosser 1958 = *welwitschii*

adpressa Salzm. ex A. St.-Hil. & Girard 1838; sect. *Oligocista*; Central Am.–Braz.

affinis Wight 1849 = *uliginosa*

afromontana R. E. Fries 1924 = *livida*

alata Benj. 1845 = *bifida*

albiflora R. Br. 1810; sect. *Pleiochasia*; NE Austral. (Queensl.)

albina Ridl. 1923 = *caerulea*

albocaerulea Dalz. 1851; sect. *Oligocista*; Ind.

Utricularia continued

alpina Jacq. 1763; sect. *Orchidoides*; Antilles, north. S Am.

alutacea Tutin 1934 = *amethystina*

amazonasana Steyerm. 1953 = *hydrocarpa*

amethystina Salzm. ex A. St.-Hil. & Girard 1838; sect. *Foliosa*; trop.–subtrop. Central–S Am.

amoena Pilg. 1914 = *myriocista*

andicola Benj. 1847 = *livida*

andongensis Welw. ex Hiern. 1900; sect. *Oligocista*; trop. Afr.

angolensis Kamienski 1902 = *subulata*

angulosa Poir. 1808 = *juncea*

angustifolia Benj. 1847 = *hispida*

anomala A. St.-Hil. & Girard 1838 = *gibba*

antennifera P. Taylor 1986; sect. *Pleiochasia*; W Austral.

anthropophora Rid. 1915 = *striatula*

aphylla Ruiz & Pav. 1798 = *gibba*

appendiculata E. A. Bruce 1934; sect. *Oliveria*; Afr., Madag.

arcuata Wight 1849; sect. *Oligocista*; Ind.

arenaria A. DC. 1844; sect. *Calpidisca*; trop.–south. Afr., Madag., Ind.

arenicola Tutin 1934 = *nana*

arnhemica P. Taylor 1986; sect. *Pleiochasia*; N Austral.

asplundii P. Taylor 1975; sect. *Orchidoides*; Col., Ecua.

aurea Lour. 1790; sect. *Utricularia*; Ind.–Jap., Austral.

aureola Blake 1917 = *adpressa*

aureolimba Steyerm. 1953 = *adpressa*

aureomaculata Steyerm. 1953; sect. *Steyermarkia*; Venez.

australis R. Br. 1810; sect. *Utricularia*; Euras., S Afr., Austral.

ayacuchae Steyerm. 1953 = *cucullata*

babui S. R. Yadav, Sardesai & Gaikwad 2005; sect. *Oligocista*; Ind.

baldwinii Steyerm. 1952 = *hispida*

bangweolensis R. E. Fries 1916 = *reflexa*

baoulensis A. Chev. 1912 = *foveolata*

barbata R. Br. 1810 = *chrysantha*

baueri R. Br. 1810 = *biloba*

baumii Kamienski 1902 = *spiralis*

beaugleholei Gassin 1993; sect. *Pleiochasia*; SE Austral. (Vict.)

benjaminiana Oliv. 1860; sect. *Utricularia*; Afr., Madag., Central–north. S Am.

benthamii P. Taylor 1986; sect. *Pleiochasia*; SW Austral.

bicolor A. St.-Hil. & Girard 1838 = *amethystina*

bifida L. 1753; sect. *Oligocista*; SE Asia (Ind.–Jap.), Austral.

bifidocalcar Good 1924 = *gibba*

biflora Lam. 1791 = *gibba*

billardieri F. Muell. 1868 = *dichotoma*

biloba R. Br. 1810; sect. *Nelipus*; SE Austral.

biovularioides (Kuhlm.) P. Taylor 1986; sect. *Utricularia*; Braz.

bipartita Elliott 1816 = *gibba*

bisquamata Schrank 1824; sect. *Calpidisca*; S Afr., Madag.

blanchetii A. DC. 1844; sect. *Aranella*; Braz.

bolivarana Steyerm. 1953 = *amethystina*

bosminifera Ostenf. 1906; sect. *Oligocista*; Thail.

botecudorum A. St.-Hil. & Girard 1838 = *foliosa*

brachiata (Wight) Oliv. 1859; sect. *Phyllaria*; Him.

brachyceras Schltr. 1899 = *bisquamata*

bracteata Good 1924; sect. *Nigrescentes*; S Afr.

bradei Markgr. 1955 = *subulata*

bramadensis Merl 1923 = *longifolia*

bremii Heer 1830; sect. *Utricularia*; central–W Eur.

brevicaulis Benj. 1847 = *bifida*

brevicornis Celak. 1886 = *ochroleuca*

brevilabris Lace 1915 = *minutissima*

breviscapa Wright ex Griseb. 1866; sect. *Utricularia*; Antilles, S Am.

buntingiana P. Taylor 1975; sect. *Orchidoides*; Venez.

butanensis Merl ex Luetzelb. 1923 = *foliosa*

caerulea L. 1753; sect. *Nigrescentes*; SE Asia (Ind.–Jap.), Madag., Austral.

calliphysa Stapf 1914 = *minutissima*

calumpitensis Llanos 1851 = *aurea*

calycifida Benj. 1847; sect. *Psyllosperma*; Venez., Guai., Surinam, Braz.

campbelliana Oliv. 1887; sect. *Orchidoides*;
   Venez., Guai., Braz.

canacorum Pellegr. 1920 = *dichotoma*

capensis Spreng. 1824 = *bisquamata*

capilliflora F. Muell. 1890; sect. *Pleiochasia*;
   N Austral.

cavalerii Stapf 1910 = *caerulea*

cearana Steyerm. 1952 = *erectiflora*

cecilii P. Taylor 1984; sect. *Oligocista*; Ind.

cervicornuta H. Perrier 1955 = *benjaminiana*

chamissonis G. Weber ex Benj. 1847 = *tricolor*

charnleyensis W. Fitzg. 1918 = *caerulea*

charoidea Stapf 1906 = *reflexa*

cheiranthos P. Taylor 1986; sect. *Pleiochasia*;
   N Austral.

chiakiana Komiya & C. Shibata 1997; sect.
   Utricularia; Venez.

chiribiquetensis A. Fernandez 1964; sect. *Oligocista*; Col., Venez.

choristotheca P. Taylor 1986; sect. *Choristothecae*; Surinam

christopheri P. Taylor 1986; sect. *Phyllaria*;
   Him.

chrysantha R. Br. 1810; sect. *Enskide*; New G.,
   NW Austral.

circumvoluta P. Taylor 1986; sect. *Oligocista*;
   N Austral.

clandestina Nutt. ex A. Gray 1848 = *geminiscapa*

cleistogama Britton 1889 = *subulata*

coccinea Benj. 1847 = *hydrocarpa*

colensoi Hook. f. 1853 = *dichotoma*

colorata Benj. 1847 = *laxa*

concinna N. E. Br. 1901 = *jamesoniana*

congesta Steyerm. 1953 = *simulans*

connellii N. E. Br. 1901 = *pubescens*

cornuta Michx. 1803; sect. *Stomoisia*; N Am.,
   Baham., Cuba

corynephora P. Taylor 1986; sect. *Phyllaria*;
   Myanmar, Thail.

costata P. Taylor 1986; sect. *Aranella*; Venez.,
   Braz.

cucullata A. St.-Hil. & Girard 1838; sect. *Vesiculina*; S Am.

cuspidata Steyerm. 1953 = *calycifida*

cutleri Steyerm. 1953 = *viscosa*

cyanea R. Br. 1819 = *uliginosa*

cymbantha Welw. ex Oliv. 1865; sect. *Utricularia*; trop.–S Afr.

damazioi Beauverd 1907 = *amethystina*

dawsonii Steyerm. 1953 = *amethystina*

deightonii F. E. Lloyd & G. Taylor 1947 = *pubescens*

delicata Kamienski 1902 = *bisquamata*

delicatula Cheeseman 1906; sect. *Australes*;
   New Zeal.

delphinioides Thorel ex Pellegr. 1920; sect.
   Oligocista; Indoch., Thail.

denticulata Benj. 1847 = *livida*

determannii P. Taylor 1986; sect. *Choristothecae*;
   Surinam

dichotoma Labill. 1804; sect. *Pleiochasia*;
   Austral.

dimorphantha Makino 1906; sect. *Utricularia*;
   Jap.

diploglossa Welw. ex Oliver 1865 = *reflexa*

dissectifolia Merl ex Luetzelb. 1923 = *flaccida*

dregei Kamienski 1902 = *livida*

dunlopii P. Taylor 1986; sect. *Pleiochasia*; NW
   Austral.

dunstaniae F. E. Lloyd 1936; sect. *Pleiochasia*;
   NW Austral.

dusenii Sylven 1909 = *nephrophylla*

eburnea R. E. Fries 1916 = *livida*

ecklonii Spreng. 1827 = *bisquamata*

elachista Goebel 1891 = *uliginosa*

elephas Luetzelb. 1910 = *cucullata*

elevata Kamienski 1902 = *livida*

emarginata Benj. 1847 = *gibba*

endresii Rchb. f. 1874; sect. *Orchidoides*; Costa
   Rica, Pan., Col., Ecua.

engleri Kamienski 1902 = *livida*

equiseticaulis Blatter & McCann 1931 =
   graminifolia

erectiflora A. St.-Hil. & Girard 1838; sect. *Oligocista*; Central Am.–Braz.

evrardii Pellegr. 1930 = *minutissima*

exigua Merl ex Luetzelb. 1923 = *subulata*

exoleta R. Br. 1810 = *gibba*

falcata Good 1924 = *tortilis*

fernaldiana F. E. Lloyd & G. Taylor 1820 =
   pubescens

fibrosa Walter 1788 = *gibba*

Utricularia continued

filiformis Roem. & Schult. 1817 = *subulata*

fimbriata Kunth 1818; sect. *Aranella*; Venez.,
Col.

firmula Welw. ex Oliv. 1865; sect. *Calpidisca*;
trop.–S Afr., Madag.

fistulosa P. Taylor 1986; sect. *Pleiochasia*; NW
Austral.

flaccida A. DC. 1844; sect. *Setiscapella*; Braz.

flava R. Br. 1810 = *chrysantha*

flexuosa Vahl 1804 = *aurea*

floridana Nash 1896; sect. *Utricularia*; SE
U.S.A.

fluitans Ridl. 1912 = *punctata*

fockeana Miq. 1850 = *hydrocarpa*

foliosa L. 1753; sect. *Utricularia*; SE U.S.A.,
Carib., Central to S Am., Afr., Madag.

fontana A. St.-Hil. & Girard 1838 = *tricolor*

forgetiana Sander 1897 = *longifolia*

forrestii P. Taylor 1986; sect. *Phyllaria*; W
China, Burma

foveolata Edgew. 1847; sect. *Oligocista*; trop.
Afr.–Asia, Austral.

fulva F. Muell. 1858; sect. *Enskide*; NW
Austral.

furcata Pers. 1805 = *gibba*

furcellata Oliv. 1859; sect. *Phyllaria*; Ind.

fusiformis Warm. 1874 = *tricolor*

galloprovincialis J. Gay ex Webb 1876 =
australis

garrettii P. Taylor 1986; sect. *Phyllaria*; Thail.

gayana A. DC. 1844 = *gibba*

geminiloba Benj. 1847; sect. *Iperua*; Braz.

geminiscapa Benj. 1847; sect. *Utricularia*; E
Can., E U.S.A.

genliseoides Benj. 1847 = *amethystina*

gentryi Standl. 1940 = *livida*

geoffrayi Pellegr. 1920; sect. *Meionula*; Indoch.

georgei P. Taylor 1986; sect. *Pleiochasia*; NW
Austral.

gibba L. 1753; sect. *Utricularia*; worldwide in
tropics and subtropics

gibbsiae Stapf 1906 = *scandens*

giletii Wildem. & Th. Dur. 1900 = *benjaminiana*

glazioviana Warm. 1911 = *neottioides*

globulariifolia Mart. ex Benj. 1847 = *tricolor*

glueckii Luetzelb. 1910 = *hispida*

goebelii Merl ex Luetzelb. 1923 = *purpureocaerulea*

gomezii A. DC. 1844 = *tricolor*

graminifolia Vahl 1804; sect. *Oligocista*; Ind.,
Sri Lanka, Thail., China

grandivesiculosa Czech 1952 = *reflexa*

graniticola A. Cheval. 1917 = *pubescens*

guyanensis A. DC. 1844; sect. *Stylotheca*; Central–S Am.

gyrans Suesseng. 1951 = *tortilis*

hamiltonii F. E. Lloyd 1936; sect. *Pleiochasia*;
N Austral.

harlandi Oliver ex Benth. 1861 = *striatula*

helix P. Taylor 1986; sect. *Pleiochasia*; SW
Austral.

herzogii Luetzelb. 1909 = *neottioides*

heterochroma Steyerm. 1953; sect. *Mirabiles*;
Venez.

heterosepala Benj. 1847; sect. *Oligocista*; Philip.

hians A. DC. 1844 = *prehensilis*

hintonii P. Taylor 1986; sect. *Psyllosperma*; Mex.

hirta Klein ex Link 1820; sect. *Meionula*; Ind.,
SE Asia

hirtella A. St.-Hil. & Girard 1838 = *amethystina*

hispida Lam. 1791; sect. *Psyllosperma*; Mex.–
Braz.

hoehnei Kuhlm. 1923 = *warmingii*

holtzei F. Muell. 1893; sect. *Pleiochasia*; N
Austral.

hookeri Lehm. 1844 = *inaequalis*

humboldtii R. H. Schomb. 1841; sect. *Iperua*;
Venez., Braz., Guia.

huntii P. Taylor 1986; sect. *Psyllosperma*; Braz.

hydrocarpa Vahl 1804; sect. *Utricularia*; trop.
Am.

hydrocotyloides F. E. Lloyd & G. Taylor 1947 =
pubescens

ibarensis Baker 1885 = *livida*

imerinensis H. Perrier 1955 = *reflexa*

inaequalis A. DC. 1844; sect. *Pleiochasia*; SW
Austral.

incerta Kamienski 1902 = *australis*

incisa (A. Rich.) Alain 1956; sect. *Utricularia*;
Cuba

inflata Walter 1788; sect. *Utricularia*; U.S.A.

inflexa Forssk. 1775; sect. *Utricularia*; Afr.,
    Madag., Ind.
intermedia Hayne 1800; sect. *Utricularia*; N
    Euras., Can., N U.S.A.
involvens Ridl. 1895; sect. *Oligocista*; SE Asia,
    N Austral.
jackii J.Parn. 2005; sect. *Oligocista*; Thail.
jamesoniana Oliv. 1860; sect. *Orchidoides*;
    Antilles, Central Am.
janarthanamii S. R. Yadav, Sardesai & Gaikwad
    2000; sect. *Oligocista*; Ind.
jankae Velen. 1886 = *australis*
janthina Hook. f. 1896 = *reniformis*
japonica Makino 1914 = *australis*
jaquatibensis Merl ex Luetzelb. 1923 = *longi-
    folia*
juncea Vahl 1804; sect. *Stomoisia*; N–Central
    Am., W Afr.
kaieteurensis Steyerm. 1948 = *amethystina*
kalmaloensis A. Cheval. 1932 = *gibba*
kamienskii F. Muell. 1893; sect. *Pleiochasia*;
    N Austral.
kenneallyi P. Taylor 1986; sect. *Pleiochasia*; NW
    Austral.
kerrii Craib 1911 = *caerulea*
khasiana J. Joseph & J. Mani 1983 = *gibba*
kimberleyensis C. A. Gardner 1930; sect. *Pleio-
    chasia*; NW Austral.
kirkii Stapf 1904 = *arenaria*
kuhlmanni Merl 1915 = *trichophylla*
kumaonensis Oliv. 1859; sect. *Phyllaria*; Him.
laciniata A. St.-Hil. & Girard 1838; sect.
    Aranella; Braz.
lagoensis Warm. 1874 = *breviscapa*
lasiocaulis F. Muell. 1885; sect. *Pleiochasia*;
    N Austral., Tasm.
lateriflora R. Br. 1810; sect. *Australes*; SE
    Austral.
lawsonii F. E. Lloyd 1936 = *biloba*
laxa A. St.-Hil. & Girard 1838; sect. *Oligocista*;
    Arg., Urug., Parag., Braz.
lazulina P. Taylor 1984; sect. *Oligocista*; Ind.
lehmanni Benj. 1845 = *bisquamata*
leptoplectra F. Muell. 1885; sect. *Nelipus*; NW
    Austral.
leptorhyncha O. Schwarz 1927; sect. *Pleiochasia*;
    NW Austral.

letestui P. Taylor 1989; sect. *Oligocista*; C Afr.
    Rep.
lilacina Griff. 1854 = *uliginosa*
lilliput Pellegr. 1920 = *minutissima*
limosa R. Br. 1810; sect. *Nelipus*; SE Asia, N
    Austral.
linarioides Welw. ex Oliver 1865 = *welwitschii*
lindmanii Sylven 1909 = *amethystina*
livida E. Mey. 1837; sect. *Calpidisca*; trop.–S
    Afr., Madag., Mex.
lloydii Merl ex F. E. Lloyd 1932; sect. *Oligocista*;
    S Am.
lobata Fernald 1904 = *livida*
longecalcarata Benj. 1847 = *livida*
longeciliata A. DC. 1844; sect. *Aranella*; Col.,
    Venez., Braz., Guai., Surinam
longifolia Gardner 1842; sect. *Psyllosperma*;
    Braz.
luetzelburgii Merl ex Luetzelb. 1923 = *pocon-
    ensis*
lundii A. DC. 1844 = *praelonga*
macerrima S. F. Blake 1917 = *hispida*
macrocheilos (P. Taylor) P. Taylor 1986; sect.
    Oligocista; trop. W Afr.
macrophylla Masam. & Syozi 1944 = *uliginosa*
macrorhiza J. Le Conte 1824; sect. *Utricularia*;
    N Am., E Asia
macrorhyncha Barnhart 1898 = *gibba*
madagascariensis A. DC. 1844 = *livida*
magnavesica Good 1924 = *reflexa*
magnifica Pilg. 1914 = *myriocista*
maguirei Steyerm. 1948 = *calycifida*
mairii Cheeseman 1906 = *protrusa*
malabarica Janarth. & A. N. Henry 1989; sect.
    Oligocista; Ind.
malmeana Sylven 1909 = *cucullata*
mannii Oliv. 1865; sect. *Chelidon*; Guin.,
    Camer., Nig.
marcelliana Merl ex Luetzelb. 1923 = *subulata*
mauroyae H. Perrier 1955 = *livida*
maxima G. Weber ex Benj. 1847 = *reniformis*
menziesii R. Br. 1810; sect. *Pleiochasia*; SW
    Austral.
meyeri Pilg. 1901; sect. *Oligocista*; Braz.
micrantha Benj. 1847 = *erectiflora*
microcalyx (P. Taylor) P. Taylor 1971; sect. *Calp-
    idisca*; trop. Afr. (Congo, N Zambia)

Utricularia continued

micropetala Sm. 1819; sect. *Oligocista*; trop. W Afr.

minima Warm. 1874 = *olivacea*

minor L. 1753; sect. *Utricularia*; N Am. & Euras.

minutissima J. Vahl 1804; sect. *Meionula*; Ind.–Jap., Austral.

mirabilis P. Taylor 1986; sect. *Mirabiles*; Venez.

mixta Barnhart 1920 = *foliosa*

modesta A. DC. 1844 = *amethystina*

monanthos Hook. f. 1860; sect. *Pleiochasia*; S Austral., Tasman., New Zeal.

moniliformis P. Taylor 1986; sect. *Phyllaria*; Sri Lanka

monophylla Dinter 1928 = *arenaria*

montana Jacq. 1763 = *alpina*

moorei F. E. Lloyd 1936 = *dichotoma*

muelleri Kamienski 1894; sect. *Utricularia*; Austral., New Guin.

multicaulis Oliv. 1859; sect. *Phyllaria*; Him.

multifida R. Br. 1810; sect. *Polypompholyx*; SW Austral.

muricata Weber 1894 = *breviscapa*

muscosa Benj. 1847 = *calycifida*

mutata L. Leiner 1859 = *australis*

myriocista A. St.-Hil. & Girard 1838; sect. *Vesiculina*; S Am.

nagurai Makino 1913 = *gibba*

naikii S. R. Yadav, Sardesai & S. P. Gaikwad 2000; sect. *Oligocista*; Ind.

nana A. St.-Hil. & Girard 1838; sect. *Benjaminia*; Venez., Braz., Guai., Surinam, Parag.

naviculata P. Taylor 1967; sect. *Utricularia*; S Am.

nayarii Janarth. & A. N. Henry 1986 = *uliginosa*

nelumbifolia Gardner 1852; sect. *Iperua*; Braz.

neottioides A. St.-Hil. & Girard 1838; sect. *Avesicaria*; Braz., Venez., Col.

nepalensis Kitamura 1954 = *minor*

nephrophylla Benj. 1847; sect. *Iperua*; Braz.

nervosa G. Weber ex Benj. 1847; sect. *Setiscapella*; Col., Venez.

nigrescens Sylven 1909; sect. *Setiscapella*; Braz.

nigricaulis Ridl. 1908 = *minutissima*

nipponica Makino 1906 = *minutissima*

novae-zelandiae Hook. f. 1853; sect. *Pleiochasia*; New Zeal., New Caled.

obsoleta Merl ex Luetzelb. 1923 = *subulata*

obtusa Sw. 1788 = *gibba*

obtusiloba Benj. 1847 = *caerulea*

occidentalis A. Gray 1883 = *ochroleuca*

ochroleuca R. W. Hartm. 1857; sect. *Utricularia*; U.S.A., Can., Euras.

odontosepala Stapf 1912; sect. *Calpidisca*; trop. Afr.

odorata Pellegr. 1920; sect. *Oligocista*; SE Asia, N Austral.

ogmosperrna Blatter & McCann 1931 = *arcuata*

oligocista Benj. 1847 = *subulata*

olivacea Wright ex Griseb. 1866; sect. *Utricularia*; E U.S.A., Antilles, Central–S Am.

oliveriana Steyerm. 1953; sect. *Avesicaria*; Braz., Col., Venez.

ophirensis Ridl. 1895 = *caerulea*

orbiculata Wall. 1844 = *striatula*

orinocensis Steyerm. 1953 = *simulans*

osteni Hicken 1913 = *tridentata*

pachyceras O. Schwarz 1927 = *singeriana*

palatina G. Weber ex Benj. 1847 = *cucullata*

pallens A. St.-Hil. & Girard 1838 = *gibba*

panamensis Steyerm. ex P. Taylor 1986; sect. *Psyllosperma*; Pan.

papillosa Stapf 1916 = *pubescens*

parkeri Baker 1883 = *bisquamata*

parkeriana A. DC. 1844 = *gibba*

parthenopipes P. Taylor 1986; sect. *Aranella*; Braz.

pauciflora Blume 1826 = *gibba*

paulineae Lowrie 1998; sect. *Pleiochasia*; SW Austral.

peckii S. F. Blake 1917 = *guyanensis*

pectinata Splitg. ex De Vriese 1848 = *longeciliata*

peltata Spruce ex Oliver 1860 = *pubescens*

peltatifolia A. Cheval. & Pellegr. 1917 = *pubescens*

pentadactyla P. Taylor 1954; sect. *Calpidisca*; trop. Afr.

peranomala P. Taylor 1986; sect. *Kamienskia*; China

perpusilla A. DC. 1955 = *foveolata*

perversa P. Taylor 1986; sect. *Utricularia;* Braz.,
  Arg., Boliv., Mex.

petersoniae P. Taylor 1986; sect. *Psyllosperma;*
  Mex.

petertaylorii Lowrie 2002; sect. *Pleiochasia;* SW
  Austral.

philetas Good 1924 = *striatula*

physoceras P. Taylor 1986; sect. *Setiscapella;*
  Braz.

picta Warm. 1874 = *hispida*

pierrei Pellegr. 1920; sect. *Oligocista;* Indoch.

pilifera A. Chevalier 1912 = *reflexa*

pilosa (Makino) Makino 1897 = *aurea*

platensis Speg. 1899; sect. *Utricularia;* Braz.,
  Arg., Urug., Parag.

platyptera Stapf 1906 = *reflexa*

pobeguinii Pellegr. 1914; sect. *Oligocista;* Guin.

poconensis Fromm 1985; sect. *Utricularia;*
  Braz., Arg., Boliv.

podadena P. Taylor 1964; sect. *Candollea;* trop.
  Afr. (Malawi, Moz.)

pollichii F. Schultz 1871 = *australis*

polygaloides Edgew. 1847; sect. *Oligocista;* Ind.,
  Sri Lanka

polyschista Benj. 1847 = *praelonga*

porphyrophylla Wright ex Griseb. 1866 =
  incisa

praelonga A. St.-Hil. & Girard 1838; sect. *Psyllo-*
  sperma; S Braz., Parag., Arg.

praeterita P. Taylor 1983; sect. *Oligocista;* Ind.

praetermissa P. Taylor 1976; sect. *Orchidoides;*
  Central Am.

prehensilis E. Mey. 1837; sect. *Oligocista;* trop.–
  S Afr., Madag.

protrusa Hook. f. 1853 = *australis*

puberula Benj. 1847 = *pubescens*

pubescens Sm. 1819; sect. *Lloydia;* trop. Afr.,
  Ind., Central–S Am.

pulcherrima Sylven 1909 = *myriocista*

pulchra P. Taylor 1977; sect. *Phyllaria;* Indones.

pumila Benj. 1847 = *subulata*

punctata Wall. ex A. DC. 1844; sect. *Utricu-*
  laria; Myanmar–China, Born.

punctifolia Benj. 1847 = *amethystina*

purpurascens Graham 1839; sect. *Oligocista;*
  Ind.

purpurea Walter 1788; sect. *Vesiculina;* N–Central Am.

purpureocaerulea A. St.-Hil. & Girard 1838;
  sect. *Aranella;* Braz.

pusilla Vahl 1804; sect. *Setiscapella;* Antilles,
  Central–S Am.

pygmaea R. Br. 1810 = *minutissima*

quadricarinata Suesseng. 1951 = *prehensilis*

quelchii N. E. Br. 1901; sect. *Orchidoides;*
  Venez., Guai., Braz.

quinquedentata F. Muell. ex P. Taylor 1986;
  sect. *Pleiochasia;* N Austral.

radiata Small 1903; sect. *Utricularia;* E U.S.A.,
  Can. (Nova Scotia)

raynalii P. Taylor 1986; sect. *Utricularia;* trop.
  Afr.

reclinata Hassk. 1855 = *aurea*

recta P. Taylor 1986; sect. *Oligocista;* Ind.,
  Nepal, Bhutan, China

recurva Lour. 1790 = *bifida*

reflexa Oliv. 1865; sect. *Utricularia;* Afr.,
  Madag.

regnellii Sylven 1909 = *pubescens*

rehmannii Kamienski 1902 = *bisquamata*

reniformis A. St.-Hil. 1830; sect. *Iperua;* Braz.

resupinata B. D. Greene 1840; sect. *Lecticula;*
  E Can., E U.S.A., Cuba

reticulata Sm. 1805; sect. *Oligocista;* Ind.

rhododactylos P. Taylor 1986; sect. *Pleiochasia;*
  N Austral.

riccioides A. Chevalier 1912 = *gibba*

rigida Benj. 1847; sect. *Avesicarioides;* trop.
  W Afr.

robbinsii (A. W. Wood) A. W. Wood 1870 =
  macrorhiza

rogersiana Lace 1915 = *minor*

roraimensis N. E. Br. 1901 = *amethystina*

rosea Edgew. 1847 = *caerulea*

roseo-purpurea Stapf ex Gamble 1924 =
  caerulea

rosulata Benj. 1937 = *striatula*

rotundifolia Merl ex Luetzelb. 1923 = *tricolor*

rubra Larranaga 1923 = *tridentata*

rubricaulis Tutin 1934 = *guyanensis*

sacciformis Benj. 1847 = *australis*

Utricularia continued

salwinensis Hand.-Mazz. 1936; sect. *Phyllaria*;
China (Yunnan)

salzmanni A. St.-Hil. & Girard 1838 = *hydro-carpa*

sampathii K. Subramanyam & S. N. Yoganara-simhan 1981 = *caerulea*

sandersonii Oliv. 1865; sect. *Calpidisca*; S Afr.

sandwithii P. Taylor 1967; sect. *Aranella*;
Venez., Guai., Surinam, Braz.

sanguinea Oliver 1902 = *livida*

saudadensis Merl ex Luetzelb. 1923 = *gemini-loba*

scandens Benj. 1847; sect. *Oligocista*; trop.
Afr.–Asia

schimperi Schenk 1887 = *jamesoniana*

schinzii Kamienski 1902 = *bisquamata*

schultesii A. Fernandez 1964; sect. *Psyllo-sperma*; Col., Venez.

schweinfurthii Baker 1906 = *scandens*

sciaphila Tutin 1934 = *pubescens*

sclerocarpa Wright 1869 = *juncea*

secunda Benj. 1847 = *gibba*

selloi G. Weber ex Benj. 1847 = *amethystina*

sematophora Stapf 1907 = *livida*

siakujiiensis Nakajima 1948 = *australis*

siamensis Ostenfeld 1906 = *minutissima*

simplex R. Br. 1810; sect. *Australes*; SW Austral.

simulans Pilg. 1914; sect. *Aranella*; trop. Afr.,
trop. Am., Fla.

singeriana F. Muell. 1891; sect. *Pleiochasia*;
NW Austral.

sinuata Benj. 1847 = *livida*

smithiana Wight 1849; sect. *Oligocista*; Ind.

sootepensis Craib 1911 = *caerulea*

spartea Baker 1883 = *livida*

spatulifolia Pilg. 1914 = *amethystina*

spicata Sylven 1909 = *erectiflora*

spiralis Sm. 1819; sect. *Oligocista*; trop. Afr.

spirandra Wright ex Griseb. 1866 = *gibba*

sprengelii Kamienski 1902 = *bisquamata*

spruceana Benth. ex Oliv. 1860; sect. *Lecticula*;
Braz., Venez.

squamosa Benj. 1845 = *caerulea*

stanfieldii P. Taylor 1963; sect. *Setiscapella*;
trop. Afr.

steenisii P. Taylor 1986; sect. *Phyllaria*; Indones.
(Sum.)

stellaris L. f. 1781; sect. *Utricularia*; Afr.,
Madag., trop. Asia, Austral.

steyermarkii P. Taylor 1967; sect. *Steyermarkia*;
Venez.

stolonifera Benj. 1847 = *amethystina*

striata J. Le Conte ex Torr. 1819; sect. *Utricu-laria*; N Am.

striatula Sm. 1819; sect. *Phyllaria*; trop. Afr.–
SE Asia

stricticaulis Stapf ex Gamble 1924 = *poly-galoides*

stygia G. Thor 1988 = *ochroleuca*

subpeltata Steyerm. 1953 = *pubescens*

subramanyamii Janarth. & A. N. Henry 1989;
sect. *Oligocista*; Ind.

subrecta Lace 1915 = *graminifolia*

subsimilis Colenso 1884 = *dichotoma*

subulata L. 1753; sect. *Setiscapella*; worldwide
in subtropics and tropics

taikankoensis Yamamoto 1931 = *striatula*

tayloriana J. Joseph & J. Mani 1983 = *hirta*

tenella R. Br. 1810; sect. *Polypompholyx*; S
Austral.

tenerrima Merr. 1912 = *foveolata*

tenuicaulis Miki 1935 = *australis*

tenuifolia Benj. 1847 = *gibba*

tenuis Cav. 1799 = *gibba*

tenuiscapa Pilg. 1914 = *subulata*

tenuissima Tutin 1934; sect. *Martinia*; Antilles,
Braz., Col., Venez., Guai.

tepuiana Steyerm. 1953 = *amethystina*

ternata Sylven 1909 = *tridentata*

terrae-reginae P. Taylor 1986; sect. *Pleiochasia*;
NE Austral. (Queensl.)

tetraloba P. Taylor 1963; sect. *Avesicarioides*;
trop. W Afr.

thomasii F. E. Lloyd & G. Taylor 1947 =
pubescens

tinguensis Merl 1923 = *gibba*

tortilis Welw. ex Oliv. 1865; sect. *Oligocista*;
trop. Afr.

transrugosa Stapf 1904 = *livida*

tribracteata Hochst. ex A. Rich. 1851 = *are-naria*

trichophylla Spruce ex Oliv. 1860; sect. *Setiscapella*; Central–S Am.

trichoschiza Stapf 1906 = *stellaris*

tricolor A. St.-Hil. 1833; sect. *Foliosa*; S Am.

tricrenata Baker ex Hiern 1900 = *gibba*

tridactyla P. Taylor 1986; sect. *Pleiochasia*; NW Austral.

tridentata Sylven 1909; sect. *Foliosa*; S Am.

triflora P. Taylor 1986; sect. *Pleiochasia*; N Austral.

triloba Benj. 1847; sect. *Setiscapella*; Central–S Am.

trinervia Benj. 1847 = *amethystina*

triphylla Ule 1898 = *geminiloba*

troupinii P. Taylor 1971; sect. *Calpidisca*; trop. Afr. (Rwanda, Burundi)

tubulata F. Muell. 1875; sect. *Pleiochasia*; N Austral.

turumiquirensis Steyerm. 1953 = *amethystina*

uliginosa J. Vahl 1804; sect. *Oligocista*; Asia (China, Ind., Malays.), Austral.

uniflora R. Br. 1810; sect. *Pleiochasia*; SW Austral.

unifolia Ruiz & Pav. 1797; sect. *Orchidoides*; Central–S Am. (Andes)

uxoris Gómez-Laur. 2005; sect. *Orchidoides*; Costa Rica

vaga Griseb. 1866 = *hydrocarpa*

velascoensis Kuntze 1898 = *amethystina*

venezuelana Steyerm. 1953 = *pubescens*

verapazensis Morong 1893 = *jamesoniana*

verticillata Benj. 1847 = *limosa*

villosula Stapf 1906 = *benjaminiana*

violacea R. Br. 1810; sect. *Pleiochasia*; SE Austral.

virgatula Barnhart 1908 = *juncea*

viscosa Spruce ex Oliv. 1860; sect. *Sprucea*; Central–S Am.

vitellina Ridl. 1923; sect. *Oligocista*; Malays.

volubilis R. Br. 1810; sect. *Pleiochasia*; SW Austral.

vulcanica Colenso 1894 = *dichotoma*

vulgaris L. 1753; sect. *Utricularia*; Euras., N Afr.

warburgii Goebel 1891; sect. *Nigrescentes*; SE China

warmingii Kamienski 1894; sect. *Utricularia*; Braz., Venez., Boliv.

welwitschii Oliv. 1865; sect. *Calpidisca*; trop.– S Afr., Madag.

westonii P. Taylor 1986; sect. *Tridentaria*; SW Austral.

wightiana P. Taylor 1986; sect. *Oligocista*; Ind.

williamsii Steyerm. 1950 = *amethystina*

yakusimensis Masam. 1934 = *uliginosa*

Glossary

abaxial located on the side facing away from the stem axis, for example, the leaf underside

adaxial located on the side facing toward the stem axis, for example, the leaf upperside

adventitious roots roots that develop on the stem axis or leaves

alternate leaves leaves that emerge singly from each leaf node

angiosperms flowering plants; a derived major group of the higher plants that develop seeds enclosed within an ovary, in contrast to gymnosperms, which include the conifers

annual a plant that goes through its entire life cycle during the course of a year

anther the pollen-bearing tip of the male flower organ (stamen)

anthesis the period during flower development from the opening of the bud to the end of flowering

basal emerging from the base of an organ

bract subtending leaf in whose axil a flower develops

calyx outermost ring of a dual perianth, mostly consisting of green sepals

carpel in flowering plants, the carpels—either singly or fused together—form closed hollow cavities, the ovaries

chasmogamic open-flowered, accessible for cross-pollination; the opposite of *cleistogamic*

circinate rolled up in a tight coil with the leaf tip at its center

cleistogamic closed-flowered, subject to self-pollination; the opposite of *chasmogamic*

commensalism an association between two kinds of organisms in which one obtains food or other benefits without harming or benefiting the other

corolla inner ring of a dual perianth, consisting of petals

cosmopolitan having a worldwide, rather than a limited, distribution; the opposite of *endemic*

dimorphism the presence of two different forms in the same plant species

edaphic relating to the soil

endemic native to only a very restricted area; the opposite of *cosmopolitan*

endosperm the nutrient tissue in the plant seed

ephemeras short-lived plants

epiphyte a plant that grows on other plants, using them as a support but without deriving nutrition from them

form (f.) the lowest systematic category, below that of variety, including plants within a homogeneous group that generally differ from one another with respect to only one feature

furcate forked

gemmae fruit bodies emerging from the stipules and serving vegetative reproduction; found in pygmy sundews

genus (gen.; pl. genera) systematic category above that of the species; closely related species with common features are members of one genus

hibernacles see *turions*

hybrids plants originating from a cross between parents of different species

inflorescence the shoot or stem serving flower development; usually quite distinct from the vegetative part of the shoot or stem

internode the part of the shoot or stem axis that lies between two stem nodes

involute rolled inward

lamina see *leaf blade*

leaf axil the upper angle between the leaf and the stem or shoot

leaf blade (lamina) the mostly flat, widened part of the leaf

mimicry resemblence, in terms of coloration or form, of an animal or plant to its surroundings

neophyte a plant that has become established in an area in which it is not native

node the thickened part of a stem or shoot (leaf joint) from which a leaf emerges

olfactory relating to the sense of smell

opposite leaves two leaves emerging at the same level, or at the same or parallel nodes, on opposite sides of a shoot or stem

ovary the basal part of a pistil formed from one or (mostly) several carpels, whose hollow cavities contain the ovules

ovule the structure in the hollow cavity of an ovary containing the egg cell within the embryo sac; the ovule develops into the seed following fertilization

peltate shaped like a shield

perennial a plant that lives for more than 2 years and typically flowers annually

perianth the calyx and corolla of a flower, in which each flower-leaf (tepal) is the same size and color as neighboring tepals

peristome toothed, collarlike margin of pitfall traps, such as those in *Nepenthes, Cephalotus*

petals in flowers, the generally brightly colored modified leaves of the corolla

pistil the female reproductive organ of a flower; composed of one to several carpels, fused at their margins, and comprising the ovary, style, and stigma

reniform kidney-shaped

rhizome a shoot or stem that mostly grows underground and often bears roots; distinguished from roots by the presence of tiny scale leaves

savanna sandy and (during rainy seasons) wet grasslands in subtropical to tropical regions, dominated by grasses, sedges, and widely scattered trees (such as pine savanna)

sepals in flowers, the modified leaves of the calyx

species (sp.) the basic unit of the taxonomic system; includes all individuals whose essential features are the same and that can be crossed with one another

staminoids rudimentary, sterile stamens

stigma in flowering plants, the uppermost tip of the carpel, which receives pollen grains

stolon a prostrate or trailing stem that takes root and gives rise to plantlets at its apex or sometimes its nodes

style in flowers, the elongated stalk section between the ovary and the stigma

subspecies (subsp.) a systematic category below that of the species; designates a population of a particular geographic region genetically distinguishable from other such populations of the same species

synonym (syn.) an invalid plant name

taxon (pl. taxa) a systematic unit of any rank, such as genus or species

tentacles stalked glands

testa the seed coat

tuber a thickened stem or root

turgor cell internal pressure

turions dormant or winter buds (hibernacles)

umbraculate umbrella-shaped

variety (var.) a systematic category below subspecies; varieties within a species can be distinguished by a few features and are not geographically separated from one another

zonobiome a large, climatically uniform habitat; a climatic zone

zygomorphic bilaterally symmetrical flowers that have only one plane of symmetry

Bibliography

Adamec, L. 1995. Ecological requirements and recent European distribution of the aquatic carnivorous plant *Aldrovanda vesiculosa* L.: a review. *Folia Geobotanica and Phytotaxonomica* 30, 53–61.

Adamec, L. 1997. Mineral nutrition of carnivorous plants: a review. *Botanical Review* 63, 273–299.

Adamec, L. 1999. The biology and cultivation of red Australian *Aldrovanda vesiculosa*. *Carnivorous Plant Newsletter 28, 128–132.*

Adamec, L. 2006. Respiration and photosynthesis of bladders and leaves of aquatic *Utricularia* species. *Plant Biology* 8, 765–769.

Adamec, L., and Lev, J. 1999. The introduction of the aquatic carnivorous plant *Aldrovanda vesiculosa* to new potential sites in the Czech Republic: a five-year investigation. *Folia Geobotanica and Phytotaxonomica* 34, 299–305.

Airy Shaw, H. K. 1951. On the Dioncophyllaceae, a remarkable new family of flowering plants. *Kew Bulletin* 6, 327–347.

Akeret, B. 1993. Ein neuer Fundort von *Aldrovanda vesiculosa* L. in der Nordschweiz und einige Bemerkungen zu *Stratiotes aloides* L. *Botanica Helvetica* 103, 193–199.

Albert, V. A., Williams, S. E., and Chase, M. W. 1992. Carnivorous plants: phylogeny and structural evolution. *Science* 257, 1491–1495.

Alcala, R. E. and Dominguez, C. A. 2003. Patterns of prey capture and prey availability among populations of the carnivorous plant *Pinguicula moranensis* (Lentibulariaceae) along an environmental gradient. *American Journal of Botany.* 90, 1341–1348.

Anderberg, A. A., Rydin, C., and Källersjö, M. 2002. Phylogenetic relationships in the order Ericales s.l.: analyses of molecular data from five genes from the plastid and mitochondrial genomes. *American Journal of Botany* 89, 677–687.

Anderson, B. 2005. Adaptations to foliar absorption of faeces: a pathway in plant carnivory. *Annals of Botany* 95, 757–761.

Anderson, B. 2006. Inferring evolutionary patterns from the biogeographical distributions of mutualists and exploiters. *Biological Journal of the Linnean Society* 89, 541–549.

Anderson, B., and Midgley, J. J. 2002. It takes two to tango but three is a tangle: mutualists and cheaters on the carnivorous plant *Roridula*. *Oecologia* 132, 369–373.

Anderson, B. and Midgley, J. J. 2003. Digestive mutualism, an alternate pathway in plant carnivory. *Oikos* 102, 221–224.

Andrikovics, S., Forró, L., and Zsunics, E. 1988. The zoogenic food composition of *Utricularia vulgaris* in the Lake Ferto, Hungary. *Opuscula Zoologica* (Budapest) 23, 65–70.

Angerilli, N. P., and Beirne, B. P. 1980. Influences of aquatic plants on colonization of artificial ponds by mosquitoes and their insect predators. *Canadian Entomologist* 112, 793–796.

Arx, B. von, Schlauer, J., and Groves, M. 2002. *CITES Carnivorous Plant Checklist: For the Genera Dionaea, Nepenthes and Sarracenia.* Royal Botanic Gardens Kew, Kew.

Ashida, J. 1934. Studies of leaf movement of *Aldrovanda vesiculosa* L. 1. Process and mechanism of the movement. *Memoirs of the College of Sciences, Kyoto Imperial University* 9, 141–246.

Atwater, D. Z, Butler, J. L., and Ellison, A. M. 2006. Spatial distribution and impacts of moth herbivory on northern pitcher plants. *Northeastern Naturalist* 13, 43–56.

Baffray, M., Brice, F., and Danton, P. 1992. *Les plantes carnivores: des pièges au détour de l'image.* Nathan Editions, Paris.

BAFU (Swiss Federal Agency for the Environment [Bundesamtes für Umwelt]) 1999. Merkblätter Artenschutz. Blütenpflanzen und Farne. http://www.umwelt-schweiz.ch; http://www.cjb.unige.ch/rsf/deu/fiches/pdf/aldr_vesi_dx.pdf.

Baker, K. S., Steadman, K. J., Plummer, J. A., Merritt, D. J., and Dixon, K. W. 2005. Dormancy release in Australian fire ephemeral seeds during burial increases germination response to smoke water or heat. *Seed Science Research* 15, 339–348.

Barthlott, W. 1988. *Meisterwerke der Evolution. Fleischfressende Pflanzen.* Bonner Universitätsblätter, 14–29.

Barthlott, W. 1992. *Mimikry. Nachahmung und Täuschung im Pflanzenreich.* Bonner Universitätsblätter, 49–61.

Barthlott, W., and Porembski, S. 2000. Vascular plants on inselbergs: systematic overview. In: Porembski, S., and Barthlott, W. (eds.): *Inselbergs: Biotic Diversity of Isolated Rock Outcrops in Tropical and Temperate Regions.* Ecological Studies 146, Springer, Berlin, 103–116.

Barthlott, W., Porembski, S., Fischer, E., and Gemmel, B. 1998. First protozoa-trapping plant found. *Nature* 392, 447.

Barthlott, W., Fischer, E., Frahm, J.-P., and Seine, R. 2000. First experimental evidence for zoophagy in the hepatic *Colura. Plant Biology* 2, 93–97.

Barthlott, W., Mutke, J., Rafigpoor, M. D., Kier, G., and Kreft, H. 2005. Global centres of vascular plant diversity. *Nova Acta Leopoldina* 342, 61–83.

Bartram, W. 1791. *Travels in North and South Carolina, Georgia and Florida.* James and Johnson, Philadelphia.

Bayer, R. J., Hufford, L., and Soltis, D. E. 1996. Phylogenetic relationships in Sarraceniaceae based on rbcL and ITS sequences. *Systematic Botany* 21, 121–134.

Beaver, R. A. 1985. Geographical variation in food web structure in *Nepenthes* pitcher plants. *Ecological Entomology* 10, 241–248.

Bentham, G. 1840. On the *Heliamphora nutans*, a new pitcher plant from British Guiana. *Transactions of the Linnean Society of London* 18, 429–433.

Benzing, D. H. 1980. *The Biology of the Bromeliads.* Mad River Press, Eureka, Calif.

Benzing, D. H., Givnish, T. J., and Bermudes, D. 1985. Adsorptive trichomes in *Brocchinia reducta* (Bromeliaceae) and their evolutionary and systematic significance. *Systematic Botany* 10, 81–91.

Bergland, A. O., Agotsch, M., Mathias, D., Bradshaw, W. E., and Holzapfel, C. M. 2005. Factors influencing the seasonal life history of the pitcher-plant mosquito, *Wyeomyia smithii. Ecological Entomology* 30, 129–137.

Bosser, J. 1958. Sur deux nouvelles Lentibulariacée de Madagascar. *Op Cit* 10, 21–29.

Bradshaw, W. E. 1983. Interaction between the mosquito *Wyeomyia smithii*, the midge *Metriocnemus knabi*, and their carnivorous host *Sarracenia purpurea.* In: Frank, J. H., and Lounibos, L. P. (eds.): *Phytotelmata: Terrestrial Plants as Hosts for Aquatic Insect Communities.* Plexus, Medford, N.J., 161–190.

Bradshaw, W. E., and Creelmann, R. A. 1984. Mutualism between the carnivorous purple pitcher plant and its inhabitants. *American Midland Naturalist* 112, 294–304.

Braem, G. 2002. *Fleischfressende Pflanzen*. 2nd ed. Augustus, München.

Brewer, J. S. 1999. Effects of competition, litter, and disturbance on an annual carnivorous plant (*Utricularia juncea*). *Plant Ecology* 140, 159–165.

Brewer, J. S. 2006. Resource competition, and fire-regulated nutrient demand in carnivorous plants of wet pine savannas. *Applied Vegetation Science* 9, 11–16.

Bringmann, G., and Pokorny, F. 1995. The naphtylisoquinoline alkaloids. *Alkaloids* 46, 127–271.

Buchen, B., Henzel, D., and Sievers, A. 1983. Polarity in mechanorezeptor cells of trigger hairs of *Dionaea muscipula* Ellis. *Planta* 158, 458–468.

Cameron, K. M., Wurdack, K. J., and Jobson, R. W. 2002. Molecular evidence for the common origin of snap-traps among carnivorous plants. *American Journal of Botany* 89, 1503–1509.

Carow, T., and Fürst, R. 1990. *Fleischfressende Pflanzen*. Thomas Carow, Nüdlingen.

Casper, S. J. 1966. *Monographie der Gattung Pinguicula L*. Bibliotheca Botanica 127/128, E. Schweizerbart'sche Verlagsbuchhandlung, Stuttgart.

Catesby, M. 1754. *The Natural History of Carolina, Florida and the Bahama Islands*. C. Marsh and T. Wilcox, London.

Cheek, M., and Jebb, M. 2001. Nepenthaceae. In: Steenis, C. (ser. ed.): *Flora Malesiana*, Series 1, Vol. 15, National Herbarium of the Netherlands, Leiden, 1–164.

Cheers, G. 1992. A Guide to the Carnivorous Plants of the World. Collins-Angus & Robertson, Pymble, New South Wales.

Chia, T. F., Aung, H. H., Osipov, A. N., Goh, N. K., and Chia, L. S. 2004. Carnivorous pitcher plant uses free radicals in the digestion of prey. *Redox Report* 9, 255–261.

China, W. E., and Carvalho, J. C. M. 1951. A new ant-like species of mirid from Western Australia. *The Western Autralian Naturalist* (12th ser.) 4, 221–225.

Christensen, K. 1976. The role of carnivory in *Sarracenia flava* L. with regard to specific nutrient deficiencies. *Journal of the Elisha Mitchell Scientific Society* 92, 144–147.

Chrtek, J., and Slavikova, Z. 1996. Comments on the families Drosophyllaceae and Droseraceae. *Casopis Národního Muzea Rada prírodovedná* 165, 139–141.

Chrtek, J., Slavikova, Z., and Studnicka, M. 1989. Beitrag zur Leitbündelanordnung in den Kronblättern ausgewählter Arten der fleischfressenden Pflanzen. *Preslia* 61, 107–124.

Cieslack, T., Polepalli, J. S., White, A., Müller, K., Borsch, T., Barthlott, W., Steiger, J., Marchant, A., and Legendre, L. 2005. Phylogenetic analysis of *Pinguicula* (Lentibulariaceae) chloroplast DNA sequences and morphology support several geographically distinct radiations. *American Journal of Botany* 92, 1723–1736.

Clarke, C. 1997. *Nepenthes of Borneo*. Natural History Publications Borneo, Kota Kinabalu, Sabah, Malaysia.

Clarke, C. M., and Kitching, R. L. 1993. The metazoan food-webs from six Bornean *Nepenthes* species. *Ecological Entomology* 18, 7–16.

Cohn, F. 1850. Über *Aldrovanda vesiculosa* Monti. *Flora* 43, 673–685.

Cohn, F. 1875. Über die Funktion der Blasen von *Aldrovanda* und *Utricularia*. *Cohn's Beiträge zur Biologie der Pflanzen* 1, 71–92.

Conran, J. G. and Christophel, D. 2004. A fossil Byblidaceae seed from Eocene South Australia. *International Journal of Plant Sciences* 165, 691–694.

Conran, J. G., and Dowd, J. M. 1993. The phylogenetic relationships of *Byblis* and *Roridula* (Byblidaceae-Roridulaceae) inferred from partial 18S ribosomal RNA sequences. *Plant Systematics and Evolution* 188, 73–86.

Conran, J. G., Lowrie, A., and Moyel-Croft, J. 2002. A revision of *Byblis* (Byblidaceae) in south-western Australia. *Nuytsia* 15, 11–19.

Cooke, R. C., and Godfrey, B. E. S. 1964. A key to the nematode-destroying fungi. *Transactions of the British Mycological Society* 47, 61–74.

Correia, E., and Freitas, H. 2002. *Drosophyllum lusitanicum*, an endangered west Mediterranean endemic carnivorous plant: threats and its ability to control available resources. *Botanical Journal of the Linnean Society* 140, 383–390.

Cronquist, A. 1988. *The Evolution and Classification of Flowering Plants*. 2nd ed. The New York Botanical Garden, New York.

D'Amato, P. 1998. *The Savage Garden: Cultivating Carnivorous Plants*. Ten Speed Press, Berkeley, Calif.

Danser, B. H. 1928. The Nepenthaceae of the Netherlands Indies. *Bulletin du Jardin Botanique de Buitenzorg* III, 9, 249–438.

Darnowski, D. W. 2003. Triggerplants (*Stylidium*, Stylidiaceae): a new floral horticultural crop with preliminary analysis of hardiness. *Acta Horticulturae* 624, 93–101.

Darnowski, D. W., Carroll, D. M., Plachno, B., Kabanoff, E., and Cinnamon, E. 2006. Evidence of protocarnivory in triggerplants (*Stylidium* spp.; Stylidiaceae). *Plant Biology* 8, 805–812.

Darwin, C. 1875. *Insectivorous Plants*. John Murray, London.

Darwin, F. 1878. Experiments on the nutrition of *Drosera rotundifolia*. *Botanical Journal of the Linnean Society* 17, 17–32.

De Buhr, L. E. 1976. Field notes on *Cephalotus follicularis* in Western Australia. *Carnivorous Plant Newsletter* 3, 8–9.

Diderot, D. 1774–1784. Éléments de physiologie. Reprint 1964. Mayer, J. (ed.). Didier, Paris. [Originally published in Assézat, J., and Tourneux, M., eds. 1875. Oeuvres complètes, Vol. 11. Paris.]

Diels, L. 1906. Droseraceae. In: Engler, A. (ed.): *Das Pflanzenreich*, Vol. 4 (112, 26). W. Engelmann, Weinheim, 1–128.

Dixon, K. W. 1975. The biology of a cormaceous *Drosera*: *Drosera erythrorhiza* Lindl. Ph.D. dissertation, University of Western Australia, Perth.

Dixon, K. W., Pate, J. S., and Bailey, W. J. 1980. Nitrogen nutrition of the tuberous sundew *Drosera erythrorhiza* (Lindl.) with special reference to the catch of arthropod fauna by its glandular leaves. *Australian Journal of Botany* 28, 283–297.

Dixon K. W, Roche, S., and Pate, J. S. 1995. The promotive effect of smoke derived from burnt native vegetation on seed germination of Western Australian plants. *Oecologia* 101, 185–192.

Dodoens, R. 1554. *Cruydeboeck*. Leyden.

Dolling, W. R., and Palmer, J. M. 1991. *Pameridea* (Hemiptera: Miridae): predaceous bugs specific to the highly viscid plant genus *Roridula*. *Systematic Entomology* 16, 319–328.

Dörrstock, S., Seine, R., Porembski, S., and Barthlott, W. 1996. First record of the American *Utricularia juncea* (Lentibulariaceae) from Africa. *Kew Bulletin* 51, 579–583.

Dowe, A. 1987. *Räuberische Pilze*. 2nd ed. A. Ziemsen, Wittenberg.

Drechsler, C. 1933. Morphological diversity among fungi capturing and destroying nematodes. *Journal of the Washington Academy of Sciences* 23, 138–141.

Drude, O. 1891. Droseraceae. In: Engler, A., and Prantl, K. (eds.): *Die Natürlichen Pflanzenfamilien*, Vol. III, Part 2. Engelmann, Leipzig, Abt. 261–272.

Ellis, A. G., and Midgley, J. J. 1996. A new plant-animal mutualism involving a plant with sticky leaves and a resident hemipteran insect. *Oecologia* 106, 478–481.

Ellis, J. 1768. To the printer of the St. James Chronicle. *The St. James Chronicle*, September 2, No. 1172.

Ellis, J. 1770. Directions for bringing over seeds and plants from the East-Indies and other distant countries, in a state of vegetation: together with a catalogue of such foreign plants as are worthy of being encouraged in our American colonies, for the purposes of medicine, agriculture, and commerce. To which is added, the figure and botanical description of a new sensitive plant, called *Dionaea muscipula*: or Venus's fly-trap. Davis, London.

Ellison, A. M. 2006. Nutrient limitation and stoichiometry of carnivorous plants. *Plant Biology* 8, 740–747.

Ellison, A. M. and Farnsworth, E. J. 2005. The cost of carnivory for *Darlingtonia californica* (Sarraceniaceae): evidence from relationships among leaf traits. *American Journal of Botany* 92, 1085–1093.

Ellison, A. M., Gotelli, N. J., Brewer, J. S., Cochran-Stafira, D. L., Kneitel, J. M., Miller, T. E., Worley, A. C., and Zamora, R. 2003. The evolutionary ecology of carnivorous plants. *Advances in Ecological Research*. Vol. 33. Academic Press, London, 1–74.

Engler, A., and Gilg, E. 1924. Roridulaceae. In: Engler, A. (ed.): *Syllabus der Pflanzenfamilien*, 9th/10th ed. Borntraeger, Berlin, 226.

Englund, G., and Harms, S. 2001. The functional response of a predatory plant preying on swarming zooplankton. *Oikos* 94, 175–181.

Erber, D. 1979. Untersuchungen zur Biozonos und Nekrozonos in Kannenpflanzen auf Sumatra. *Archiv für Hydrobiologie* 87, 37–48.

Fabian-Galan, G., and Salageanu, N. 1968. Considerations on the nutrition of certain plants (*Drosera capensis* and *Aldrovanda vesiculosa*). *Revue Roumaine de Biologie, series Botanique* 34, 295–330.

Fashing, N. J. 1981. Arthropod associates of the cobra lily (*Darlingtonia californica*). *Virginia Journal of Science* 32, 92.

Fenner, C. A. 1904. Beiträge zur Kenntnis der Anatomie, Entwicklungsgeschichte und Biologie der Laubblätter und Drüsen einiger Insektivoren. *Flora* 93, 335–434.

Fermi, C., and L. Buscaglione. 1899. Die proteolytischen Enzyme im Pflanzenreiche. *Zentralblatt für Bakteriologie, Parasitenkunde und Infektionskrankheiten, Abt. 2, Allgemeine, landwirtschaftliche, technische Nahrungsmittelbakteriologie und Mykologie, Protozoologie, Pflanzenkrankheiten und Pflanzenschutz sowie Tierkrankheiten* 5, 24–33.

Field, C., and Mooney, H. A. 1986. The photosynthesis-nitrogen relationship in wild plants. In: Givnish, T. J. (ed.): *On the Economy of Plant Form and Function*. Cambridge University Press, Cambridge, 25–55.

Fineran, B. A., and Lee, M. S. L. 1975. Organisation of quadrifid and bifid hairs in the trap of *Utricularia monanthos*. *Protoplasma* 84, 43–70.

Fischer, E., Porembski, S., and Barthlott, W. 2000. Revision of the genus *Genlisea* A.St.-Hil. (Lentibulariaceae) in Africa and Madagascar with notes on ecology and phytogeography. *Nordic Journal of Botany* 20, 291–318.

Fischer, E., Barthlott, W., Seine, R., and Theisen, I. 2004. Lentibulariaceae. In: Kubitzki, K. (ed.): *The Families and Genera of Vascular Plants*. Vol. 7. Springer, Heidelberg, 276–282.

Forterre, Y., Skotheim, J. M., Dumais, J., and Mahadevan, L. 2005. How the Venus flytrap snaps. *Nature* 433, 421–425.

Frahm, J. P. 2001. Tierfangende Lebermoose. *Taublatt* 41, 27–31.

Friday, L. E. 1989. Rapid turnover of traps in *Utricularia vulgaris* L. *Oecologia* 80, 272–277.

Friday, L. E. 1992. Measuring investment in carnivory: seasonal and individual variation in trap numbers and biomass in *Utricularia vulgaris* L. *New Phytologist* 121, 439–445.

Friday, L. E., and Quarmby, C. 1994. Uptake and translocation of prey-derived ^{15}N and ^{32}P in *Utricularia vulgaris* L. *New Phytologist* 126, 273–281.

Froebe, H. A., and Baur, N. 1988. Die Morphogenese der Kannenblätter von *Cephalotus follicularis* Labill. *Akad. Wiss. Lit. Mainz, Math.-Naturwiss. Klasse, Trop. Subtrop. Pflanzenwelt* 3, 1–19.

Fromm-Trinta, E. 1977. Tayloria, new section of the genus *Genlisea* from Brazil. *Boletim do Museu Nacional Rio de Janeiro/Botânica* 44, 1–4.

Fromm-Trinta, E. 1981. Revisao do genero *Genlisea* A. St.-Hil. (Lentibulariaceae) do Brasil. *Boletim do Museu Nacional Rio de Janeiro/Botânica* 61, 1–21.

Fromm-Trinta, E. 1984. Genliseas americanas. *Sellowia*, 36, 55–62.

Frosch T., Schmitt, M., Schenzel, K., Faber, J. H., Bringmann, G., Kiefer, W., and Popp, J. 2006. In vivo localization and identification of the antiplasmodial alkaloid dioncophylline A in the tropical liana *Triphyophyllum peltatum* by a combination of fluorescence, near infrared Fourier transform Raman microscopy, and density functional theory calculations. *Biopolymers* 82, 295–300.

Fürsch, H. 2001. *Sarracenia purpurea* im Bayerischen Wald. *Berichte der Bayerischen Botanischen Gesellschaft* 71, 169–170.

Galek, H., Osswald, W. F., and Elstner, E. F. 1990. Oxidative protein modification as predigestive mechanism of the carnivorous plant *Dionaea muscipula*—an hypothesis based on invitro experiments. *Free Radical Biology and Medicine* 9, 427–434.

Garrido, B., Hampe, A. Maranon, T., and Arroyo, J. 2003. Regional differences in land use affect population performance of the threatened insectivorous plant *Drosophyllum lusitanicum* (Droseraceae). *Diversity and Distributions* 9, 335–350.

Gaume, L., Perret, P., Gorb, E., Gorb, S., Labat, J. J., and Rowe, N. 2004. How do plant waxes cause flies to slide? Experimental tests of wax-based trapping mechanisms in three pitfall carnivorous plants. *Arthropod Structure & Development* 33, 103–111.

Gibson, M., and Warren, K. S. 1970. Capture of *Schistosoma mansoni*, miracidia and cercariae by carnivorous aquatic plants of the genus *Utricularia*. *Bulletin of the World Health Organization* 42, 833–835.

Givnish, T. J. 1989. Ecology and evolution of carnivorous plants. In: Abrahamson, W. G. (ed.): *Plant-Animal Interactions*. McGraw-Hill, New York, 243–290.

Givnish, T. J., Burkhardt, E. L., Happel, R. E., and Weintraub, J. D. 1984. Carnivory in the bromeliad *Brocchinia reducta*, with a cost/benefit model for the general restriction of carnivorous plants to sunny, moist, nutrient poor habitats. *American Naturalist* 124, 479–497.

Glossner, F. 1992. Ultraviolet patterns in the traps and flowers of some carnivorous plants. *Botanische Jahrbücher Syst.* 113, 577–587.

Goebel, K. 1889. Der Aufbau von *Utricularia*. *Flora* 72, 291–297.

Goebel, K. 1891. *Pflanzenbiologische Schilderungen*. 2, V. *Insektivoren*. Elwert, Marburg, 121–127.

Goebel, K. 1893. Zur Biologie von *Genlisea*. *Flora* 77, 208–212.

Goncalves, S., Jesus, J., and Romano, A. 2003. In vitro production of *Drosophyllum lusitanicum* plants. *Revista de Biologia* (Lisbon) 21, 17–27.

Goncalves, S. and Romano, A. 2005. Micropropagation of *Drosophyllum lusitanicum* (Dewy pine), an endangered West Mediterranean endemic insectivorous plant. *Biodiversity and Conservation* 14, 1071–1081.

Gonzalvez, J. M., Jaffe, K., and Michelangeli, F. 1991. Competition for prey between the carnivorous Bromeliaceae *Brocchinia reducta* and Sarraceniaceae *Heliamphora nutans*. *Biotropica* 23, 602–604.

Gorb, E. V. and Gorb, S. N. 2006. Physicochemical properties of functional surfaces in pitchers of the carnivorous plant *Nepenthes alata* Blanco (Nepenthaceae). *Plant Biology* 8, 841–848.

Gorb, E., Haas, K., Henrich, A. Enders, S., Barbakadze, N., and Gorb, S. 2005. Composite structure of the crystalline epicuticular wax layer of the slippery zone in the pitchers of the carnivorous plant *Nepenthes alata* and its effect on insect attachment. *Journal of Experimental Biology* 208, 4651–4662.

Gorb, E., Kastner, V., Peressadko, A., Arzt, E., Gaume, L., Rowe, N., and Gorb, S. 2004. Structure and properties of the glandular surface in the digestive zone of the pitcher in the carnivorous plant *Nepenthes ventrata* and its role in insect trapping and retention. *Journal of Experimental Biology* 207, 2947–2963.

Gordeev, M. I., and Sibataev, A. K. 1995. Influence of predatory plant bladderwort (*Utricularia vulgaris*) on the process of selection in malaria mosquito larvae. *Russian Journal of Ecology* 26, 216–220.

Gore, A. J. P. 1983. *Ecosystems of the World*. Vol. 4A, *Mires: Swamp, Bog, Fen and Moor*. Elsevier, Amsterdam.

Green, S. 1967. Notes on the distribution of *Nepenthes* species in Singapore. *Gardens Bulletin* 22, 53–65.

Green, S., Green, T. L., and Heslop-Harrison, Y. 1979. Seasonal heterophylly and the leaf gland features in *Triphyophyllum* (Dioncophyllaceae), a new carnivorous plant genus. *Botanical Journal of the Linnean Society* 78, 99–116.

Greilhuber, J., Borsch, T., Müller, K., Worberg, A., Porembski, S., and Barthlott, W. 2006. Smallest angiosperm genomes found in Lentibulariaceae, with chromosomes of bacterial size. *Plant Biology* 8, 770–777.

Grudger, E. W. 1947. The only known fish-eating plant *Utricularia* the bladderwort. *Scientific Monthly* 64, 369–384.

Guisande, C., Andrade, C., Granado-Lorencio, C., Duque, S. R., and Nunez-Avellaneda, M. 2000. Effects of zooplankton and conductivity on tropical *Utricularia foliosa* investment in carnivory. *Aquatic Ecology* 34, 137–142.

Hambler, D. J. 1964. The vegetation of granitic outcrops in western Nigeria. *Journal of Ecology* 52, 573–594.

Hanslin, H. M., and Karlsson, P. S. 1996. Nitrogen uptake from prey and substrate as affected by prey capture level and plant reproductive status in four carnivorous plant species. *Oecologia* 106, 370–375.

Harder, R. 1970. *Utricularia* als Objekt für Heterotrophieuntersuchungen bei Blütenpflanzen. *Zeitschrift für Pflanzenphysiologie* 63, 181–184.

Harder, R., and Zemlin, I. 1968. Blütenbildung von *Pinguicula lusitanica* in vitro durch Fütterung mit Pollen. *Planta* 78, 72–78.

Harms, S., and Johansson, F. 2000. The influence of prey behaviour on prey selection of the carnivorous plant *Utricularia vulgaris*. *Hydrobiologia* 427, 113–120.

Hegner, R. W. 1926. The interrelationships of protozoa and the utricles of *Utricularia*. *Biological Bulletin* 50, 271–276.

Hepburn, J. S., St. John, E. Q., and Jones, F. M. 1920. The absorption of nutrients and allied phenomena in the pitchers of Sarraceniaceae. *Journal of the Franklin Institute* 189, 147–184.

Hepburn, J. S., Jones, F. M., and St. John, E. Q. 1927. The biochemistry of the American pitcher plants: biochemical studies of the North American Sarraceniaceae. *Transactions of the Wagner Free Institute of Science in Philadelphia* 11, 1–95.

Heslop-Harrison, Y. 1975. Enzyme release in carnivorous plants. In: Dingle, J. T., and Dean, R. T. (eds.): *Lysozymes in Biology and Pathology*. North Holland Publishing, Amsterdam, 525–578.

Heslop-Harrison, Y., and Knox, R. B. 1971. A cytochemical study of the leaf-gland enzymes of insectivorous plants of the genus *Pinguicula*. *Planta* 96, 183–211.

Hess, S., Frahm, J.-P., and Theisen, I. 2005. Evidence of zoophagy in a second liverwort species; *Pleurozia purpurea*. *Bryologist* 108, 212–218.

Heubl, G., Bringmann, G., and Meimberg, H. 2006. Molecular phylogeny and character evolution of carnivorous plant families in Caryophyllales – revisited. *Plant Biology* 8, 821–830.

Hobbhahn, N., Küchmeister, H., and Porembski, S. 2006. Pollination biology of mass flowering terrestrial *Utricularia* species (Lentibulariaceae) in the Indian Western Ghats. *Plant Biology* 8, 791–804.

Hodick, D., and Sievers, A. 1986. The influence of Ca^{2+} on the action potential in mesophyll cells of *Dionaea muscipula* Ellis. *Protoplasma* 133, 83–84.

Hodick, D., and Sievers, A. 1988. The action potential of *Dionaea muscipula* Ellis. *Planta* 174, 8–18.

Hodick, D., and Sievers, A. 1989. On the mechanism of trap closure of Venus flytrap (*Dionaea muscipula* Ellis). *Planta* 179, 32–41.

Hooker, J. D. 1873. Nepenthaceae. In: De Candolle, A. *Prodromus Systematis Naturalis Regni Vegetabilis* 17, 90–105.

Horres, R., Zizka, G., Kahl, G., and Weising, K. 2000. Molecular phylogenetics of Bromeliaceae: evidence from trnL (UAA) intron sequences of the chloroplast genome. *Plant Biology* 2, 306–315.

Iijima, T., and Sibaoka, T. 1985. Membrane potentials in excitable cells of *Aldrovanda vesiculosa* trap-lobes. *Plant and Cell Physiology* 26, 1–13.

Istock, C. A., Tanner, K., and Zimmer, H. 1983. Habitat selection by the pitcher-plant mosquito, *Wyeomyia smithii*: behavioral and genetic aspects. In: Frank, J. H., and Lounibos, L. P. (eds.): *Phytotelmata: Terrestrial Plants as Hosts for Aquatic Insect Communities*. Plexus, Medford, N.J., 191–204.

Jaffe K., Michelangeli, F., Gonzalez, J. M., Miras, B. and Ruiz, M. C. 1992. Carnivory in pitcher plants of the genus *Heliamphora* (Sarraceniaceae). *New Phytologist* 122, 733–744.

Jang, G. W., Kim, K. S., and Park, R. D. 2003. Micropropagation of Venus fly trap by shoot culture. *Plant Cell Tissue & Organ Culture* 72, 95–98.

Jebb, M., and Cheek, M. 1997. A skeletal revision of *Nepenthes* (Nepenthaceae). *Blumea* 42, 1–106.

Jobson, R. W., Playford, J., Cameron, K. M., and Albert. V. A. 2003. Molecular phylogenetics of Lentibulariaceae inferred from plastid rps16 intron and trnL-F DNA sequences: implications for character evolution and biogeography. *Systematic Botany* 28, 157–171.

Joel, D. M. 1986. Glandular structures in carnivorous plants; their role in mutual exploitation of insects. In: Juniper, B. E., and Southwood, T. R. E. (eds.): *Insects and the Plant Surface*. Edward Arnold, London, 219–234.

Joel, D. M. 1988. Mimicry and mutualism in carnivorous pitcher plants (Sarraceniaceae, Nepenthaceae, Cephalotaceae, Bromeliaceae). *Biological Journal of the Linnean Society* 35, 185–197.

Joel, D. M., Juniper, B. E., and Dafni, A. 1985. Ultraviolet patterns in the traps of carnivorous plants. *New Phytologist* 101, 585–593.

Juniper, B. E. 1986. The path to plant carnivory. In: Juniper, B. E., and Southwood, R. (eds.): *Insects and the Plant Surface*. Edward Arnold, London, 195–218.

Juniper, B. E., Robins, R. J., and Joel, D. M. 1989. *The Carnivorous Plants*. Academic Press, London.

Kameyama, Y. and Ohara, M. 2006. Predominance of clonal reproduction, but recombinant origins of new genotypes in the free-floating aquatic bladderwort *Utricularia australis* f. *tenuicaulis* (Lentibulariaceae). *Journal of Plant Research* 119, 357–362.

Kerner von Marilaun, A. 1922. *Pflanzenleben*. 3rd ed. Vol. 1. Leipzig, Vienna.

Kim, K. S. and Jang, G. W. 2004. Micropropagation of *Drosera peltata*, a tuberous sundew, by shoot tip culture. *Plant Cell Tissue & Organ Culture* 77, 211–214.

Knight, S. E. 1992. Cost of carnivory in the common bladderwort *Utricularia macrorhiza*. *Oecologia* 89, 348–355.

Knight, S. E., and Frost, T. M. 1991. Bladder control in *Utricularia macrorhiza*: lake-specific variation in plant investment in carnivory. *Ecology* 72, 728–734.

Krenn, L., Beyer, G., Pertz, H. H., Karall, E., Kremser, M., Galambosi, B., and Melzig, M. F. 2004. In vitro antispasmodic and anti-inflammatory effects of *Drosera rotundifolia*. *Arzneimittel-Forschung* 54, 402–405.

Kubitzki, K. 2002a. Droseraceae. In: Kubitzki, K. (ed.): *The Families and Genera of Vascular Plants*. Vol. 5. Springer, Heidelberg, 198–202.

Kubitzki, K. 2002b. Drosophyllaceae. In: Kubitzki, K. (ed.): *The Families and Genera of Vascular Plants*. Vol. 5. Springer, Heidelberg, 203–205.

Kubitzki, K. 2002c. Nepenthaceae. In: Kubitzki, K. (ed.): *The Families and Genera of Vascular Plants*. Vol. 5. Springer, Heidelberg, 320–324.

Kurata, S. 1976. *Nepenthes of Mount Kinabalu*. Sabah National Parks Trustees, Kota Kinabalu, Sabah, Malaysia.

Laakkonen, L., Jobson, R. W., and Albert, V. A. 2006. A new model for the evolution of carnivory in the bladderwort plant (*Utricularia*): adaptive changes in cytochrome c oxidase (COX) provide respiratory power. *Plant Biology* 8, 758–764.

Labat, J.-J. 2003. *Fleischfressende Pflanzen*. Eugen Ulmer, Stuttgart.

Labillardière, J. J. 1806. Novae Hollandiae Plantarum Specimen. Vol. 2, 7.

Lang, F. X. 1901. Untersuchung über Morphologie, Anatomie und Samenentwicklung von *Polypompholyx* und *Byblis gigantea*. *Flora* 88, 149–206.

Lauber, K., and Wagner, G. 2001. *Flora Helvetica*. 3rd ed. Haupt, Berne.

Legendre, L. 2000. The genus *Pinguicula* L. (Lentibulariaceae): an overview. *Acta Botanica Gallica* 147, 77–95.

Linnaeus, C. 1753. *Species Plantarum*. Stockholm.

Linnaeus, C. 1764. *Genera Plantarum*. 6th ed. Stockholm.

Lloyd, F. E. 1942. *The Carnivorous Plants*. Chronica Botanica, Waltham, Mass.

Lobova T. A. 1999. Seed morphology and anatomy in *Roridula* species (Roridulaceae). XVI International Botanical Congress; Abstract No. 3277.

Lowrie, A. 1998a. *Carnivorous Plants of Australia*. Vol. 3. University of Western Australia Press, Nedlands.

Lowrie, A. 1998b. A new species of *Utricularia* (Lentibulariaceae) from the south-west of Western Australia. *Nuytsia* 12, 37–41.

Lowrie, A. 2002. *Utricularia petertaylorii* (Lentibulariaceae), a new species from the south-west of Western Australia. *Nuytsia* 14, 405–410.

Lowrie, A., and Conran, J. G. 1998. A taxonomic revision of the genus *Byblis* (Byblidaceae) in northern Australia. *Nuytsia* 12, 59–74.

Luhrs, H. 1993. Corrections to the nomenclatural synopsis of the genus *Pinguicula*. *International Pinguicula Study Group Newsletter* 4, 28.

Lüttge, U. 1965. Untersuchungen zur Physiologie der Carnivoren-Drüsen: IV. Die Kinetik der Chloridsekretion durch das Drüsengewebe von *Nepenthes*. *Planta* 68, 269–285.

Lysek, G., and Nordbring-Hertz, B. 1983. Die Biologie nematodenfangender Pilze. *Forum Mikrobiologie* 6, 201–208.

Macfarlane, J. M. 1908. Nepenthaceae. In: Engler, A. (ed.): *Das Pflanzenreich*, Vol. 4 (111, 36). W. Engelmann, Weinheim, 1–92.

Marburger, J. E. 1979. Glandular leaf structure of *Triphyophyllum peltatum* (Dioncophyllaceae): a "fly-paper" insect trapper. *American Journal of Botany* 66, 404–411.

Marloth, R. 1903. Some recent observations on the biology of *Roridula*. *Annals of Botany* 17, 151–157.

Martin, J. T., and Juniper, B. E. 1970. *The Cuticles of Plants*. Edward Arnold, London.

Matusikova, I., Salaj, J., Moravcikova, J., Mlynarova, L., Nap, J. P., and Libantova, J. 2005. Tentacles of in vitro-grown round-leaf sundew (*Drosera rotundifolia* L.) show induction of chitinase activity upon mimicking the presence of prey. *Planta* 222, 1020–1027.

Mazrimas, J. A. 1972. *Drosophyllum lusitanicum*. *Carnivorous Plant Newsletter* 1, 5–6.

McPherson, S. 2006. *Pitcher Plants of the Americas*. McDonald & Woodward Publishing Company, US, Granville.

Meimberg, H., Dittrich, P., Bringmann, G., Schlauer, J., and Heubl, G. 2000. Molecular phylogeny of Caryophyllales s.l. based on matK sequences with special emphasis on carnivorous taxa. *Plant Biology* 2, 218–228.

Meimberg, H. and Heubl, G. 2006. Introduction of a nuclear marker for phylogenetic analysis of Nepenthaceae. *Plant Biology* 8, 831–840.

Meimberg, H., Wistuba, A., Dittrich, P., and Heubl, G. 2001. Molecular phylogeny of Nepenthaceae based on cladistic analysis of plastid trnK intron sequence data. *Plant Biology* 3, 164–175.

Melzig, M. F., Pertz, H. H., and Krenn, L. 2001. Anti-inflammatory and spasmolytic activity of extracts from Droserae Herba. *Phytomedicine* 8, 225–229.

Mendez, M. and Karlsson, P. S. 1999. Costs and benefits of carnivory in plants: insights from the photosynthetic performance of four carnivorous plants in a subarctic environment. *Oikos* 86, 105–112.

Mendez, M. and Karlsson, P. S. 2004. Between-population variation in size-dependent reproduction and reproductive allocation in *Pinguicula vulgaris* (Lentibulariaceae) and its environmental correlates. *Oikos* 104, 59–70.

Mendez, M. and Karlsson, P. S. 2005. Nutrient stoichiometry in *Pinguicula vulgaris*: nutrient availability, plant size, and reproductive status. *Ecology* 86, 982–991.

Menzel, R. 1979. Spectral sensitivity and colour vision in invertebrates. *Handbook of Sensory Physiology*. Vol. VII/6a. Springer, Berlin.

Merbach, M. A., Zizka, G., Fiala, B., Merbach, D., and Maschwitz, U. 1999. Giant nectaries in the peristome thorns of the pitcher plant *Nepenthes bicalcarata* Hooker f. (Nepenthaceae): anatomy and functional aspects. *Ecotropica* 5, 45–50.

Merbach, M. A., Zizka, G., Fiala, B., Maschwitz, U., and Booth, W. E. 2001. Patterns of nectar secretion in five *Nepenthes* species from Brunei Darussalam, north-west Borneo, and implications for ant-plant relationships. *Flora* 196, 153–160.

Merbach, M. A., Merbach, D. J., Maschwitz, U., Booth, W. E., Fiala, B., and Zizka, G. 2002. Mass march of termites into deadly trap. *Nature* 415, 36–37.

Metcalfe, C. R. 1951. The anatomical structure of the Dioncophyllaceae in relation to the taxonomic affinities of the family. *Kew Bulletin* 6, 351–368.

Mette, N., Wilbert, N., and Barthlott, W. 2000. Food composition of aquatic bladderworts (*Utricularia*, Lentibulariaceae) in various habitats. *Beiträge zur Biologie der Pflanzen* 72, 1–13.

Meyers, D. G., and Strickler, J. R. 1978. Morphological and behavioral interactions between a carnivorous aquatic plant (*Utricularia vulgaris* L.) and a chydorid cladoceran (*Chydorus sphaericus* O.F.M.). *Verh. Internat. Verein. Limnol.* 20, 2490–2495.

Meyers, D. G., and Strickler, J. R. 1979. Capture enhancement in a carnivorous aquatic plant: function of antennae and bristles in *Utricularia vulgaris*. *Science* 203, 1022–1025.

Midgley, J. J., and Stock, W. D. 1998. Natural abundance of delta ^{15}N confirms insectivorous habit of *Roridula gorgonias*, despite it having no proteolytic enzymes. *Annals of Botany* 82, 387–388.

Moran, J. A. 1996. Pitcher dimorphism, prey composition and the mechanisms of prey attraction in the pitcher plant *Nepenthes rafflesiana* in Borneo. *Journal of Ecology* 84, 515–525.

Moran, J. A., Merbach, M. A., Livingston, N. J., Clarke, C. M., and Booth, W. E. 2001. Termite prey specialization in the pitcher plant *Nepenthes albomarginata*—evidence from stable isotope analysis. *Annals of Botany* 88, 307–311.

Müller, J. 1981. Fossil pollen records of extant angiosperms. *Botanical Review* 47, 10–145.

Müller, J., and Deil, U. 2001. Ecology and structure of *Drosophyllum lusitanicum* (L.) Link populations in the south-western of the Iberian Peninsula. *Acta Botanica Malacitana* 26, 47–68.

Müller, K., and Borsch, T. 2005. Phylogenetics of *Utricularia* (Lentibulariaceae) and molecular evolution of the trnK intron in a lineage with high substitutional rates. *Plant Systematics and Evolution* 250, 39–67.

Müller, K., Borsch, T., Legendre, L., Porembski, S., and Barthlott, W. 2000. A phylogeny of Lentibulariaceae based on sequences of matK and adjacent non-coding regions. *American Journal of Botany* 87 (Suppl.), 145–146.

Müller, K., Borsch, T., Legendre, L., Porembski, S., Theisen, I., and Barthlott, W. 2004. Evolution of carnivory in Lentibulariaceae and the Lamiales. *Plant Biology* 6, 477–490.

Müller, K., Borsch, T., Legendre, L., Porembski, S., and Barthlott, W. 2006. Recent progress in understanding the evolution of carnivorous Lentibulariaceae (Lamiales). *Plant Biology* 8, 748–757.

Muravnik, L. E., Vassilyev, A. E. and Potapova, Y. Y. 1995. Ultrastructural aspects of digestive gland functioning in *Aldrovanda vesiculosa*. *Russian Journal of Plant Physiology* 42, 1–8.

Murza, G. L., Heaver, J. R., and Davis, A. R. 2006. Minor pollinator-prey conflict in the carnivorous plant, *Drosera anglica*. *Plant Ecology* 184, 43–52.

Ne'eman, G., Ne'eman, R., and Ellison, A. M. 2006. Limits to reproductive success of *Sarracenia purpurea* (Sarraceniaceae). *American Journal of Botany* 93, 1660–1666.

Nelson, E. C. 1990. *Venus's Flytrap: Aphrodite's mousetrap: a biography of Venus's Flytrap with facsimiles of an original pamphlet and the manuscripts of John Ellis, F.R.S.* Boethius Press, Aberystwyth, Wales.

Nielsen, D. W. 1990. Arthropod communities associated with *Darlingtonia californica*. *Annals of the Entomological Society of America*. 83, 189–200.

Okabe, T., Iwakiri, Y., Mori, H., Ogawa, T., and Ohyama, T. 2005. An S-like ribonuclease gene is used to generate a trap-leaf enzyme in the carnivorous plant *Drosera adelae*. *Febs Letters* 579, 5729–5733.

Oliver, F. W. 1944. A mass catch of cabbage whites by sundews. *Proceedings of the Royal Entomological Society of London* 19, 5.

Olvera Garcia, M., and Martinez, S. E. 2002. Primer registro de *Genlisea* (Lentibulariaceae) para Mexico. *Acta Botanica Mexicana* 59, 71–73.

Ortega-Olivencia, A., Carrasco, J. P., and Devesa, J. A. 1995. Floral and reproductive biology of *Drosophyllum lusitanicum* (L.) Link (Droseraceae). *Botanical Journal of the Linnean Society* 118, 331–351.

Owen, T. P., Benzing, D. H., and Thomson, W. W. 1988. Apoplastic and ultrastructural characterizations of the trichomes from the carnivorous bromeliad *Brocchinia reducta*. *Canadian Journal of Botany* 66, 941–948.

Panessa, B. J., Kuptsis, J., Piscopa-Rodgers, I., and Gennaro, J. 1976. Ion and uranium transport in the carnivorous pitcher plant: studies by SEM, TEM and X-ray microanalysis. In: Johri, O. (ed.): *Workshop on Plant Science Applications of the SEM*. Illinois Institute of Technology, Chicago, 461–468.

Parnell, J. A. N. 2005. An account of the Lentibulariaceae of Thailand. *Thai Forest Bulletin* (Botany) 33, 101-144.

Pate, J. S. 1986. Economy of symbiotic nitrogen fixation. In: Givnish, T. J. (ed.): *On the Economy of Plant Form and Function*. Cambridge University Press, Cambridge, 299–325.

Phillipps, A., and Lamb, A. 1996. *Pitcher Plants of Borneo*. Natural History Publications Borneo, Kota Kinabalu, Sabah, Malaysia.

Picado, C. 1913. Les Bromeliacées epiphytes considérée comme milieu biologique. *Bull. Soc. France Belg.* 47, 215–360.

Pietropaolo, J., and Pietropaolo, P. A. 1996. *Carnivorous Plants of the World*. 2nd ed. Timber Press, Portland, Ore.

Plachno, B., Adamec, L., Lichtscheidl, I. K., Peroutka, M., Adlassnig, W., and Vrba, J. 2006. Fluorescence labelling of phosphatase activity in digestive glands of carnivorous plants. *Plant Biology* 8, 813–820.

Ponte-Sucre, A., Faber, J. H., Gulder, T., Kajahn, I., Pedersen, S. E. H., Schultheis, M., Bringmann, G., and Moll, H. 2007. Activities of naphthylisoquinoline alkaloids and synthetic analogs against *Leishmania major*. *Antimicrobial Agents and Chemotherapy* 51, 188–194.

Porembski, S., and Barthlott, W., eds. 2000. *Inselbergs: Biotic Diversity of Isolated Rock Outcrops in Tropical and Temperate Regions*. Ecological Studies 146. Springer, Berlin.

Porembski, S., and Barthlott, W. 2002. Dioncophyllaceae. In: Kubitzki, K. (ed.): *The Families and Genera of Vascular Plants*. Vol. 5. Springer, Heidelberg, 178–181.

Porembski, S, and Barthlott, W. 2006. Advances in carnivorous plants research. *Plant Biology* 8, 737–739.

Porembski, S., Theisen, I., and Barthlott, W. 2006. Biomass allocation patterns in terrestrial, epiphytic and aquatic species of *Utricularia* (Lentibulariaceae). *Flora* 201, 477–482.

Prior, S. 1939. *Carnivorous Plants and "The Man-Eating Tree."* Field Museum of Natural History, Chicago.

Quintanilha, A. 1926. O problema das plantas carnivoras. *Boletim Sociedade Broteriana* (2a ser.) 4, 44–129.

Rauh, W. 1995. *Succulent and Xerophytic Plants of Madagascar*. 2 Vols. Strawberry Press, Mill Valley, Calif.

Ravikumar, V. R., Sudha, M., and Joseph, V. M. 2003. Antimicrobial activity of *Drosera peltata*. *Indian Journal of Natural Products*. 19, 29–30.

Reichle, D. E., Shanks, M. H., and Crossley, D. A. 1969. Calcium, potassium and sodium content of forest floor arthropods. *Annals of the Entomological Society of America* 62, 57–62.

Reifenrath, K., Theisen, I., Schnitzler, J., Porembski, S., and Barthlott, W. 2006. Trap architecture in carnivorous *Utricularia* (Lentibulariaceae). *Flora* 201, 597–605.

Rice, B. A. 2006. *Growing Carnivorous Plants*. Timber Press, Portland.

Richards, P.W. 1957. Ecological notes on West African vegetation. I. The plant communities of the Idanre Hills, Nigeria. *Journal of Ecology* 45, 563–577.

Ridder, F. de and Dhondt, A. A. 1992. The reproductive behaviour of a clonal herbaceous plant, the longleaved sundew *Drosera intermedia*, in different heathland habitat. *Ecogeography* 15, 144–153.

Riedel, M., Eichner, A., and Jetter, R. 2003. Slippery surfaces of carnivorous plants: composition of epicuticular wax crystals in *Nepenthes alata* Blanco pitchers. *Planta* 218, 87–97.

Riley, C. V. 1873. Description and natural history of two insects which brave the dangers of *Sarracenia variolaris*. *Transactions of the Academy of Sciences of St. Louis* 3, 235–240.

Rivadavia, F., Kondo, K., Kato, M., and Hasebe, M. 2003. Phylogeny of the sundews, *Drosera* (Droseraceae), based on chloroplast rbcL and nuclear 18S ribosomal DNA sequences. *American Journal of Botany* 90, 123–130.

Robins, R. J. 1978. Studies in secretion and absorption in *Dionaea muscipula* Ellis. Ph.D. dissertation, University of Oxford.

Rutishauser, R., and Sattler R. 1989. Complementary and heuristic value of contrasting models in structural botany. III Case study on shoot-like "leaves" and leaf-like "shoots" in *Utricularia macrorhiza* and *U. purpurea* (Lentibulariaceae). *Botanische Jahrbücher Syst.* 111, 121–137.

Sakamoto, K., Nakamoto, H., and Kaneko, Y. 2006. Development of protease activity in carnivorous leaves of *Aldrovanda vesiculosa*, an aquatic carnivorous plant. *Plant and Cell Physiology* 47, S118–S118.

Sanabria-Aranda, L., Gonzalez-Bermudez, A., Torres, N. N., Guisande, C., Manjarres-Hernandez, A., Valoyes-Valois, V., Diaz-Olarte, J., Andrade-Sossa, C., and Duque, S. R. 2006. Predation by the tropical plant *Utricularia foliosa*. *Freshwater Biology* 51, 1999–2008.

Sasago, A., and Sibaoka, T. 1985a. Water extrusion in the trap bladders of *Utricularia vulgaris*. 1. A possible pathway of water across the bladder wall. *Botanical Magazine* 98, 55–66.

Sasago, A., and Sibaoka, T. 1985b. Water extrusion in the trap bladders of *Utricularia vulgaris*. 2. A possible mechanism of water outflow. *Botanical Magazine* 98, 113–124.

Schlauer, J. 2000. Global carnivorous plant diversity a contribution from the Carnivorous Plant Specialist Group (GPSG) of the International Union for the Conservation of Nature (IUCN, SSC). *Carnivorous Plant Newsletter* 29, 75–82.

Schlauer, J. 2007. The World Carnivorous Plant List—A Nomenclatural Synopsis of the Carnivorous Phanerogamous Plants. http://www.omnisterra.com/bot/cp_home.cgi.

Schmid, R. 1964. Die systematische Stellung der Dioncophyllaceae. *Botanische Jahrbücher Syst.* 83, 1–56.

Schnell, D. E. 2002. *Carnivorous Plants of the United States and Canada*. 2nd ed. Timber Press, Portland, Ore.

Schnepf, E. 1960. Zur Feinstruktur der Drüsen von *Drosophyllum lusitanicum*. *Planta* 54, 641–674.

Schuiteman, A., and de Vogel, E. F. 2002. *Nepenthes vogelii* (Nepenthaceae): a new species from Sarawak. *Blumea* 47, 537–540.

Schulze, E. D., Gebauer, G., Schulze, W., and Pate, J. S. 1991. The utilization of nitrogen from insect capture by different growth forms of *Drosera* from southwest Australia. *Oecologia* 87, 240–246.

Schulze, W., Schulze, E. D., Pate, J. S., and Gillison, A. N. 1997. The nitrogen supply from soils and insects during growth of the pitcher plants *Nepenthes mirabilis*, *Cephalotus follicularis* and *Darlingtonia californica*. *Oecologia* 122, 464–471.

Schulze, W., Schulze, E. D., Schulze, I., and Oren, R. 2001. Quantification of insect nitrogen utilization by the Venus fly trap *Dionaea muscipula* catching prey with highly variable isotope signatures. *Journal of Experimental Botany* 52, 1041–1049.

Seine, R., and Barthlott, W. 1992. Ontogeny and morphological quality of the marginal bristles of *Dionaea muscipula* Ellis (Droseraceae Salisb.). *Beiträge zur Biologie der Pflanzen* 67, 289–294.

Seine, R., and Barthlott, W. 1993. On the morphology of trichomes and tentacles of Droseraceae Salisb. 345–366.

Seine, R., and Barthlott, W. 1994. Some proposals on the infrageneric classification of *Drosera* L. *Taxon* 43, 583–589.

Seine, R., Porembski, S., and Barthlott, W. 1995. A neglected habitat of carnivorous plants: inselbergs. *Feddes Repertorium* 106, 7–12.

Seine, R., Porembski, S., Balduin, M., Theisen, I., Wilbert, N., and Barthlott, W. 2002. Different prey strategies of terrestrial and aquatic species in the carnivorous genus *Utricularia* (Lentibulariaceae). *Botanische Jahrbücher Syst.* 124, 71–76.

Sibaoka, T. 1966. Action potentials in plant organs. *Symposium for the Society for Experimental Biology* 20, 49–74.

Slack, A. 2000. *Carnivorous Plants*. MIT Press, Cambridge, Mass.

Smith, L. B., and Till, W. 1998. Bromeliaceae. In: Kubitzki, K. (ed.): *The Families and Genera in Vascular Plants*. Vol. 4, Springer, Berlin, 74–99.

Sorrenson, D. R., and Jackson, W. T. 1968. The utilization of *Paramecia* by the carnivorous plant *Utricularia gibba*. *Planta* 83, 166–179.

Sparg, S. G., Kulkarni, M. G., and van Staden, J. 2006. Aerosol smoke and smoke-water stimulation of seedling vigor of a commercial maize cultivar. *Crop Science* 46, 1336–1340.

Speta, F., and Fuchs, F. 1982. Neue *Pinguicula*-Arten (Lentibulariaceae) aus Mexiko. *Stapfia* 10, 111–119.

Speta, F., and Fuchs, F. 1989. Drei neue *Pinguicula*-Arten der Sektion Orcheosanthus DC. aus Mexiko. *Phyton* 29, 93–103.

Splett, S. 1996. Pflanzenökologische Untersuchungen auf Weisssandfeldern in Zentral- und Südostbrasilien. Ph.D. dissertation, University of Bonn.

Spomer, G. G. 1999. Evidence of protocarnivorous capabilities in *Geranium viscosissimum* and *Potentilla arguta* and other sticky plants. *International Journal of Plant Sciences* 160, 98–101.

Steenis, C. G. van. 1969. Plant speciation in Malesia, with special reference to the theory of non-adaptive saltatory evolution. *Biological Journal of the Linnaean Society* 1, 97–133.

Steenis, C. G. van. 1971. Byblidaceae. In: Steenis, C. G. van (ed.): *Flora Malesiana*, Series 1, Vol. 7. Noordhoff International Publishing, Leyden, 135–137.

Succow, M., and Jeschke, L. 1990. *Moore in der Landschaft. Entstehung, Haushalt, Lebewelt, Verbreitung, Nutzung und Erhaltung der Moore*. 2nd ed. Harri Deutsch, Frankfurt am Main.

Sydenham, P. H., and Findlay, G. P. 1973. The rapid movements of the bladder of *Utricularia* sp. *Australian Journal of Biological Sciences* 26, 1115–1126.

Sydenham, P. H., and Findlay, G. P. 1975. Transport of solutes and water by resetting bladders of *Utricularia*. *Australian Journal of Plant Physiology* 2, 335–351.

Taylor, P. 1989. *The Genus Utricularia*. Kew Bulletin Additional Series 14. Royal Botanic Gardens, Kew, London.

Thoren, L. M., Karlsson, P. S., and Tuomi, J. 1996. Somatic cost of reproduction in three carnivorous *Pinguicula* species. *Oikos* 76, 427–434.

Thum, M. 1988. The significance of carnivory for the fitness of *Drosera* in its natural habitat. 1. The reactions of *Drosera intermedia* and *Drosera rotundifolia* to supplementary feeding. *Oecologia* 75, 472–480.

Torrey, J. 1853. On the *Darlingtonia californica*, a new pitcher plant from northern California. *Smithsonian Contributions to Knowledge* 6, 1–8.

Treat, M. 1876. Is the valve of *Utricularia* sensitive? *Harper's New Monthly Magazine* 52, 382–387.

Troll, W., and Dietz, H. 1954. Morphologische und histogenetische Untersuchungen an *Utricularia*-Arten. *Österreichische Botanische Zeitschrift* 101, 165–207.

Trzcinski, M. K., Walde, S. J., and Taylor, P. D. 2005. Stability of pitcher-plant microfaunal populations depends on food web structure. *Oikos* 110, 146–154.

Varadarajan, G. S. 1986. Habitats of *Brocchinia*, a descriptive account. *Journal of the Bromeliad Society* 36, 209–216.

Vintejoux, C. 1974. Ultrastructural and cytochemical observations on the digestive glands of *Utricularia neglecta* L. (Lentibulariaceae): distribution of protease and acid phosphatase activities. *Portugaliae Acta Biologica Series A* 14, 463–471.

Wager, V. A. 1928. The resting buds of *Utricularia stellaris* Linn. f. *Transaction of the Royal Society of South Africa* 16, 204.

Walter, H., and Breckle, S.-W. 1983. *Ökologie der Erde*. Vol. 1. *Ökologische Grundlagen in globaler Sicht*. UTB, Fischer, Stuttgart.

Watson, A. P., Matthiessen, J. N., and Springett, B. P. 1982. Arthropod associates and macronutrient status of the red-ink sundew (*Drosera erythrorhiza* Lindl.). *Australian Journal of Ecology* 7, 13–22.

Williams, S. E. 1976. Comparative sensory physiology of the Droseraceae: the evolution of a plant sensory system. *Proceedings of the American Philosophical Society* 120, 187–204.

Williams, S. E., Albert, V. A., and Chase, M. W. 1994. Relationships of Droseraceae: a cladistic analysis of rbcL sequence and morphological data. *American Journal of Botany* 81, 1027–1037.

Worley, A. C., and Harder, L. D. 1996. Size-dependent resource allocation and costs of reproduction in *Pinguicula vulgaris* (Lentibulariaceae). *Journal of Ecology* 84, 195–206.

Zamudio, S. 1988. Dos nuevas especies de *Pinguicula* (Lentibulariaceae) del centro y norte de Mexico. *Acta Botanica Mexicana* 3, 21–28.

Zamudio, S. 2005. Dos especies nuevas de *Pinguicula* (Lentibulariaceae) de la Sierra Madre oriental, Mexico. *Acta Botanica Mexicana* 70, 69–83.

Zamudio, S., and Rzedowski, J. 1986. Tres especies nuevas de *Pinguicula* (Lentibulariaceae) de Mexico. *Phytologia* 60, 255–265.

Zamudio, S., and Rzedowski, J. 1991. Dos especies nuevas de *Pinguicula* (Lentibulariaceae) del estado de Oaxaca, México. *Acta Botanica Mexicana* 14, 23–32.

Zeeuw, J. de. 1934. Versuche über die Verdauung von Nepentheskannen. *Biochemische Zeitschrift* 269, 187–195.

Index

Carnivorous Plant Societies and Sources

Societies

Gesellschaft für fleischfressende Pflanzen im deutschsprachigen Raum
Zitterhuck 6a
D-47608 Geldern, Germany
phone 49 (0) 2838 778187
www.omnisterra.com/bot/cp_home.cgi
Society journal: *Das Taublatt*

International Carnivorous Plant Society, Inc.
PMB 322
1564-A Fitzgerald Drive
Pinole, California 94564-2229
www.carnivorousplants.org
Society journal: *Carnivorous Plant Newsletter*

Sources

California Carnivores
2833 Old Gravenstein Highway South
Sebastopol, California 95472
phone (707) 824-0433
fax (707) 824-2839
www.californiacarnivores.com

Hampshire Carnivorous Plants
Allington Lane
West End
Southampton SO30 3HQ
England
phone 44 (0) 23 80 473314
fax 44 (0) 23 80 473314
www.hampshire-carnivorous-plants.co.uk

Meadowview Biological Research Station
8390 Fredericksburg Turnpike
Woodford, Virginia 22580
phone/fax (804) 633-4336
www.pitcherplant.org

PJ-Plants (formerly Marston Exotics)
www.pj-plants.co.uk (European Union only)

Sarracenia Northwest
P.O. Box 12
Eagle Creek, Oregon 97022-0012
phone (503) 630-7522
www.cobraplant.com

Triffid Park
257 Perry Road
Keysborough, Victoria 3173
Australia
phone 61 (0) 3 9769 1663
fax 61 (0) 3 9769 1663
www.triffidpark.com.au

Wistuba Exotische Pflanzen
Dr. Hermann Wistuba
Mudauer Ring 227
68259 Mannheim
Germany
www.wistuba.com (ships worldwide)

title page: *Nepenthes alata*. Arco Digital Images/ P. Wegner, Germany

English language edition copyright © 2007 by Timber Press. All rights reserved.

Translation by Michael L. C. Ashdown

First published with the title *Karnivoren: Biologie und Kultur Fleischfressender Pflanzen* by Eugen Ulmer GmbH & Co., Stuttgart, Germany

© 2004 Eugen Ulmer GmbH & Co., Stuttgart, Germany

Published in 2007 by
Timber Press, Inc.
The Haseltine Building
133 S.W. Second Avenue, Suite 450
Portland, Oregon 97204-3527, U.S.A.
www.timberpress.com
For contact information regarding editorial, marketing, sales, and distribution in the United Kingdom, see www.timberpress.co.uk.

Second printing 2008

Printed in China

Library of Congress Cataloging-in-Publication Data
Karnivoren. English.
   The curious world of carnivorous plants : a comprehensive guide to their biology and cultivation / by Wilhelm Barthlott ... [et al.] ; translation by Michael L.C. Ashdown. — English language ed.
      p. cm.
   "First published with the title Karnivoren: biologie und kultur fleischfressender pflanzen by Eugen Ulmer GmbH & Co., Stuttgart, Germany, c2004."
   Includes bibliographical references and index.
   ISBN-13: 978-0-88192-792-4
   1. Carnivorous plants. I. Barthlott, Wilhelm. II. Ashdown, Michael. III. Title.
   QK917.K2813 2007
   583'.75—dc22
                                        2006026242
A catalog record for this book is also available from the British Library.